Global Perspectives on Financial Inclusion

Global Perspectives on Financial Inclusion: Case Studies in Microfinance and Women's Empowerment

BY

NISHI MALHOTRA
Indian Institute of Management (IIM) Sambalpur, India

emerald
PUBLISHING

United Kingdom – North America – Japan – India – Malaysia – China

Emerald Publishing Limited
Emerald Publishing, Floor 5, Northspring, 21-23 Wellington Street, Leeds LS1 4DL.

First edition 2025

British Library Cataloguing in Publication Data
A catalogue record for this book is available from the British Library

ISBN: 978-1-83708-081-6 (Print)
ISBN: 978-1-83708-080-9 (Online)
ISBN: 978-1-83708-082-3 (Epub)

Printed and bound by CPI Group (UK) Ltd, Croydon, CR0 4YY

INVESTOR IN PEOPLE

I would like to dedicate this book to the people in rural India and in other parts of the globe, who are excluded from microfinance due to the lack of access to the physical collateral.

Contents

List of Abbreviations

ACTBRW	Active borrowers
ALBG	Average loan per borrower
APMAS	Mahila Abhivruddhi Society, Andhra Pradesh
ASA	Association for Social Advancement
ATM	Automated teller machine
BRAC	Bangladesh Rural Advancement Committee
BSS	Bittaheen Samabaya Samity
CAR	Capital asset ratio
CBO	Collective bank organization
CGAP	Consultative Group to Assist the Poor
CIDA	Canadian International Development Agency
CPB	Cost per borrower
CVF	Competing value framework
DAY	Deen Dayal Antodaya Yojana
DBTEQ	Debt to equity
FINCA	Foundation for International Community Assistance
FSS	Financial self-sustainability
GDP	Gross domestic product
GLP	Gross loan portfolio
GLPTA	Gross loan portfolio to total assets
GMM	Generalized methods of moments
ICT	Information communication technology
IPO	Initial public offering
KSS	Krishak Samabaya Samity
MAC	Mutual-aided cooperative
MBS	Mahila Bittaheen Samity
MFI	Microfinance institution
MSME	Micro, small, and medium enterprise
MUDRA	Micro Unit Development and Refinance Agency Limited
MYRADA	Mysore Resettlement and Development Agency
MYWO	Maendeleo Ya Wanawake Organization
NAB	Net active borrowers
NABARD	National Bank for Agriculture and Rural Development
NBFC	Non-banking finance company
NGO	Non-government organization
NPA	Non-performing asset
NRLM	National Rural Livelihood Mission

OECD	Organisation for Economic Co-operation and Development
OPELP	Operating expenses to loan portfolio
PMJDY	Pradhan Mantri Jan Dhan Yojana
PPP	Public–private partnership
PRADAN	Professional Assistance for Development Action
PRTRSK	Portfolio at risk
RBV	Resource-based view
ROA	Return to asset
ROE	Return on equity
ROI	Return on investment
ROSCA	Rotating Savings and Credit Association
RRB	Regional Rural Bank
SEWA	Self-Employed Women's Association
SFB	State finance bank
SHPI	Self-help promotion institution
SLBC	State-level banking committee
UN	United Nations
VLE	Village-level entrepreneur
VPO	Village phone service provider
VPP	Village pay phone
VRIO	Valuable, rare, imitable, and organization
WBR	Woman borrower ratio
YDGLP	Yield on gross loan portfolio

Preface

Microfinance is the lifeblood of rural banking in India, and it plays an important role in supporting economic activities for the marginalized and the poor at the bottom of the pyramid. The underprivileged at the bottom of the pyramid do not have collateral, due to which they find it difficult to borrow money for the business. Most of the studies in this book are conducted using the case study method and the data have been collected using the semi-structured interview approach. In this regard, community lending provides a viable option to access finance through the use of social capital or social collateral. Though there are earlier studies that have explored the impact of community lending on the financial health of micro-enterprises, there is a dearth of studies that explore the international best practices in community lending. Group lending has now existed for a fairly long period in the form of Rotating Savings and Credit Associations, German cooperatives, Guanxi Chinese group lending, Grameen Bank, Bangladesh, and Savings banks in Kenya that have played an extremely important role in the development of the microfinance. This book aims to explore the impact of the various international best practices in community lending on economic growth and the development of the global economy. Developing nations like India have adopted various best practices from the different economic and financial models of community lending across the globe. The book provides a glimpse and snapshot of the various international case studies in the domain of microfinance. It provides valuable insights for the researchers and the policymakers to design various microfinance programmes to facilitate financial access and support to the people at the bottom of the pyramid. I would like to thank various self-help groups across the globe for their valuable time and feedback.

Acknowledgements

I would like to thank Emerald Publishing, Editor Daniel Ridge, and his team for their support and cooperation. I also take this opportunity to thank the members of various community lending programmes who have spared their valuable time for this initiative. I would like to thank my parents and younger sister, without whom this would not have been possible.

Chapter 1

UN Sustainable Development Goals and Importance of Microfinance

Abstract

The chapter delves into the significant shift among emerging economies towards embracing the UN Sustainable Development Goals, particularly focusing on poverty reduction and women's empowerment. This transformation reflects a departure from conventional donor-driven and subsidy-centric models towards sustainable finance frameworks. The chapter underscores the escalating emphasis on microfinance and social finance within this evolving landscape. By leveraging the theoretical constructs of critical mass and sustainable finance, the chapter aims to elucidate the critical role of financial intermediation in facilitating access to microfinance for impoverished segments globally. It delineates how bottom-up strategies, such as collective endeavours and savings groups, can catalyse sustainable finance initiatives to advance the UN Sustainable Development Goals. Employing a research framework that combines expert interviews with grounded theory analysis of existing literature, the chapter endeavours to provide a nuanced understanding of the intersection between the UN Sustainable Development Goals and poverty alleviation through microfinance. Furthermore, it offers insights into the policy initiatives spearheaded by the World Bank to propel the realization of the Sustainable Development Goals through diverse microfinance interventions. Overall, this chapter serves as a comprehensive exploration of the synergies between sustainable finance, microfinance, and the UN Sustainable Development Goals, shedding light on the pivotal role of financial inclusion strategies in fostering socio-economic progress and empowerment at the grassroots level.

Keywords: Sustainable Development Goals; poverty reduction; financial inclusion; microfinance; group lending

Global Perspectives on Financial Inclusion: Case Studies in Microfinance and Women's Empowerment, 1–15

doi:10.1108/978-1-83708-080-920251001

1. Introduction

Microfinancing and rural financing history in India can be segregated into three different eras. The first phase was post-independence from 1950 till the nationalization of banks, during which the cooperative banks were set up to ensure financial inclusion of the poor underserved and unbanked. Initially, till the 1970s, to ensure financial deepening and access to finance, donor-based, and subsidized finance appeared as a panacea to the problem of financial exclusion. Donor-based models were not found to be sustainable due to deteriorating asset quality and undermining of the credit behaviour leading to insufficient credit allocations (Ledgerwood, 2000). The financial system in India in the post-independence era was extremely shallow and lop-sided as most of the credit creation was by informal players such as money lenders, shopkeepers, and relatives. Money lenders having access to the local information and knowledge about the client could profitably expand into the rural hinterlands (Rosenberg et al., 2009). Due to the lack of institutional sustainability supply of credit was extremely weak. In 1969, the nationalization of banks took place and there was a major thrust on the expansion of rural banking and social finance aimed at providing a positive impact through microfinancing and social banking emerged as major areas. During the post-nationalization phase after 1969, bank branches were expanded in rural India. This initiative was aimed at rural development and poverty reduction (Burgess et al., 2005). It was the beginning of the first phase when the focus was the priority lending mandate of 1971 for the commercial banks for the poor. It led to the setting up of the regional rural banks in 1975. Various policy measures such as priority lending mandate to be implemented by the commercial banks to lend to the underbanked and unbanked were designed to facilitate financial inclusion and upliftment of the poor through improved consumption and productivity. This phase also witnessed the setting up of the supervisory and regulatory body National Bank for Agriculture and Rural Development (NABARD) in 1982 to regulate and ensure financial inclusion in rural India. The financial crisis of 1991 paved the way for the financial sector reforms which were based on the recommendation of the Narasimhan committee. These reforms included the dismantling of the sectoral mandates and the introduction of BASEL and capital adequacy norms, which further led to the decline in the credit deposit ratios in rural India. This heralded the end of the era of donor-based and social banking and the failure of the donor-based credit model, which was not sustainable and exacerbated the problem of moral hazard leading to increasing non-performing assets (NPAs) and impacting the financial sustainability of the banks and financial systems. In 1992, in the aftermath of the recession and economic reforms, the government-based formal credit declined rapidly and the dependence of rural households on non-institutional finance increased rapidly. Further as per the recommendations of the C Rangarajan Committee on Financial Inclusion (2008), Usha Thorat Panel (2007), Nachiket Mor Panel (2013), the Central Bank of India, Reserve Bank of India laid out the detailed vision for financial inclusion and financial deepening in India through universal access to banking services including bank accounts, payment services, deposit services, credit services, and insurance based on principle of stability, transparency, neutrality, and responsibility.

Microfinance interventions by private players such as microfinance institutions and non-banking finance corporations were not financially viable due to lower repayment rates, high transaction costs, NPAs, and exorbitant transaction costs. The programme started as the Integrated Rural Development Programme and then was graduated to Swarna Jayanti Gram Swarozgar Yojana. This scheme was fraught with increasing NPAs and deteriorating asset loan portfolios. And, in 2012, this scheme was transformed into Deen Dayal Antodaya Yojana, National Rural Livelihoods Mission (DAY NRLM) which resulted in the withdrawal of the capital subsidy and disbursement of credit to the poorer states (Government of India Ajeevika, 2020). In the form of grants, funds are provided by the institutions to the rural poor and then these funds are passed on to the self-help group (SHG) member. The third reform period started in the 1990s, which was marked by the launch of the *SHG bank linkage* in 1992 and establishment of the small industries development bank in 2000 and the establishment of the Small Industries Development Bank of India and Micro Unit Development and Refinance Agency Limited in 2016 (Fisher et al., 2002). It was started as an Action Research Project in 1989 by NABARD, which sanctioned Rs. 10,00,000 crores to Mysore Resettlement and Development Agency for testing credit management groups. In Rajasthan, on an experimental basis, Professional Assistance for Development Action was established by the Ministry of Rural Development. The project was approved in 1992, reviewed by the Working Group in 1995, and the Reserve Bank of India issued the guidelines in 1995. In 1992, SHG bank linkage appeared as a unique approach to financial intermediation and aimed at providing last-mile connectivity to the underbanked and underserved at the bottom of the pyramid. A SHG has been defined as a group of homogenous set of people concerning social and economic backgrounds, who come together for the achievement of financial goals such as the promotion of thrift and savings habits and ensuring access to credit to the people at the bottom of the pyramid (Micro Credit Innovation Department, NABARD, 2018; Shri & Kalia, 1994). The landmark model of SHG linkage provides membership to approximately 1.02 crore groups and 12.4 crore households. This scheme has generated savings of Rs. 26,152 crore savings and credit of Rs. 1,08,075 crores. Total NPAs under this scheme have declined from 5.06% to 4.92% in 2020 (Fernandez & Gómez, 2007; NABARD, 2019–2020). The SHG linkage programme was the result of a series of studies conducted by NABARD in the aftermath of financial reforms. The Central Bank of India, the Reserve Bank of India wanted to cater to the demand for small ticket sizes and frequent loans to the microborrowers. To encourage the poorest of the poor to undertake forced savings and provide a substitute for the physical collateral, NABARD envisaged a SHG linkage programme. Moreover, regarding the achievement of the Sustainable Development Goal of financial inclusion as per the UN Agenda, 2030, the Government of India has adopted SHG linkage as an indicator of financial inclusion. Financial inclusion in India is jettisoned by various barriers on the supply and demand sides. An initiative like SHG bank linkage which is aimed at driving banking from 'class banking' to 'mass banking' is fraught with various supply-side factors such as the requirement of physical collateral, information asymmetry (Aravind, 2018), access exclusion in the form of distance from the banks and automated teller machines (Morduch, 1999).

Expansion of the SHG bank linkage programme in the form of an increase in credit linkage and credit deepening is marred with barriers such as lack of financial literacy and lack of financial planning and attitude among the members of SHGs (Dev, 2006). Financial literacy is an important component of financial inclusion and social intermediation through training and human capacity building. However, specifically in the context of the SHG linkage issue of financial literacy is severe and many members are not proficient in the financial concepts and financial knowledge (Drexler et al., 2010). Within the purview of *Microfinanciarization*, which is the process of financial inclusion, banking reforms, and regulation of informal institutions of finance to reach financially excluded people (Fouillet & Augsburg, 2007), falls the improvization of Swarna Jayanti Gram Swarozgar Yojana (1999) into Deendayal Antodaya Yojana (2013, DAY NRLM). Under DAY NRLM, banks are made responsible by the Central Bank, Reserve Bank of India to undertake capacity building and training for the members of SHG bank linkage (Bhanot & Bapat, 2019). The success of this wave of SHG linkage programmes hinges on ability and financial literacy among the SHG members and social norms are the major reasons for the lack of credit generation and financial inclusion under this initiative.

2. SHGs in India

The microfinance revolution in India started with SEWA, the landmark group lending model which started in 1974 as a unique approach to financial intermediation through peer monitoring and joint liability. A collaborative movement of self-employed women emerged as a dominant driving force behind social banking. *Microfinance* can be described as a measure to render financial services to unbanked and underserved microenterprises and microborrowers that are excluded from the formal financial sector (World Bank Group, 2015). A total of 1.7 billion people worldwide are financially excluded and unbanked (Demirguc-Kunt et al., 2017). Most of these unbanked people live in the emerging economies of the world (Demirgüç-Kunt et al., 2017). These people lack physical collateral and suffer from information asymmetry. India has adopted the goal of financial inclusion to provide access to financial services to all as part of the Sustainable Development Goals Agenda, 2030. *Financial inclusion* has been defined as access to financial services and credit at an affordable cost to the marginalized poor at the bottom of the pyramid. Achievement of the Sustainable Development Goals of women empowerment and poverty reduction is impacted by access to microcredit and level of financial inclusion (Pitt et al., 2006). *Joint liability* through social collateral and *social capital* which refers to the set of institutionalized relationships and social networks facilitates access to formal finance for the financially excluded microborrowers (Rankin, 2002). Characterized by glaring social and economic inequalities the path to financial inclusion is chequered with barriers and challenges on the supply and demand side (Kempson & Whyley, 2000). Concerns are raised regarding how financial exclusion interacts with information asymmetry to create price exclusion, condition exclusion, self-exclusion, and access exclusion. Several factors on the demand side impact the nature and extent of financial inclusion through the SHG bank linkage initiative, including the information asymmetry and lack of physical collateral. Social capital and collateral offer a panacea against the problem of information asymmetry and lack of collateral by making use of peer monitoring and group liability (Ito, 1998). Overall joint liability groups or SHGs groups. Described as a 'landmark model' of financial intermediation, SHG linkage facilitates higher recovery of loans, better loan repayment, better savings, and reduction of transaction costs by peer mechanism and joint liability (Basu et al., 2005). There is a lack of studies that highlight the importance of group mechanism, peer monitoring, and financial literacy or social intermediation, that is, investment in social capital or human resources to facilitate the sustainability of the microfinance initiative like SHG linkage. While SHG bank linkage is lauded for its massive outreach, it suffers from financial and institutional unsustainability. Over the period, various studies have emphasized that the members do not adhere to the group norms in terms of preparation of books of accounts, savings register, loan register, and minutes of meetings (Beaman et al., 2014). Peer mechanisms and joint liability play an extremely important role in ensuring financial and organizational sustainability (Ito, 1998). As per the extant literature, social innovation such as group lending, which lacks information asymmetry, and financial and institutional sustainability can be a successful initiative with social intermediation and investment in human capital and institutional capital. In the lack of a viable financial model for group lending and monitoring, peer monitoring can be an enabler that facilitates the supervision of group lending and there is a need for theorizing this process.

3. Overview of Existing Literature

A SHG has been defined as a homogenous group of 10–20 people, who are homogenous concerning their social and economic background. These people come together to promote savings, intra-lending, and external credit for the welfare of the members of the group (Micro Credit Innovation Department, NABARD, 2018). Besides, other characteristics of SHGs are that they carry out multiple socio-economic goals (Brody et al., 2016). The extant literature substantiates that groups provide additional benefits by operationalizing peer pressure commitment or sanctions but none of the studies validate the mechanism through which groups achieve desired outcomes in terms of financial empowerment. Most of the studies highlight, 'What', the financial outcomes of a group mechanism in the form of promoting saving mechanisms (Gugerty, 2007), increased access to credit (Deininger & Liu, 2009) and asset ownership (Greaney et al., 2013), recovery performance, and reduced transaction costs (Puhazhendhi, 2000). However, there is a lack of studies in the domain of 'How' the group mechanism facilitates financial discipline and sustainability, in a lack of physical collateral and information asymmetry. SHG linkage has emerged as a unique approach to financial intermediation and is lauded for its ability to extend access to credit to the poorest of poor who are unbanked and underbanked due to the lack of physical collateral and information asymmetry (Arora & Singh, 2015). Most of the literature in the domain of Agency theory discusses how lack of financial contract and information asymmetry leads to the problem of moral hazard and adverse selection (Jensen & Meckling, 1976), and these studies highlight the importance of monitoring and incentive compatibility, but there is lack of studies in domain of social capital or social collateral that provides a substitute to physical collateral and group liability in Indian context (Armendariz & Morduch, 2010). SHG bank linkage was introduced by NABARD to bridge the investment gap and give impetus to entrepreneurship (Beaman et al., 2014). In a group lending mechanism such as a SHG linkage programme, social capital, and peer monitoring facilitate better repayments, even if there is a lack of physical collateral (Besley, 1995; de Aghion, 1999; Stiglitz, 1990). Against this backdrop, the concept of social capital and peer monitoring has become extremely relevant for policymakers, academicians, and practitioners. From the perspective of financial viability of the group lending initiative, Guinnane and Ghatak (1999) argue that peer monitoring leads to better financial behaviour in terms of repayment of loans, per capita savings and generation, reduced transaction costs, and better social capital. Considerable evidence shows that banks cannot apply financial sanctions against individual clients due to financial incentives, but the members of the group or neighbours can impose financial sanctions to counter the problem of moral hazard. The literature identifies the self-selection of the members of the group and information asymmetry as the reasons for loan defaults. However, in these joint liability groups, the members have access to private information about the creditworthiness of the members which can resolve the problem of adverse selection (Morduch, 1999). The extant literature in the domain of group lending touts peer monitoring and social capital which refer to the institutionalized relationship among the members of the group as the reason for the success of group lending. The concept of social capital overrides the basic premise behind conventional banking that credit contracts are impossible without adequate physical collateral. By joint liability, the social capital ensures solvency for the insolvent borrowers or members of the SHGs by resolving the problem of information asymmetry, moral hazard, and adverse selection (Ito, 1998; Putnam & Nanetti, 1993). A seminal paper by Stiglitz (1990), a representative moral hazard model, suggests that in a heterogenous risk group, safe borrowers will not be ready to cross-subsidize the risky borrowers leading to peer mechanism (Banerjee et al., 1994). The use of group meetings and peer screening for sanctioning the loans reduces transaction costs and promotes good financial behaviour through peer pressure and peer dynamics. This model has been hailed as a dominant driving force behind sustainable banking aimed at ameliorating the challenges in banking by the formal banking institutions. In recent literature, an attempt has been made to explain whether group lending through peer monitoring, selection, and enforcement provides an integrated microfinancing institutional framework to ensure financial inclusion but there is still a lack of theories or process view on peer monitoring (Conning & Morduch, 2011). In a paper by Chee (2002), the author discusses the free rider problem whereby a safe borrower will have to cross-subsidize the risky borrower in a joint liability scenario. They highlight the relevance of peer monitoring and institutional sustainability through peer mechanisms to improve project outcomes. Also, through the theoretical lens of information asymmetry, the authors highlight that the borrowers can mitigate the risk of loss by cross-monitoring each other through reports to the lenders. From the study of literature, it becomes apparent that there is a lack of theory on peer monitoring and social capital and mechanisms underlying SHG mechanism and its impact on developmental outcomes (Gugerty et al., 2019). Besides that, the extant literature (Schmidt, 2004) points out that supervision and regulation of the SHGs become important because the majority of members do not conform to the group norms or Panchsutras, that is, maintenance of Savings register, loan register, and minutes of meeting, and there is lack of standardization in reporting. Moreover, groups are supposed to violate the basic tenets of peer monitoring, social inclusion, discipline, and refrain (Ashta, 2010). SHG linkage is a unique approach to financial intermediation and provides access to finance at the doorsteps of citizens of India. The literature discusses the supply and demand side factors (Fisher et al., 2002; Kempson & Whyley, 2000). Supply-side factors impacting financial inclusion have been identified as infrastructure, financial technology, connectivity, and information asymmetry. Demand-side factors include demographic factors, age, gender, financial literacy, income, and access to financial technology. Despite the stupendous success in terms of repayment, there are concerns regarding the sustainability of the groups impacted by factors such as inability to access credit, lack of adherence to the group norms such as maintenance of the books of record such as savings register, loan register, etc. (Schmidt & Reinhardt, 2004). The sustainability of this unique approach to financial intermediation is a matter of national importance for policymakers, academicians, and practitioners. As per the literature, sustainability can be financial sustainability and organizational sustainability (Bhuiya et al., 2016). From the analysis of the literature, financial and organizational sustainability appear to be the major concern in the domain of SHG bank linkage. Financial sustainability of SHG bank linkage refers to the financial ability of the groups and can be operationalized through indicators about the financial health of this programme regarding the amount of credit, frequency of credit, amount of savings and thrift, meetings conducted, etc. (Das et al., 2018). The main reason cited for the lack of institutional sustainability defined as a stable institutional framework is the mismanagement of funds and lack of commitment to group activities and social intermediation (Parida & Sinha, 2010). Despite innumerable different ways of studying the issue of sustainability of SHGs, there is a lack of a comprehensive framework to analyse the sustainability of these group lending financial intermediaries (Masum & Fernandez, 2008). In extant literature, financial sustainability has been operationalized through various group interaction variables (Isern et al., 2007). Indicators of financial sustainability include indicators such as intra-lending, frequency of bank credit which refers to the progressive loans (Piotroski & Srinivasan, 2008), amount of loan, group loans, maintaining financial records and books of accounts (Misra & Lee, 2007), and human capacity building and training (Mann & Randhawa, 2015). Lack of maintenance of books, irregular savings, and loan repayment are some of the additional problems faced by the members of SHG bank linkage, due to the low investment in human capacity development and training of the SHG members (Baland et al., 2008; Parida & Sinha, 2010). Though there are studies on sustainability indicators, none of the studies capture the construct of institutional and financial sustainability in the form of an index. Lack of financial literacy and skills required for financial technology leads to a lack of financial discipline and a lack of credit discipline leading to credit starvation (Basu et al., 2005; Reserve Bank of India, 2018). The intervention that has touched the lives of millions of poor people is not sufficient to meet the credit requirement of the poor people at the bottom of the pyramid. Within the rural financial system, commercial banks suffer from mission drift and are unwilling to provide credit to the members due to the lack of financial returns and return on investment. To further answer the question regarding financial sustainability, there is a need to answer the questions regarding the cost structures and delivery methodologies (Ryne, 2009). Banks and formal financial institutions lack the motivation to finance and provide loans to the underbanked and unbanked due to the credit risk and risk of deterioration of asset quality. Small banks and specialized institutions for rural financing are keen to extend credit to the microborrowers due to lack of availability of local information (Berger & Berger, 2011). According to the extant literature, all these variables impact group monitoring and social cohesion. Marginalized poor or the underbanked and unbanked who are catered to by the SHG bank linkage face various barriers in accessing financial services such as lack of information or information asymmetry, which further leads to the moral hazard and adverse selection (de Aghion & Gollier, 2000), is the biggest challenge in serving the marginalized poor. Social intermediation and institutional human capacity building have a vast impact on changing the financial attitudes of the members and have a positive impact on the sustainability of groups and there is a need to undertake research in this domain (Bali Swain, 2013). Despite a grading system put in place to assess the workings of the institution of SHGs and implementation of various government schemes, there are lacunae in monitoring this initiative, due to the lack of adherence to the governance norms by the stipulated vigilance and monitoring committees (Krahnen & Harper, 2002).

4. Discussion and Importance

The success of the group lending model is due to the higher rate of repayment of loans sanctioned by the groups, which is made possible due to peer pressure and social pressure. Group or joint liability lending institutions can pool savings, which can be used as collateral for credit creation and this has been lauded as a panacea and solution to the problem of microborrowers. Due to the smaller size of the loans and higher frequency of borrowing, lending to the people at the bottom of the pyramid is not viable. Higher transaction costs due to the cost of screening, monitoring, and microlending are not viable for large commercial banks. Microborrowers do not have collateral and this acts as a hindrance in access to finance. The principle of joint liability provides an incentive for microlending to the poor people at the bottom of the pyramid (Gine & Karlan, 2005). Due to the massive social capital embedded in the initiative monitoring of the SHG linkage scheme becomes important. Most of the literature is limited to increasing the availability of finance to unbanked and financial inclusion rather than financial sustainability. However, despite the banks being wary of monitoring SHGs, peer-to-peer monitoring has emerged as a main factor behind the success of SHGs. Despite being important, neither is there any theory on how peer-to-peer monitoring operates, nor there is any process of peer-to-peer monitoring (CGAP, 2002; Armendáriz & Morduch, 2005). India is committed to the achievement of poverty reduction and SHG linkage has been adopted as an indicator of financial inclusion. While SHG linkage is lauded for its massive outreach, it suffers from financial and institutional unsustainability. These groups suffer from the problem of non-adherence to the group norms such as maintenance of savings, loan register, and minutes of meetings (EDA Rural Systems & APMAS, 2006). The extant literature does not address the problem of non-adherence to group norms and what factors impact the adherence to the governance norms. Also, there is a need to study how financial literacy impacts group financial discipline through thrifts and savings and adherence to group norms and disclosures, reporting and governance mechanisms (Bhuiya et al., 2016). This study aims to explore the dynamics of social capital, and how it is important for the sustainability of the group lending mechanism.

4.1. Case Studies

Interviewer: How does the self-help promoting institution (SHPI) help the SHGs to come together?

Respondent: Over the past 12 years, we have been actively collaborating with the terracotta artisans' community in the Chittoor district of Andhra Pradesh, which comprises 640 artisan families engaged in pottery work. Initially, we introduced SHGs among these artisans – both men and women – to address their savings and thrift needs as well as to facilitate inter-lending for working capital loans needed for their handicraft production. However, we noticed that these SHGs were not functioning effectively. Many of the groups consisted of homogenous members who were close relatives such as parent–child duos. This proximity led to a lack of enthusiasm for attending meetings and participating in thrift activities since the original concept of SHGs – working together towards shared goals – was not being realized under these circumstances. To address these challenges, we transitioned to forming mutual-aided cooperative (MAC) societies, allowing membership on a family basis instead. This new structure has proven successful, enabling members to engage in thrift and credit activities as a formal legal entity. Through the MAC societies, members can borrow funds from scheduled banks, which are then equitably distributed among them. Notably, there has been no misuse of these funds, and as of now, there are no NPAs within the two societies. Each MAC society has achieved a remarkable turnover of over 7 crores per annum, reflecting the effectiveness of this new approach.

Interviewer: In this society, are members from the same family or the same vocation?

Respondent: In each MAC society, membership is structured so that one family corresponds to one membership. These members come from nearby villages, with approximately 350 families participating in each society, organized based on a cluster approach to ensure proximity.

While the SHGs are unregistered entities that open joint accounts in the name of the group, MAC societies are registered organizations that maintain accurate accounting records and undergo annual audits. These audit reports and financial records are essential for membership renewal. SHGs typically consist of small groups of 10–12 individuals, but they suffer from a lack of homogeneity and activity focus. The SHG guidelines allow for a mix of members engaged in different trades, such as pottery, weaving, and small-scale businesses. This diversity can lead to loan repayment issues, as one member may take out a loan for pottery while another focuses on weaving, complicating accountability and repayment. In contrast, homogenous groups allow for better mutual monitoring, which is crucial for effective loan management. In MAC societies, although members possess varied skills, they are still better able to oversee each other's activities. The societies offer two types of loans: one for purchasing raw materials and another for working capital needed to construct assets. Unfortunately, many SHG members struggle with financial literacy, which hampers their ability to maintain proper books of accounts. The SHGs are typically initiated by government agencies, such as the District Rural Development Agency, and are structured under a framework called Sangh Mitra, which federates 10–15 SHGs into larger village organizations.

The NRLM places responsibility for bookkeeping on SHG members, but participation in these groups is often low due to the additional burdens placed on the Sangh Mitra. While some well-organized SHGs successfully maintain their financial records under capable leadership, overall financial literacy remains a significant barrier. Accurate bookkeeping demands a basic level of education, and many residents at the bottom of the economic pyramid face challenges with digital and financial literacy.

Within these clusters, responsibility for loan utilization is collective, and the establishment of showrooms often involves loans, with shared accountability for repayment. Joint liability groups, although unregistered, allow a group leader to take responsibility for loan repayment, creating an additional layer of oversight. Within these groups of 10–15 members, master craftsmen play a pivotal role in quality control and monitoring. All master craftsmen have formed an apex body that enhances accountability across the groups, leveraging their skills to exert influence and ensure adherence to high standards.

The MAC society model and the micro, small, and medium enterprises framework provide significant advantages, including registration under the Companies Act, facilitating access to loans from scheduled banks. Effective support from SHPI enables members to engage in various crafts, including pottery and weaving. Ultimately, skill-building and hands-on support are critical, alongside enhanced financial literacy, to promote craftsmanship among group members and ensure the sustainability of their enterprises.

5. Social Capital and Group Lending

Table 1 provides the codes for social capital and group lending. Thus, from the analysis of the literature, SHGs leverage social capital that plays an important role in ensuring sustainability of these groups.

Table 1. Coding for Social Capital and Group Lending.

Line-by-Line Analysis	In Vivo Code	Descriptive Code	Analytical Code
Social capital captures the networks, norms, and social trust that facilitate coordination and cooperation for mutual benefit	Networking, norms, and social trust define social capital	Social capital enables coordination through networks, norms, and social trusts	Social capital is defined as a set of networks, norms, and social trusts
It is the engine that fuels coordination and cohesion between family, friends, associates, and stakeholders to achieve a given goal or outcome that would not otherwise be possible in its absence	Social capital facilitates coordination and social cohesion between friends, associates, and stakeholders	Social capital enables coordination and cohesion between family members, friends, and stakeholders	Social capital as an enabler
Trust, norms of reciprocity, group membership, goodwill fellowship, mutual sympathy, and social engagement are all components in the generation, maintenance, and utilization of social capital	Social capital comprises norms, reciprocity, group membership, fellowship, mutual sympathy, and social engagement	Social capital comprises norms, reciprocity, group membership, fellowship and engagement	Components of social capital
Researchers have categorized social capital into three main categories: bonding, bridging, and linking social capital	Social capital can be bonding, bridging, and linking	Social capital can be of three types: bonding, bridging, and linking types	Types of social capital
Bonding ties help us explain close, tight-knit communities that share a similar background, race, ethnicity, or religion	Bonding ties refer to the close tight knit communities among similar background	Bonding refers to the close knit communities with similar background	Bonding ties refer to the similar type group together
Bridging social capital is inclusive. The term helps us explain ties that bring people together across a wide array of backgrounds, whether it be age, race, ethnic, political, social, economic, or otherwise	Bridging capital refers to heterogenous groups	Bridging refers to heterogenous groups	Bridging refers to heterogenous groups of members from different background

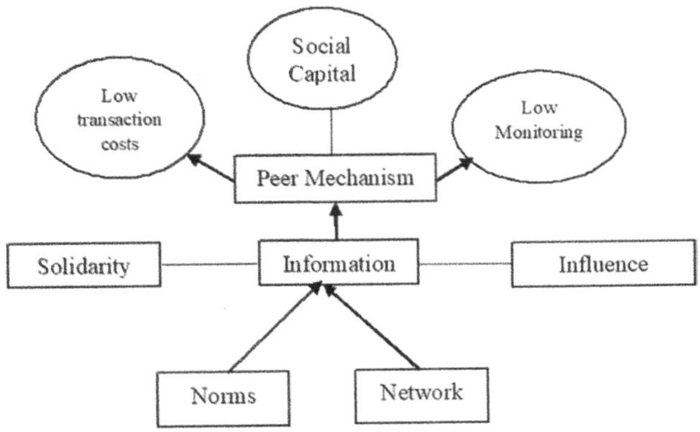

Fig. 1. Social Capital and Role in Microfinance.

As per Fig. 1 the presence of social capital, which is the aggregate of norms, networks, information, and peer mechanisms, reduces the cost of monitoring and transaction costs for the organization. Peer mechanism comprises peer selection, monitoring, and sanction and enforcement. Banks and formal financial institutions are unwilling to lend to the poor due to the lack of collateral. Peer mechanism replaces the physical collateral with social collateral, reducing the information asymmetry and making financing to the group lending institutions viable.

6. Conclusion

This study provides a detailed analysis of how the network ties and network structure impact the financial outcomes in SHGs. As per the study, the network analysis was done to identify the structure of the SHGs. As per the study, the data establish that various SHGs depend on shared norms and networks impact social capital and the financial outcomes of the social organization through social means. Besides, multiple factors such as solidarity, influence, and information impact the financial outcomes of the social organization. From the analysis of the codes generated in the process, it becomes clear that social capital improves the financial outcome by lowering the transaction cost and monitoring the cost of the group. Peer mechanism plays a vital role in operationalizing the social capital through peer monitoring, selection, and enforcement. Thus, the role of social capital and peer mechanisms in motivating marginalized people to join the cooperative movement through group lending is extremely vital. Governments and banks across the merging economies are working to tap this hidden social innovation to realize the dream of social and financial inclusion.

References

Aravind, A. (2018). *Advanced technologies for microfinance solution & challenges*. Business Science Reference.

Armendariz, B., & Morduch, J. (2010). *Economics of microfinance*. MIT Press.

Arora, M., & Singh, S. (2015). An evaluation of the non performing assets of public and private sector banks under the SHG bank linkage programme. *Indian Journal of Finance*, *9*(6), 41–50.

Ashta, A. (2010). *Advanced technologies for microfinance: Solutions and challenges*. IGI Global.

Baland, J. M., Somanathan, R., & Vandewalle, L. (2008). Microfinance lifespans: A study of attrition and exclusion of the self help groups in India. *India Policy Forum*, *4*(1), 159–210.

Bali Swain, R. (2013). *The microfinance impact*. Routledge.

Banerjee, A. V., Besly, T., & Guinnane, T. W. (1994). Thy neighbour keeper the design for credit cooperative with theory & test. *The Quarterly Journal of Economics*, *109*(2), 491–515.

Basu, P., World Bank, & Srivastava, P. (2005). *Scaling-up microfinance for India's rural poor*. National Council of Applied Economic Research, India.

Beaman, L., Karlan, D., & Thuysbaert, B. (2014). *Saving for rainy day* [Working Paper Series]. NBER.

Berger, A. N., & Berger, L. K. (2011). Bank size lending technologies and small business finance. *Journal of Banking and Finance*, *35*(3), 724–735.

Besley, T. A. (1995). Group lending: Repayment incentives and social collateral. *Journal of Development Economics*, *6*(1), 1–18.

Bhanot, D., & Bapat, V. (2019). c. *Asia Pacific Sustainable Development Journal*, *26*(2), 25–55.

Bhuiya, M. M. M., Khanam, R., Rahman, M. M., & Nghiem, H. S. (2016). Impact of microfinance on household income & consumption in Bangladesh. *Journal of Developing*, *50*(3), 305–318.

Brody, C., de Hoop, T., Vojtkova, M., Warnock, R., Dunbar, M., Murthy, P., & Dworkin, S. L. (2016). *Economic self-help group programmes for improving women's empowerment: A systematic review* [3ie Systematic review no. 23]. International Initiative for Impact Evaluation (3ie).

Burgess, R., Pande, R., & Wong, G. (2005). Banking for the poor: Evidence from India. *Journal of Economic Association*, *3*(2–3), 268–278.

CGAP. (2002). *Microfinance and the millennium development goals* [Donor brief no. 9]. Consultative Group to Assist the Poor.

Chee, Y. k. (2002). Joint liability and peer monitoring under group lending. *Contributions in Theoretical Economics*, *2*(1), 3.

Conning, J., & Morduch, J. (2011). Microfinance and social investment. *Annual Review of Financial Economics*, *3*(1), 407–434. https://doi.org/10.1146/annurev-financial-102710-144909

Das, S., Guha, D., & Mesiar, R. (2018). Information measures in the intuitionistic fuzzy framework and their relationships. *IEEE Transactions on Fuzzy Systems*, *26*, 1626–1637. https://doi.org/10.1109/TFUZZ.2017.2738603

de Aghion, B. A. (1999). On the design of a credit agreement with peer. *Journal of Development Economics*, 79–104.

de Aghion, B. A., & Gollier, C. (2000). Peer group formation in adverse selection. *Economic Journal Royal Economic Society*, *110*, 632–643.

Deininger, K., & Liu, Y. (2009). *Economic and social impacts of self-help groups in India* [Policy research working paper no. 4884]. World Bank.

Demirguc-Kunt, A., Klapper, L., Singer, D., Ansar, A., & Hess, J. R. (2017). *The global findex database*. World Bank Group.

Dev, S. M. (2006). Financial inclusion: Issues and challenges. *Economic & Political Weekly*, *41*(41), 14–20.

Drexler, A., Fischer, G., & Schoar, A. (2010). *Keeping it simple: Financial literacy and rules of thumb*. Center for Economic Policy Research.
EDA Rural Systems & APMAS. (2006). *Self-help groups in India. A study of lights and shades, a report prepared for catholic relief services*, CARE, USAID and GTZ/NABARD.
Fernández, A., & Gómez, S. (2007). *Portfolio selection using neural networks*. Computers & operations research.
Fisher, T., Sriram, M. S., & Harper, M. (2002). *Beyond micro-credit: Putting development back into micro-finance*. Vistaar Publications.
Fouillet, C., & Augsburg, B. (2007). Spread of the Self Help Group Linkage programme in India. FAO Headquarters.
Gine, X., & Karlan, D. S. (2005). Long term evidence from micro credit lending groups and without group liability. World Development, *33*, 149–169.
Government of India Ajeevika. (2020). *SHG bank linkage: A success story*. In South Asia Agriculture and Rural Growth Discussion Series.
Greaney, B., Kaboski, J. P., & Van Leemput, E. (2013). *Can self-help groups really be "self-help"?* [Working papers no. 18970]. National Bureau of Economic Research.
Gugerty, M. K. (2007). You can't save alone: Commitment in rotating savings and credit associations in Kenya. *Economic Development and Cultural Change*, *55*(2), 251–282.
Guinnane, M., & Ghatak, T. W. (1999). The economics of lending with joint liability theory and practice. *Journal of Development Economics*, *60*, 195–228.
Gugerty, M. K., Biscaye, P., & Anderson, C. L. (2019). Delivering development? Evidence on self-help groups as development intermediaries in South Asia and Africa. *Developmental Policy Review*, *37*(1), 129–151.
Isern, J., Prakash, L. B., Pillai, A., Hashemi, S. M., Christen, R. P., Ivatury, G., & Rosenberg, R. (2007). *Sustainability of self-help groups in India: Two analyses* [Occasional paper no. 12]. Consultative Group to Assist the Poor (CGAP).
Ito, S. (1998). *The Grameen bank and peer monitoring: A sociological perspective* [Working paper 3]. University of Sussex, Institute of Development Studies.
Jensen, M. C., & Meckling, W. H. (1976). Theory of the firm: Managerial behavior, agency costs and ownership structure. *Journal of Financial Economics*, *3*(4), 305–360.
Kempson, E., & Whyley, C. (2000). *In or out? Financial exclusion: A literature and research review*. Consumer Policy and Research. Financial Services Authority.
Krahnen, J. P., & Harper, M. (2002). *Promotion of self help group under the self help group linkage programme* [Paper presentation]. Seminar on Self Help Group Bank Linkage Programme at New Delhi, NABARD, Micro Credit Innovations Department.
Ledgerwood, J. (2000). *Microfinance handbook: An institutional & financial perspective*. The World Bank.
Mann, S., & Randhawa, V. (2015). Training and capacity building of women self-help groups in Punjab. *Agricultural Update*, *10*(2), 130–133.
Masum, M., & Fernandez, A. (2008). *Internationalization process of SMEs: Strategies and methods* [Master thesis]. Mälardalen University.
Micro Credit Innovation Department, NABARD. (2018, August 23). Circular No./23Cy MCID-05/2018. 28. NABARD.
Misra, R., & Lee, N. (2007). Primary agricultural society linkage: The best remote self-help groups in India can do? *Small Enterprise Development*, *18*(1), 25–36.
Morduch, J. (1999). The microfinance promise. *Journal of Economic Literature*, *37*(4), 1569–1614.
NABARD. (2019–2020). *Status of microfinance in India*. NABARD.
Nachiket Mor Panel. (2013). *Committee on comprehensive financial services for small business and low income households*. Reserve Bank of India.
Parida, P. C., & Sinha, A. (2010). Performance and sustainability of self-help. *Asian Development Review*, *27*(1), 80–103.

Piotroski, J. D., & Srinivasan, S. (2008). Regulation and bonding: The Sarbanes-Oxley act and the flow of international listings. *Journal of Accounting Research*, *46*, 383–425. https://doi.org/10.1111/j.1475-679X.2008.00279.x

Pitt, M. M., & Khandekar, S. R. (1998). The impact of group-based credit programmes on poor households in Bangladesh: Does the gender of participant matter? *Journal of Political Economy*, *106*(5), 958–996.

Pitt, M., Khandker, S., & Cartwright, J. (2006). Empowering women with micro finance: Evidence from Bangladesh. *Economic Development and Cultural Change*, 791–831.

Puhazhendhi, V. (2000). *Evaluation study of self help groups in Tamil Nadu*. NABARD.

Putnam, R., & Nanetti, R. (1993). *Making democracy work: Civic traditions in modern Italy* [Review paper]. Princeton University Press.

Rankin, K. N. (2002). Social capital, microfinance, and the politics of development. Feminist Economics, *8*(1), 1–24.

Reserve Bank of India. (2018). *Financial literacy for self help groups*. Reserve Bank of India.

Rosenberg, R., Gonzalez, A., & Narain, S. (2009). *The new moneylenders are poor being exploited by high microcredit interest rates* [Occasional paper no. 10] (pp. 145–181). CGAP.

Ryne, E. (2009). *Microfinance for bankers & investors under challenges & opportunities*. McGraw Hill.

Schmidt, J. P. (2004). *The German financial system*. Oxford University Press.

Shri, S. K., & Kalia, W. G. (1994). *Working group on role of NGO and SHG in credit*. NABARD.

Stiglitz, J. (1990). Peer monitoring and credit markets. *The World Bank Economic Review*, *4*(3), 351–366.

Usha Thorat Panel. (2007). *Usha Thorat financial inclusion experience*. In HMT-DFID financial inclusion conference, Whitehall Place, London, UK.

World Bank Group. (2015). *Microfinance: A critical literature survey*. World Bank.

Chapter 2

Effectual Approach to Microfinance: A Case Study of ROSCAs in Ireland

Abstract

Rotating Savings and Credit Associations (ROSCAs) are the semi-formal financial institutions that have been in existence for a long time. Through internal lending, these financial institutions have ensured access to finance for the people at the bottom of the pyramid. ROSCAs are saving vehicles that are based on trust and reciprocity and ensure access to finance for the people at the bottom of the pyramid. Various kinds of models of ROSCAs exist, including random, fixed, and bidding models. These semi-formal saving vehicles have enabled the members of the society, without access to collateral to access credit and finance. Further, since historical times, various types of ROSCAs have existed in Ireland and Taiwan and these semi-financial institutions have ensured the financial inclusion of the poor without collateral. In this study, a hermeneutical approach has been adopted to oversee the development in the present while exploring the colonial past and the best practices that existed in the Western world to facilitate a meaningful discourse. The study highlights that group lending through semi-financial institutions like rotated saving groups enables a higher level of savings and repayment among the members of the group. The study describes the role of social contracts and peer mechanisms in promoting the financial inclusion of the poor through the use of peer mechanisms and social capital.

Keywords: ROSCAs; peer mechanism; group lending; financial inclusion; savings group

Global Perspectives on Financial Inclusion: Case Studies in Microfinance and Women's Empowerment, 17–41

Published under exclusive licence by Emerald Publishing Limited
doi:10.1108/978-1-83708-080-920251002

1. Introduction

A causal approach typically delineates a linear connection between a cause and its effect, such as the relationship between financial exclusion and poverty reduction in attaining the Sustainable Development Goals (SDGs). While many studies have historically adopted a causal approach to address the SDG of poverty reduction through financial inclusion, this methodology assumes that countries possess adequate resources to achieve the desired outcomes, with any gaps primarily attributed to a lack of policy interventions. However, in the context of many emerging economies facing severe resource constraints, a more pragmatic approach is often required. In contrast to the causal approach, the effectual approach focuses on leveraging the means at hand to achieve desired ends. This methodology involves tailoring initiatives based on available resources and fostering commitment towards poverty reduction goals. An example of this approach is exemplified by ROSCAs in Ireland, which functioned on principles of social commitment and mutual savings among community members. ROSCAs are one of the oldest credit associations that have been practised worldwide as a special type of financial agreement (Gugerty et al., 2014). These structures, comprising rotating groups of members who pooled and rotated funds as loans, played a pivotal role in Ireland's rural economy. Despite the historical significance of ROSCAs, existing research predominantly adopts a structuralist perspective, overlooking the operational dynamics and eventual discontinuation of these microfinance vehicles. To address this gap, a hermeneutical approach will be employed to delve into the functional aspects of these savings groups. The chapter aims to present a strategic process model alongside a root cause analysis elucidating the factors contributing to the cessation of these structures as effective microfinance mechanisms. By offering insights into the operational intricacies and contextual factors influencing ROSCAs, this study is poised to be instrumental for policymakers seeking to design effective poverty alleviation strategies tailored to the specific needs and resources of communities.

2. Research Design

In this study, we adopt a hermeneutical paradigm as our research design. The epistemology is grounded in deconstructing the colonial history of group lending through a hermeneutical lens, extending beyond Hegelian thought with the premise of 'I am because we are'. This approach is informed by a polycentric global epistemology, seeking to explore the interplay among time, place, and phenomena to identify the various factors contributing to the success of ROSCAs. As noted by Maffei, unlike traditional truth-seeking methods, our epistemology aims to empower the oppressed and marginalized communities. The study utilizes group-based lending mechanisms, specifically ROSCAs, as tools to help combat poverty. Its purpose is to forge connections between past discourses, Western knowledge, and the experiences of developing nations, thereby enriching the universal system of knowledge neutrally and objectively. The diverse experiences of various countries discussed in this text are not confined to frameworks such as experientialism, social constructivism, or feminism. Instead, we aim to shift from the problem of induction represented by 'I think I am' to the more communal understanding of 'I am because we are'. This study seeks to deconstruct and contextualize ROSCAs from the past as a collective initiative rooted in mutual agreement among their members.

3. Theoretical Lens

The iceberg of ROSCAs remains largely unexplored, often viewed merely as vehicles for financial inclusion for those at the bottom of the economic pyramid. There is currently no comprehensive theory addressing the collective savings process that leads to the emergence of ROSCAs. In this study, we employ Tuckman's stages of group formation as a theoretical framework, which includes five stages: (1) forming, (2) storming, (3) norming, (4) performing, and (5) adjourning. We examine these stages in the context of ROSCAs, utilizing a hermeneutical approach to analyse relevant texts. Additionally, we incorporate effectuation theory from entrepreneurship, highlighting how the synergies of group formation facilitate the pooling of collective resources to achieve common goals. The theory of group formation supports leveraging these resources to promote the welfare and financial inclusion of individuals at the bottom of the pyramid. Effectuation operates on several key principles, such as affordable loss – investing only what one is willing to lose – creating conditions for success, initiating financial inclusion with private capital, and fostering effective group norms like regular attendance, meetings, and periodic savings. Through optimal resource utilization and careful management of group dynamics, ROSCAs can significantly address issues of acute poverty and financial exclusion among vulnerable populations.

4. Research Problem

Indigenous financial instruments known as ROSCAs have existed for a long time, helping individuals at the bottom of the economic pyramid achieve their financial goals. These savings vehicles are deeply embedded in local ecosystems and have consistently addressed the needs of the masses. ROSCAs are primarily designed to serve those who are underserved by formal financial institutions. These associations operate under cooperative principles, governed by established norms such as regular meetings and accurate bookkeeping. This study investigates the significance of ROSCAs and the crucial role these internal savings clubs play in rural economies. Employing a hermeneutical approach, I analyse relevant texts to uncover the history and operational dynamics of ROSCAs. Additionally, the study examines a case study of ROSCAs in Ireland, which emphasizes principles of social commitment and mutual savings among community members. Through this analysis, we aim to highlight the impact of ROSCAs on local financial landscapes and community resilience. In this study, a further narrative strategy has been adopted to elucidate the developments in microfinance to understand the evolution and position of ROSCAs as a tool of microfinance (Langley, 1999).

RQ. How do ROSCAs enable the poor to get financially included in the financial system, in Ireland?

5. Literature Review

This study concentrates on exploring the operational dynamics of savings clubs called ROSCAs, a semi-financial institution that provides access to finance to the poor at the bottom of the pyramid. Lieberman and Schroeder (2020) in his research study highlights that microfinance is the financial service that serves the people at the bottom of the pyramid. Earlier literature indicates that microfinance, before 1990, relied on a poverty lending approach characterized by charity and subsidies from banks aimed at promoting financial inclusion for the poor. Poor people do not have any physical collateral and the banks and financial institutions are wary of lending to them. In this regard, the semi-financial institutions based on trust, reciprocity, and social capital play an extremely important role in the financial inclusion of the poor. With excessive dependence on charity and subsidies, the banks started facing the issue of bankruptcy and deterioration in asset quality. Following the liberalization of the 1990s, there emerged a recognized need for sustainable financial practices. To further sustainable finance, the ROSCAs were introduced to facilitate poor people to collect their savings and get access to credit based on physical collateral.

In this context, ROSCAs were identified as a viable solution to include financially marginalized individuals who lack collateral, and to whom banks are often reluctant to lend due to deteriorating asset quality and declining profits. This chapter further explores that microfinance in India is based on four main models: (1) business models focused on profitability and scalability, (2) institutional capacity building, (3) capital markets development, and (4) commercialization of finance.

This literature review starts with defining microfinance, followed by a brief history of microfinance and the historical context of ROSCAs to ensure a discourse

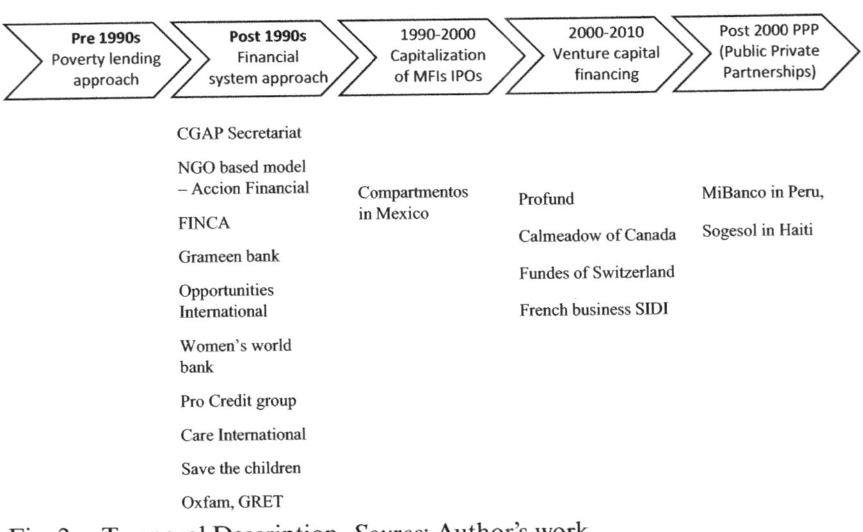

Fig. 2. Temporal Description. *Source*: Author's work.

regarding the various benefits of this semi-formal financial institution in the financial inclusion of the poor. After this, the study discusses the meaning and the history of the semi-formal finance vehicles called ROSCAs that enable poor people to get access to microfinance. Initially, it defines ROSCAs, the process of formation of ROSCAs, and the various benefits of ROSCAs. Finally, the study provides a conceptual framework to define the theory of operational dynamics of semi-formal microfinance institutions (MFIs) called ROSCAs. Microfinance refers to the credit and small ticket-size loans that are extended to the poor people at the bottom of the pyramid for their businesses. Microfinance is touted to be the panacea for poverty reduction (Armendariz et al., 2011). MFIs extend credit that enables poor people to carry out income-generating activities and help poor people to come out of poverty.

In the 1720s, microfinance emerged as a panacea to fight the evils of poverty. Initially, before the 1990s, these vehicles in Ireland were run through donations and charity. However, in the post-liberalization era, these legal institutions were turned into sustainable vehicles that could accept and lend money (Seibel, 2003). These savings vehicles disappeared in the 1950s and this kind of structure originated in Germany to provide loans to poor people. In the 1970s, Mohammed Yunus started a novel microfinance scheme to provide loans under the aegis of Grameen Bank. Grameen Bank was a great success with repayment rates of over 95%. During the era of 1970s and 1990s, many banks were given the priority mandate to lend to the poor. However, MFIs faced major issues in self-sufficiency. This further gave impetus to commercialization and use of external microfinancing in the 1990s, Bank Rakyat Indonesia was the first bank to be commercialized followed by Bancsol, which enabled the banks to achieve financial sustainability.

In 1720, ROSCAs appeared as microfinance vehicles to fight the evil of poverty. Initially, before the 1990s, these vehicles in Ireland were run through charity and donations. In a post-liberalization era, these legal institutions were turned into sustainable vehicles that could accept deposits and lend money (Seibel, 2003). In the 1970s, Mohammad Yunus started a microfinance scheme to provide loans under the aegis of the Grameen Bank. Grameen Bank was a great success with the repayment of over 95%. Many banks were given the priority mandate to lend to the poor. However, MFIs faced major self-sufficiency issue. It further gave rise to the commercialization of microfinance in the 1990s. Bank Rakyat Indonesia was the first bank to be commercialized, followed by Bancosol which emerged as a major vehicle of microfinance.

Analysis of the literature establishes that, as depicted in Fig. 2, before the 1990s, microfinance initiatives such as ROSCAs were primarily funded through charity and donations. In the post-1990s era, MFIs began to secure funding through formal loans from banks and financial institutions. Following 1990, it became common for MFIs to capitalize by raising funds from markets, venture capital, and public–private partnerships (PPPs). During this period, multinational MFIs expanded, including BRAC, Grameen Bank in the USA, the Association for Social Advancement, Compartamos, Kenya's Equity Bank, Scotiabank in the Caribbean, and Commerzbank in Germany, along with the ProCredit Investment Consortium and Citigroup. The development of the microfinance sector also led to the establishment of various institutional frameworks, including standardized financial performance metrics, longitudinal databases, peer groups, rating agencies for MFIs, and capacity-building initiatives, alongside supervisory and monitoring frameworks. With the increased capitalization and fundraising from capital markets, the phase of private venture capital raising emerged. This included the launch of ProFund, which aimed to attract capital from venture capitalists for microfinance financing. Other notable private entities contributing to impact investment include Calmeadow from Canada, Fundes from Switzerland, and the French business SIDI. A significant development in microfinance was the rise of PPPs, exemplified by MiBanco in Peru, Sogesol in Haiti, and fundraising through initial public offerings, such as Compartamos in Mexico.

Even after the commercialization of finance, the banks and financial institutions suffered from mission drift or the conflict between financial sustainability and social sustainability. Thus, the banks and financial institutions were unable to meet the needs of the people at the bottom of the pyramid without compromising the profits and financial returns. In this scenario, group lending in the form of ROSCAs and group lending emerged as the panacea to provide access to finance for the people at the bottom of the pyramid. The study recognizes the experiences of three prominent MFIs: Grameen Bank, Rakyat Indonesia, and Banco Sol in Bolivia. It underscores the significance of microfinance for individuals at the bottom of the pyramid, defining it as a bottom-up approach. Key social entrepreneurs who have made notable contributions to extending financial inclusion at lower socio-economic levels include Muhammad Yunus and BRAC in Bangladesh, Ela Bhatt of SEWA in India, Carlos Daniel and Carlos Labarthe of Compartamos in Mexico, Kimanthi Mutua of K-Rep Bank, and James Mwangi of Equity Bank in Kenya. Another significant institution lending credibility to the microfinance sector is Acleda in Cambodia. The microfinance revolution, particularly in terms of technology, relies on robust financial institutions and innovative solutions that enhance poverty reduction and promote financial inclusion for the poor by leveraging social capital. With the commercialization of microfinance, MFIs have been successful in reducing poverty and promoting better and sustainable livelihoods among the poor (Busch & Rhyne, 2006). This study highlights the factors contributing to the success of microfinance, which extends beyond credit to include services such as savings, insurance, housing rehabilitation, and education loans. The decade following the 1990s saw the emergence of various microfinance models, including the Consultative Group to Assist the Poor Secretariat, which established good practices for microfinance in India. Additionally, networks of organizations, particularly non-governmental organizations (NGOs), were formed to promote the financial and institutional sustainability of MFIs in the country. The model of NGO-supported microfinance originated in the USA and was bolstered by entities such as Accion International, FINCA, Opportunities International, Women's World Banking, and ProCredit Group, along with charitable organizations like Care International, Save the Children, Oxfam, and GRET.

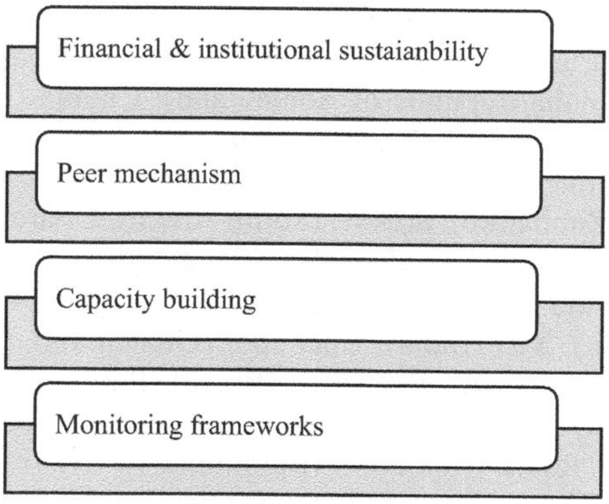

Fig. 3. Themes in ROSCAs. *Source*: Author's work.

Fig. 3 illustrates the major themes emerging in the realm of group lending through ROSCAs. These themes encompass the financial and institutional sustainability of the groups involved. Various studies highlight a notable absence of standardized performance metrics for evaluating the financial performance and institutional capabilities of these groups. Within the context of ROSCAs, peer mechanisms and monitoring are critically important. Effective leadership and supervision are essential for instilling discipline and governance within the group. These four elements – peer monitoring, leadership, discipline, and governance – are key policy drivers. Establishing shared norms and principles through mutual agreements among the members can facilitate the financial sustainability of the groups while preserving profitability and return on investment. ROSCAs imply Rotating Savings and Credit Associations (Geertz, 1962). These savings clubs as they were originally called are aimed at increasing the savings of the people and improving their attitude towards savings. These semi-formal institutions help to increase goal-based and planned savings. These organizations are also called Jesus or contribution clubs and have been aimed at promoting thrift, loan, and saving associations. Geertz is the pioneer of the role and type of ROSCAs. According to him, these semi-formal savings clubs are aimed at promoting the savings of fixed sums at regular intervals. There is a core fund to which all members agree to contribute at regular intervals. The members take turns in receiving the pot or the savings. According to the various types of literature, the oldest form of the ROSCAs existed in China, and Malaysia and were called by the terms Kongsi and hui. ROSCAs have been called by different names such as South Korean ke, Chinese (kai hui), and Taiwanese yokai (biāo huì). ROSCAs are based on solidarity, cohesion, bonds, and relationships among the members (Onda, 2021). Indeed, this method of savings has been used by women for saving all over the world for centuries. These savings methods and vehicles were called France ROSCAs are called tontines and susu in South Africa. In France ROSCAs, the members of the group contribute a fixed sum of money throughout their life, and in susu, the members also receive along with pot the amount of interest. Over time, ROSCAs have been celebrated for financial inclusion, providing access to credit, and improving trust among the members of the group. Money clubs have existed throughout the history of mankind and have been known as Adashe (Nigeria), Ajo (Nigeria), Ayuuto (South Somalia/Republic of Somaliland), Chama (East Africa), Ekub (Ethiopia and Eritrea), Esusu (Nigeria), Gameeya (Egypt), Hagbad (Somalia), Jojuma (Togo), Tontine (Côte d'Ivoire and Cameroon), Noufi (Tunisia), Stockfair (South Africa and Zimbabwe), Stokvel (South Africa), Upato (Tanzania), Arisan (Indonesia), Chit funds (Sri Lanka, Nepal, and India), Dhukuti (Nepal), Hui (China, Thailand, and Vietnam), Kye (South Korea), Paluwagan (Philippines), Tano Moshi (Japan), Visi (India), Cuchubal (Guatemala), Cundina (Mexico), Esu (Bahamas), Junta (Peru), Pandeiros (Brazil), Pardna (Caribbean), Partner head (Caribbean), Quiniela (Peru), Susu (Caribbean), Tanda (Latin America), Gun (Turkey), and Roata (Romania) (Bloommoney, 2023). In underprivileged communities, ROSCAs have emerged as the major tool for development based on a cooperative strategy (Zambrano et al., 2023). ROSCAs are an informal consensus among the members of a community or homogenous set of people to save a pot or kitty, cooperatively by paying a fee or amount periodically (Besley et al., 1993). According to the literature, ROSCAs are found all over the world but are predominant in developing nations. These institutional formats exist to increase the economic well-being of the communities, by increasing the cohesion and solidarity among the homogenous set of people.

All over the world, the ROSCAs predominantly differ according to the number of members, frequency of lending, amount, and the agreed method for the allocation of funds. ROSCAs could be of various kinds such as (1) random, (2) fixed, and (3) bidding. In the random ROSCAs, the permutation and arrangement for the allocation of the pot of savings are determined randomly at the beginning of the cycle (Ardener, 1964). The underprivileged members are unable to get access to the savings and the ROSCAs provide them the alternative to the formal financial institutions. There are various kinds of ROSCAs, which include two main varieties – random ROSCA, fixed sum money ROSCA, and bidding ROSCAs. In random allocation ROSCAs, the chits are randomly drawn to choose the winner from the given cohort. Once an individual has got the pot, he is excluded from the cohort and the process again repeats itself. In the bidding ROSCA, the individual gets the right to receive the savings or the pot based on the promise of higher savings or side payments. Most of the ROSCAs that existed in Kenya and Nairobi were mainly aimed at providing credit to the marginalized women at the bottom of the pyramid. Various studies highlight that the ROSCAs play an important role in reducing the saving time for people who want to avail the credit. The studies further highlight that the order or sequence of getting the pot is decided by the people before the social contract of savings and credit starts to take place.

Traditional banking is aimed at generating money through credit creation and deposit-taking. In this regard, ROSCAs play an extremely important role in augmenting deposit taking (Aliber, 2001). It also enables the credit creation through the rotation of the pot. Indeed, one of the most common issues faced by marginalized women is that they are unable to save money for the rainy day. In this regard, the author of the study (Aliber, 2001) highlights that the ROSCAs help the members to save money without the risk of withdrawing the money. Benda (2013) in his research study highlights that many thinkers and economists have highlighted the importance of ROSCA are self-sustaining economic system, the organizations that are used to provide livelihood to the people, and the community initiatives are based on trust, reciprocity, and integrity. These organizations serve as the common thread for people who are interested in informal, localized cooperation among the people. The simple tricks like saving the money in a cash box with a slit and saving the money in a mud pot are all examples of how money is rotated and used for lending to the members of the societies. ROSCAs play an important role in promoting voluntary savings among the people in the nations, with the complexity of the system, language barriers, negative experiences, and cultural and religious reasons (Light, 1972; Light & Zhong, 1995). Also, the savings groups are formed on the principle of relationships of trust and reciprocity (Light & Dana, 2013). Zainuddin and Yasin (2020) in their study highlight that the microfinance revolution has paved the way for access to finance for all. The study further substantiates that microfinance in several forms has existed for time immemorial and saving clubs have existed for a long time in Asia and Europe. Srnec and Hejkrlík (2005) in their research study highlight that the saving clubs and cooperative forms of groups for saving can be classified as those related to the Government, those in the private sector, NGOs, cooperatives, and informal money lenders. Bousalam and Hamzaoui (2015) in their study highlight the importance of the ROSCAs in promoting access to finance and microfinance for socially excluded minorities. Moreover, ROSCAs are based on institutional theory and these formal structures have different characteristics such as access, information, incentives, and rules and norms. Thus, ROSCAs play an important role in inculcating the habit of compulsory saving among the members of the group. Ito (2003) further highlights that the various social interactions are the main factor that impacts the formation of the savings clubs. Schreiner (2000) in his research study highlights that the informal finance ROSCAs help to lower transaction costs, supply savings services and loans, and socially self-enforced contracts.

Fig. 4 illustrates several developments in the realm of microfinance, including capacity building, digitization, financial literacy, and the use of cultural media and promotional strategies to enhance the adoption of ROSCAs for savings among marginalized communities. In the past decade, the environment for banking has

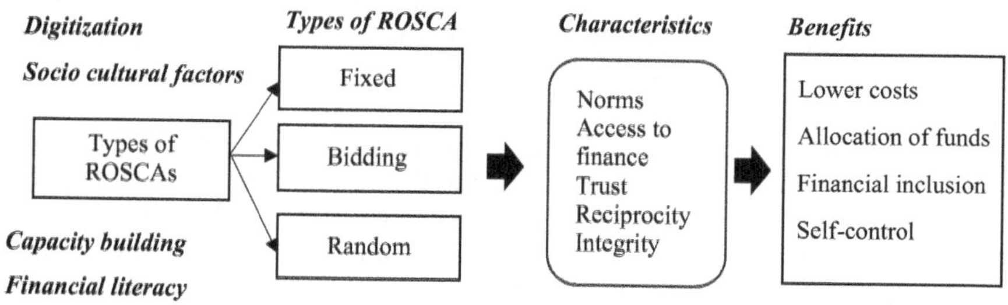

Fig. 4. Types, Characteristics, and Benefits of ROSCAs. *Source*: Author's work.

changed tremendously with the advent of technology. With the microfinance revolution and the introduction of the technology in form of digital currencies and digitization, the groups have higher resilience and institutional sustainability to combat the challenges. To achieve the objectives of sustainable growth through the deployment of ROSCAs, there is a need for capacity building and social intermediation. Also, there is a need for financial literacy and digital literacy to enable the members of the group to take advantage of group lending through ROSCAs.

There are three types of ROSCAs, each grounded in principles of trust, reciprocity, and integrity, enabling members to access microfinance by adhering to established norms. These groups contribute to lowering costs, effectively allocating funds, and promoting financial inclusion through self-control.

In the lower strata of society, Grameen banks and self-help groups play an important role in financial inclusion (Light, 2021). Misati's (2008) study highlights that the ties and relationships that exist among the members of the group lead to the success of the ROSCAs. Moreover, the social environment of the group has a vast impact on the functioning of the savings clubs and associations. Dagnelie and Lemay-Boucher (2012) in their study highlight that the ROSCAs are primarily aimed at addressing the commitment issue. Thus the people who are unable to save money and have self-control problems are helped through savings clubs and rotating savings and credit associations. Moreover, according to the author, ROSCAs help women bargain with men for their share of autonomy and wealth. Thus, ROSCAs have emerged as a tool for empowerment and autonomy. Smets (1998) highlights the importance of ROSCA for extending the psychological and socio-cultural benefits. Bouman (2016) is an example of balanced reciprocity and a vehicle to facilitate the purchase of the consumer durable. Hossein (2015) in his research work highlights that peer-to-peer lending also enables the women at the bottom of the pyramid to provide aid to their family members, friends, and community members. Smets (2000) in the research study highlights that ROSCAs provide security in accessing finance from formal sources as compared to informal sources of finance. Francis (2018) in his research study highlights the important use of savings technology like ROSCAs to promote group savings among the members of the group. It also highlights the importance of self-control to drive the demand for collective savings. Bouman (2016) in his research study has highlighted the importance of ROSCAs in mitigating various issues such as record keeping, delayed payments, collection, distribution, and the safety of money. Thus, social innovations such as ROSCAs play an extremely important role in promoting the institutional sustainability of various financial organizations. Karlan and Morduch (2010) in their research study highlight the importance of the ROSCAs to reduce the consumption of regretted items or high lifestyle goods and services. According to the study, collective savings provide convenience, reduce risk, and extend simplicity in promoting savings among the members of the group. Also, according to the author, direct marketing plays an extremely important role in promoting forced savings and collecting the deposits from the members. Further, the study argues that financial literacy has a positive impact on the saving potentials of the members, who are part of the savings clubs and ROSCAs. Also, the study argues that peer influence has an important impact on savings through the ROSCAs and the savings clubs. Moreover, the study argues that the savings in the groups are driven by social norms and macro-level policies. Further, the study argues that the technology solutions have a significant impact on savings through the savings clubs and the ROSCAs. Further, the existing literature highlights that the commitment savings products might lead to empowerment among the members of the group. Levenson and Besley (1996) in their study highlight that the income stability among the members plays an extremely important role in promoting participation in ROSCAs. Guha and Gupta (2005) in their study highlight that microcredit institutions like ROSCAs play an extremely important role in income generation, repayment of loans through adherence to group norms, peer monitoring, regular loan repayments, and reduction in the rate of default. El-Gamal et al. (2014) in their study highlight that ROSCAs enable higher repayment rates and ROSCAs that are bank-insured have a higher capability to achieve a higher rate of financial inclusion. Bauchet and Larsen (2017) have shown that ROSCAs run the risk of higher default, by availing of the pot savings early in the life cycle of the group and defaulting on payment. However, the existing social capital and homogeneity in the group enable higher profitable savings and emergency credit in the group. Fang et al. (2015) in their research study discuss the importance of credit markets in furthering the role of ROSCAs in promoting the sharing of risk. From the study, it is established that ROSCAs with a perfect credit market, where the rate of borrowing is the same as the rate of lending, leads to improvement in the financial health of members. Whereas the ROSCAs in an economic environment with imperfect markets, where the rate of borrowing is not as rate of saving, leads to improvement in the financial health of the members. Kedir and Ibrahim (2011) highlight that the ROSCAs are significantly impacted by the characteristics of the women members. Etang et al. (2011) in their research study highlight that trust plays an extremely important role in ROSCAs. Levenson and Besley (1996) in their research study highlight that ROSCA witnesses the highest level of participation by high-income households and is an alternative saving vehicle for households. Calomiris and Rajaraman (1998) in their research study emphasize that the ROSCAs play an extremely important role as the insurance providers. Fang and Ke (2006) in their research study assert that even in the presence of formal credit markets, ROSCAs provide the instrument to share the contemporaneous shocks among them. Many studies also substantiate that the ROSCAs facilitate ease in access to housing finance and also access to finance from the informal sector like money lenders. Acquah and Dahal (2018) in their research study highlight that the factors that impact the lending from the ROSCAs include the size of ROSCA and diversity in employment sectors. Rosca et al. (2020) in their research study highlight that women have a special place in promoting entrepreneurship. During the venture creation process, women entrepreneurs show a lot of resilience and transition between causation and effectuation. Adams and Von Pischke (1992) in his research study highlights that the ROSCAs are the informal finance organizations that help to overcome various challenges in this domain by economizing the transaction costs, lengthening the term structure, and managing the risk effectively. Kabuya (2015) in his research study highlights that ROSCAs play an extremely important role in poverty reduction. Various studies highlight that the concept of ROSCAs has evolved over the period and these are extremely efficient vehicles for savings (Jahangir et al., 2023). Chen (2016) in his study highlights that microfinance helps in maintaining economic stability, improving the ability of households by improving social capital, and enhancing the role of women in organizations. Nwosu (2008) in his research study highlights that the integrated model of the Grameen Bank and ROSCAs play an extremely important role in raising capital from the markets, which acts as an important vehicle in raising newer capital and reducing poverty. Altuntas et al. (2019) in their research study highlight that membership with the ROSCAs helps to augment the consumption among the members of the savings groups and leads to a higher level of trust, leading to a higher level of risk management tools in the hands of the savers. Armendariz et al. (2011) in their research study highlight that the microfinance through ROSCAs indeed helps to promote the cause of women, by designing the products that are suited to the needs of the women. Ojukwu et al. (2021) in their research study highlight that ROSCAs and the savings clubs indeed help to enhance the financial performance of the small and medium enterprises. Ahn et al. (2017) in their research study highlight that at times ROSCAs are used as vehicles for allocating disproportionate amount of capital to the rich category of people. Thompson (2016) in his research study highlights that the ROSCAs are defined by the spirit of reciprocity and social interaction. Benda (2013) in his study substantiates that the ROSCAs are more inclusive and lead to higher level of community development, reciprocity, and solidarity. Shoaib and Siddiqui (2020) in the research study highlight that the ROSCAs and savings clubs cater to the need for existence, relatedness among the people from the lower and middle-class community. Satkunasingam and Shanmugam (2006) in their research study highlight that the savings clubs and ROSCAs are mostly used by the women as the method of forced savings and insurance against the uncertainty. Ibrahim (2016) in his research study highlights the role of various factors for the low rate of participation among the members of the ROSCAs. These factors include lack of financial services, economic system, language barriers, negative experiences with financial markets, and cultural religious reasons. Tchuindjo (1999) highlights the importance of ROSCA in economies and the role they play in day-to-day functioning of the business. It also highlights the practice of use of sticks to collect and keep an account of the savings. For the purpose of savings, the study highlights the use of the sticks, long sticks, larger sticks, pointed sticks, short sticks, and thin sticks in keeping an account of the savings that are collected from the members of the group. Warnier (1985) in the research study highlights that the ROSCAs are the backbone of the financial system and economy. Ojukwu et al. (2021) in their research study highlight that the ROSCAs and the solidarity groups are based on reciprocity, solidarity, and savings to name a few. Zambrano et al. (2003) in their study highlight that the saving groups and the saving clubs enable the members of the group to access some of the financial and cultural benefits. This saving vehicle is primarily beneficial for the people from the lower section of society. Rugimbana and Spring (2009) in their research study highlight that the diversified system like ROSCAs can help to increase the alignment between MFIs and promoting global and local interface. Canup (2016) in the research study highlights that the ROSCAs are able to leverage their cultural factors and reduction of the transaction costs. Hossein (2020) in his research study highlights that the ROSCAs serve an extremely important purpose of achieving the cause of self-determination. Hamzaoui and Bousalam (2015) in their research study emphasize the role of this microfinance initiative to avail the microfinance on the basis of prior cognition, with the aid of bank as guarantor. They also emphasize the role of microfinance savings clubs as vehicle for promoting savings, risk sharing, and integration of financially excluded households. Umuhire (n.d.) in his study highlights that the individuals who affiliate to the microfinance vehicles like ROSCAs are essentially catering to the people who have been excluded by the financial system (Besley et al., 1993; Gugerty, 2005). The study also highlights the importance of the Lewis model that refers to the dualistic characteristic of developing economies. Ajija and Siddiqui (2021) in their research study highlight that the ROSCAs and other informal saving clubs indeed help in the accumulation of the durable assets and besides that the peer monitoring further helps in the regulation of the savings and finance function in a savings group. Mushuku and Mayisa (2014) in their research study highlight that the ROSCAs have enabled the members to accumulate savings and start a new business. However, as per the study these saving associations face various challenges such as defaulting members and mismanagement of the fund. Thus, in a savings club indeed the members are prone to the risk of moral hazard. Handa and Kirton (1999) further highlight the importance of the size of the ROSCA in the success of the group and the role of the leaders in promoting the sustainability of the ROSCAs. Joshi et al. (2020) further highlight the importance of the ROSCAs in enabling the poor at the bottom of pyramid to cope up with the distressing circumstances and disasters.

6. Discussion and Analysis

From the analysis of the various texts, important themes that emerged were: (1) shared norms and self-control, (2) dynamic incentives, and (3) formation of the group. The theory of group formation suggests that a group passes through various stages which include: (a) storming, (b) norming, (c) forming, and (d) performing.

6.1. Storming Stage

The goal of savings clubs, including ROSCAs, is to foster a culture of saving among individuals who struggle to save independently. These groups enable members to save collectively, with the added benefit of providing a form of financial support or insurance for those at the lower end of the economic spectrum. One of the key challenges faced by financially excluded individuals is understanding and staying motivated to save. In a pot-saving system, participants who lack saving habits come together to contribute a fixed amount of money into a communal pool.

Each member takes turns receiving the entire amount in the pool, known as the 'hand' or 'pot' at scheduled intervals. After every member has received their share, the cycle begins anew. This collective approach not only encourages saving but also provides a structured way to access lump sums of money, acting as both a savings mechanism and a support system. The individuals participate in ROSCAs to overcome difficulties in access to formal finance, conflict in personal relations, and lack of mutual insurance. Individuals generally join ROSCAs to facilitate the purchase of a high-ticket item or consumer durable product costing a certain sum of money, which they cannot afford from their income y. Besley et al. (1993) in their study from a utilitarian standpoint discuss savings as the redistribution of the income y earned during the period to consume today. In this study, I assert that individuals who affiliate with ROSCAs are individuals, who lack self-control and seem to be habitual to frittering away money. These individuals cannot access the banking and credit market, due to the lack of collateral and any credit history. In this study, I further assert that the Government of India scheme of Pradhan Mantri Jan Dhan Yojana has provided universal access to banking for all. But still, the members of the unorganized sector do not have the motivation or social disposition to save. In this regard, the study aims to explore how cultural factors in different parts of the world have facilitated incremental savings for people who lack the attitude to save. Thus, ROSCAs appear as a panacea for individuals who want to immediately purchase consumer durable but do not have the means to purchase them same. In the case of ROSCAs, the major assumption is that the members of the group do not earn any form of interest or there is no discounting. In this regard, let's assume that the utility of income y today is a logarithmic function, represented by log y. In this case, the utility function for y can be expressed as a function of consumption today and owning an asset that generates some income tomorrow. Let's assume that the individual earning income y, decides to save α today. From the analysis of the various texts, we discover that the individuals who set out to consume have an increasing utility function. This implies that the utility for consumption keeps on increasing with each additional unit of consumption but at a decreasing rate. That implies the extra unit of consumption gives less utility as compared to the previous unit. Individuals who become members of ROSCAs or rotating saving groups and credit associations, in general, are averse. That is they wish to reduce their risk from uncertain events that can take place in the future. Thus, a utility for an individual who earns y of his income today is

$$\log y = \alpha x + \gamma y$$

where α is consumption today and γ is income from an asset that generates income.

The assumption here is that

$$\gamma y = y - \alpha x \tag{1}$$

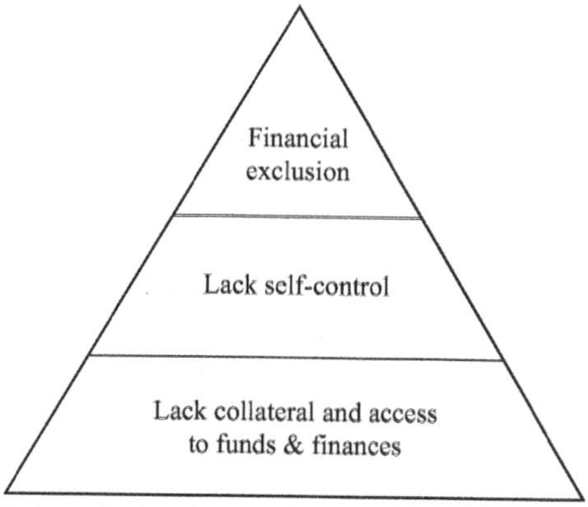

Fig. 5. Characteristics of Members Who Form ROSCAs.

Upon analysis, the evident solution is that the utility of current income is influenced by both consumption and the earning potential of income derived from assets that are partially financed by today's savings, to the extent of *yy*. This study assumes that the utility of income increases over time, even in the absence of discounting or interest payments. This is because individuals at the lower end of the income spectrum, who lack access to banking services, experience rising utility from asset ownership. In ROSCAs, members come from similar income brackets and neighbourhoods, which allows for risk sharing through diversification among the group.

The data analysis reveals that ROSCAs serve as a savings mechanism for individuals who are excluded from traditional banking services and struggle with self-control. Additionally, these individuals typically lack collateral and access to formal financial resources. Fig. 5 provides the details regarding the characteristics of the members who form ROSCAs. There are various objectives for forming the groups for savings and credit. These groups are aimed at achieving the objective of increasing the savings and wealth of the members, depending on various factors such as (1) affiliation to low-income communities and (2) affiliation to high-income communities. The members from the low-income communities join these communities to get access to credit and banking. On the other hand, the members of the high-income group join these communities to get over their addiction to excessive savings and use the money for productive purposes, including social welfare.

6.2. Norming Stage

The norming stage involves crucial decisions about membership size and the guiding principles, or 'panch sutras', necessary for the group's sustainability. Winston (1980) emphasizes the role of self-control in maintaining the viability of ROSCAs. These groups often face significant challenges related to both institutional and financial sustainability. Institutional sustainability issues arise when members fail to adhere to group norms, such as regular savings, leading to the potential dissolution of the group. Stroz's work highlights how savings clubs help members stick to their saving schedules and optimize consumption within budget constraints. In contrast, members lacking internal discipline might rely on external constraints to manage their savings and account balances. Economic models also address the role of addiction in financial management. Research indicates that ROSCAs can reduce dependence on addictive behaviours by enforcing adherence to group norms. Non-compliance with these norms is a major issue, often resulting in diminished financial autonomy and sustainability among members. Effective savings plans and adherence to these plans are essential for fostering good financial habits. The literature suggests that dynamic incentives play a key role in promoting disciplined saving. Such incentives may include stringent penalties for non-compliance and the option to access funds out of turn in times of need. John Cochrane's work on utility maximization underscores the importance of delaying consumption today for greater benefits tomorrow. ROSCAs address this by providing incentives, such as interest on savings, which encourage members to forgo immediate consumption in favour of future gains. Dynamic incentives, therefore, are crucial in ensuring financial sustainability and adherence to group norms within ROSCAs. Ambec and Treich (2007) in their research study highlight that people join the ROSCAs to address the problem of self-control and self-commitment. Most of the individual members do not have adequate self-control in order be able to save the money for the future. In this regard, the members look forward to maximizing their utility, and the aggregate utility is the sum of utilities of the different individuals discounted at a certain rate of interest. For this study, we assume that the utility of the savings and consumption for the individuals is not the same over the different periods and is different for different periods. Gugerty et al., (2014) further clarifies that since the preference for savings and consumption is not the same across the period. In his research study, he assumes four periods: period 1, period 2, period 3, and period 4. In period 4, the demand for goods by the consumer is not the same as the demand in period 3. Due to the lack of a commitment agreement, individuals find it extremely difficult to save money. This is due to the fact that the members of the group lack self-control and self-commitment. A mechanism like ROSCAs provides a commitment to provide access to funds in the period, in which they need the funds as per the time inconsistency principle. For, let's assume that there are two members in the group: member 1 and member 2. Let's assume member 1 needs the funds in period 1 and member 2 needs the fund in period 2. ROSCA will take the funds from member 1 and member 2 and provide the funds to member 1 in period 1 and to member 2 in period 2. Thus, the members in the group face time inconsistency, and the savings clubs and rotating savings and credit associations enable the members to get access to funds, when they need it the most.

From the analysis of Fig. 6, it is clear that the primary challenge individuals face is determining the optimal consumption path: deciding whether to consume now or save for future consumption. In this context, savings clubs and ROSCAs play a crucial role. Excessive saving can lead to an addiction-like behaviour, where individuals might save excessively or hoard money, potentially reducing the overall utility of their savings. In situations where special consumption needs arise,

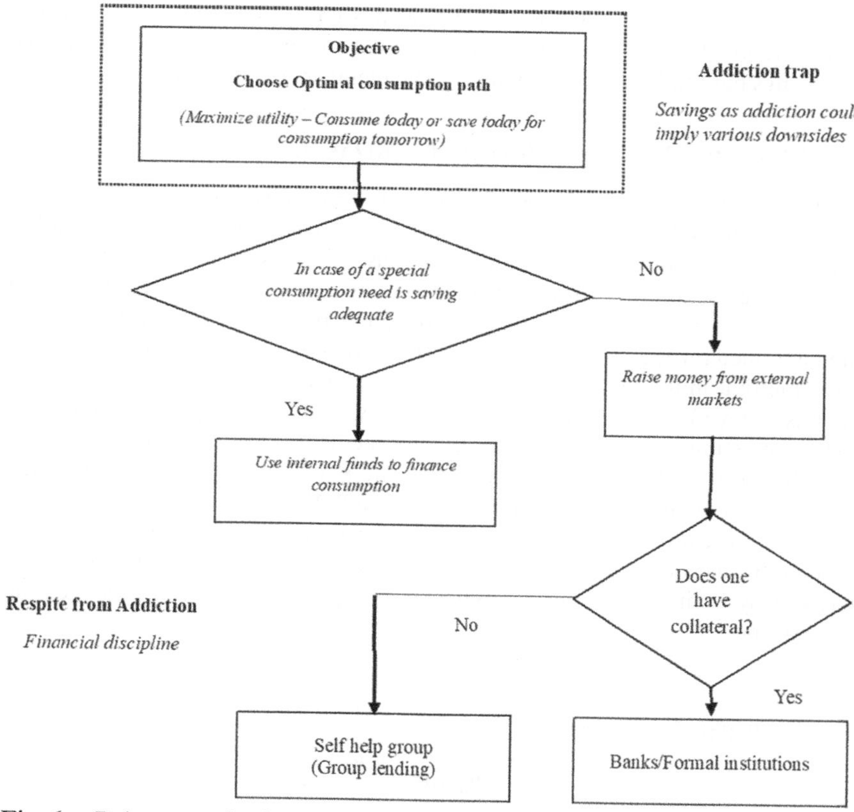

Fig. 6. Relevance of Joint Liability Groups in Optimizing Consumption.
Source: Author's work.

individuals may need to access external funds. Those without sufficient collateral often struggle to secure loans or credit from traditional financial institutions. ROSCAs and savings clubs address this gap by providing essential social capital and leveraging peer mechanisms to encourage disciplined saving and collective financial support. Many of the women from the married households might be joining the ROSCAs to avoid conflict with the other members of the households. The women in the households might be subject to some form of domestic violence, which includes the forced stealing away of the resources and money by the in-laws and the households. In this scenario, the ROSCAs come to the aid of the members of the group to promote savings.

6.3. Forming Stage

As far as forming groups is concerned, these could be formed through the (1) random method, (2) bidding method, and (3) fixed method. As per the literature, the ROSCAs or the rotating savings and credit associations are formed by the members who are known to each other in the form of relatives, friends, neighbours, or relatives. Ardener (1964) in his study highlights the importance of good leadership in the formation of the savings groups and credit associations. Stewart (2007) further adds that the members of the group mutually decide how the savings have to be distributed among the members of the group.

6.4. A Cognitive Model of Self-control in ROSCAs

In ROSCA, the members who become part of the savings groups are facing scarcity of resources. By nature, individuals are interested in consuming today rather than consuming tomorrow. Towards this cause, there is a need for psychological processes to train the automatic pathways and create controlled pathways to ensure savings by the members of the group. The pre-frontal cortex in the brain can be trained through stimulus and incentives to exercise restraint. In this model, I assume that individuals are controlled, as denoted by c, and with the control there is a payoff x that is associated. Similarly, with the temptations that arise due to the stimulus and cues in the environment, there is a negative payoff y. The objective of ROSCAs is to maximize the payoff of the members through control of the environment. The objective of the ROSCAs is to maximize the payoff given the controlled environment. The controlled environment in ROSCAs refers to the use of the agreement among the members of the group to contribute periodically to the pool of resources and by compulsion, irrespective of the time value of money:

$$P(\text{Payoff} / \text{Control}) = \frac{P\left(\dfrac{Control}{Payoff}\right)}{P\left(\dfrac{Control}{Payoff}\right) + P\left(\dfrac{Temptation}{payoff}\right)} \tag{2}$$

Temptation in the above formula refers to the automatic pathways and cues that compel the members to consume the resources today rather than saving them for tomorrow. Payoff refers to the money that is the pot savings linked with an agreement to save periodically. And negative payoff refers to the penalties that are associated with dissavings. The objective of the members in a ROSCA is to maximize *U(Payoff, Control)* and minimize *U(Negative payoff, Temptation)*, where *U* refers to the utility in the model. ROSCAs are primarily aimed at maximizing this payoff for the benefit of the members of the groups. From the analysis of the literature, it is found that ROSCAs help to increase the consumption of durable goods and thus, the ability to accumulate capital for their consumption (Besley & Levenson, 1996). These saving institutions and clubs are generally based on mutual trust and social networks, which allow them to make large capital investments or purchase capital goods (Light & Gold, 1999).

6.5. Effectual Approach to Microfinance

Fig. 7 provides the effectual model for the operation of ROSCAs.

The effectual approach is the theory of entrepreneurship based on whatever is available at hand. The collectives and the groups are based on collective efforts

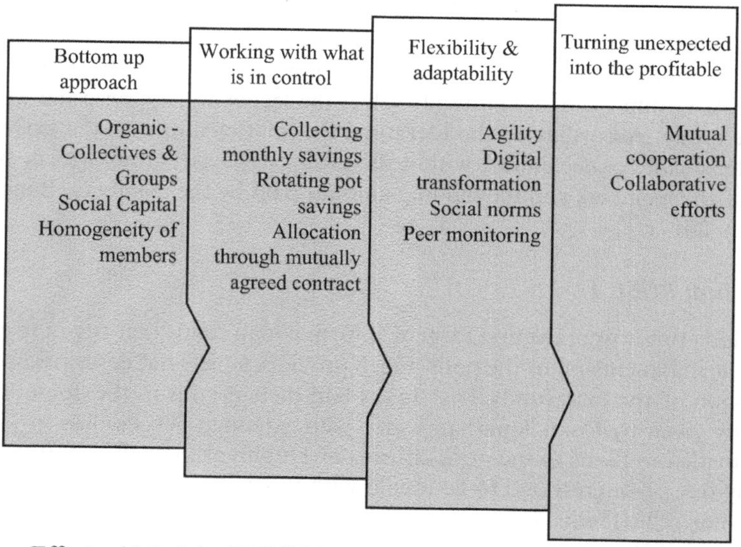

Fig. 7. Effectual Model of ROSCAs. *Source*: Author's work.

and are organic structures that enable the members with limited resources or no physical collateral to get access to resources. They use extremely innovative ways to form groups based on some form of homogeneity and social capital, such as existing relationships among the members. Based on trust and reciprocity of promise, the members come together to form groups. Most of the members are not literate, and thus, they create a mutual agreement to keep an account of all the savings and loans. One such novel mechanism is the use of sticks to keep an account of the savings and loans given to members and repayments made. Further, these groups also use the peer mechanism to monitor each other. Each member promises to pay an equal amount periodically and if one member defaults after taking the hand all the others will not be able to get their share of the hand. This moral hazard among the members is reduced through peer monitoring. Digital technologies and transformation are used to monitor the working of the groups. Through financial inclusion and training, ROSCAs have emerged as a tool for achieving the unachievable by collaborative efforts. Baland and Anderson (2002) in their study highlight that ROSCAs are mostly used by women participants to protect their savings from their husbands.

6.6. Case Studies

6.6.1. Taiwanese ROSCA

Bidding ROSCAs are most prevalent in the Asia Pacific. One such form of joint liability group exists in Taiwan. According to the various literature, ROSCAs are based on peer pressure and social sanctions, and the relationship among the members is of utmost importance for the success of group lending. Similarly, as per the literature, leaders in a joint liability group are young, less educated, individualistic, and live in rural areas. According to the literature, the social connections with the leader strongly impacted the behaviour in bidding ROSCA. Group members mutually select the leader to supervise the working of the group. According to the literature, the relationship with the leader and not the social connectedness within the group impacts the repayment behaviour of the members and the bidding amount paid by the members (Bauchet & Larsen, 2017).

6.6.2. Irish ROSCA

Irish loan funds were the first form of informal loan funds that began to ensure the financial inclusion of the poor. Fig. 8 provides a pictorial description of the evolution of the loan funds. Irish loans had their origins in the donation and subsidy given by Dean Jonathan Swift, who extended 500 Pounds in 1720 to be provided as loans to the poor citizens of Dublin at the value of 10 pounds, totally free of interest and to be repaid with the personal security of a known person or peer (Hollis & Sweetman, 1996). The Dublin Musical Society, in the 1740s and 1750s, was urged to make the loans on the same system as the Dean Jonathan. This Dublin Society started providing loans at the same terms and conditions as the Dean Jonathan Swift. This was the first stage or origin of Irish loan funds. Thus, in the first stage, the main phases of ROSCAs were: (1) small loans, (2) no physical collateral, (3) enforcement by law to recover dues, and (4) co co-signatories. This process enabled Dean Jonathan Swift to avoid the problem of information asymmetry, that is, moral hazard and adverse selection.

Yet in 1822, the other committee gave pounds 55,000 to establish the Irish Reproductive Loan fund. In 1823, a loan fund bill was passed to regulate microfinance in Ireland, with a regulation in 1824 to form joint-stock banking companies. This paved the way for banking through branches, which accepted deposits, financed short-term credit, and purchased government bonds. The legislation brought about a culture of payment of interest on deposits and standardized rules for accounting and stationary. As part of this legislation managers and trustees were freed from personal liability. The board was responsible for supervision, monitoring, and inspection of funds. Ultimately, in 1824, though the government did not financially back the board, it provided the space to the board in the Castle. Thus, in 1823, microfinance which was donation and charity-based, was regulated and the loan funds and committees started charging interest on loan extended. Thus, till the 1720s, the business of microfinance which was based on charity became formalized as a financial institution. The dream of sustainable finance seems alluring.

Moreover, in 1836 and 1838, the loan fund board, which was established to regulate and monitor the funds, became a beacon of hope to the poor. Ireland, as a country through regulation, made an immense contribution to increase the penetration of microfinance through increasing disclosure requirements and requirements for supervision and monitoring. Within the ambit of this bill, the information on loans was published in annual reports. The introduction of the preference for creditor's rights and freeing the managers from personal liability ensured better regulation of these ROSCAs. As per the literature, till the setting up of the Dublin Musical Society, most of the banks operating were private and limited in scope. Thus, 1836 was the era of the creation of the banking commission.

In 1843, the interest rate ceilings were introduced in a new interest rate legislation to reduce the interest rate on deposits from 6% to 5% and interest on loans from 13.6% to 8.8%. However, in 1845, many banks made a foray into the traditional banking business to conduit their savings. Agricultural and Commercial Bank and Provident Banks started making loans to the poor and the needy. Despite the setting up of new banks, institutions started facing defaults and deterioration in asset quality, which further led to the prominence and dominance of the loan funds in catering to the credit needs of the poor. Loan funds faced an overlap with the informal moneylenders. These loan funds were formed by the people who knew each other and catered to the needs of the borrowers who had no source of credit other than the money lenders. However, many studies indicate that though these loan funds were sufficiently regulated and there was a lack of diversification as compared to the commercial banks. In terms of the lending function of these loan funds, they had an extremely strong peer mechanism to overcome the adverse selection. All the borrowers were required to be referred by their peers and were known to each other mitigating the probability of adverse selection. The contract of lending in these loan funds was enforceable in a court of law. In addition to legal recourse, the funding charitable societies had a moral recourse on these funds through peer monitoring and peer enforcement to reduce the moral hazard among the members of the group. However, once a great source of financial inclusion, these loan funds dwindled rapidly due to reckless money lending and lack of corporate governance. Thus, 1836–1843 was the stage of the creation of the bank commission.

Post-1843, in the 1880s, the loan funds started seeing a gradual decline due to probable procyclicality. Procyclicality in the management of the loans given by these groups led to their demise. With increasing competition, the loan funds were unable to be sustainably viable. Many of these loan funds suffered from moral hazard, lack of regulations, and negligence by the managers. In 1914, the Report of the Departmental Committees on Agricultural Credit propagated that many of the loan funds were found guilty of abuse of power, lack of supervision, moral hazard, and illegal extractions and thus were recommended to be closed and their capital to be transferred to the cooperative society.

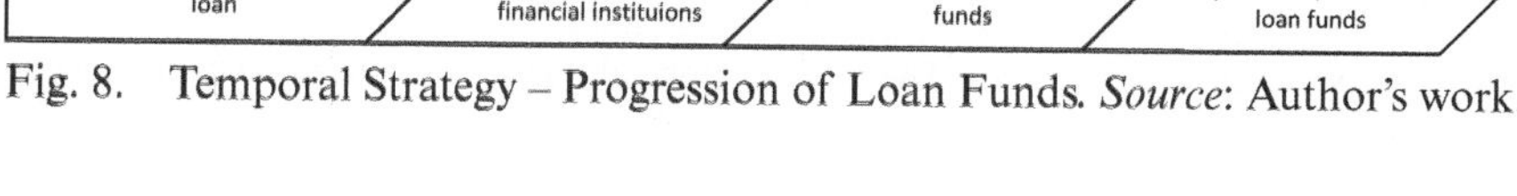

Fig. 8. Temporal Strategy – Progression of Loan Funds. *Source*: Author's work.

7. Conclusion

Group lending plays an extremely important role in promoting financial inclusion among the members of the marginalized society. ROSCAs are the oldest form of semi-financial institutions that have played an extremely important role in promoting solidarity and access to finance for the people at the bottom of the pyramid. Further, the solidarity and existence of the peer mechanism are at the heart of these semi-financial institutions. Fixed, Bidding, and Random ROSCAs have been instrumental in furthering the cause of financial inclusion in the underdeveloped part of the world. In the random ROSCAs, the members of the group are selected randomly through the chit-based system. Such ROSCAs existed in Taiwan, Ireland, and other parts of the world in these semi-financial institutions. During the 18th century, loan funds saw a decline due to the procyclicality among the bankers. This procyclicality led to the demise of the loan funds and the semi-finance institutions such as ROSCAs. However, ROSCAs have played an important role in promoting the financial inclusion of poor women through better self-control, adherence to group norms, and financial discipline.

References

Acquah, J. K., & Dahal, R. (2018). ROSCAs as lenders of last resort after financial crises: Lessons from Indonesia. *Journal of International Development*, *30*(7), 1223–1239.

Adams, D. W., & Von Pischke, J. D. (1992). Microenterprise credit programs: Déjà vu. *World Development*, *20*, 1463–1470. https://doi.org/10.1016/0305-750X(92)90066-5

Ahn, D., Kang, W., Kim, K. K., & Shin, H. (2017). Analysis and design of microfinance services: A case of ROSCA. *The Engineering Economist*, *62*(3), 197–230.

Ajija, S. R., & Siddiqui, A. I. (2021). Impact of joining Rotating Savings and Credit Association (ROSCA) on household assets in Indonesia. *The Journal of Developing Areas*, *55*(3), 205–216.

Aliber, M. (2001). Rotating savings and credit associations and the pursuit of self-discipline: A case study in South Africa. *African Review of Money Finance and Banking*, 51–73.

Altuntas, M., Erlbeck, A., & Huber, F. (2019). The effect of ROSCA participation on microinsurance purchase: Evidence from Indonesia. *Zeitschrift für die Gesamte Versicherungswissenschaft*, *108*, 141–163.

Ambec, S., & Treich, N. (2007). ROSCAs as financial agreements to cope with self-control problems. *Journal of Development Economics*, *82*(1), 120–137.

Ardener, S. (1964). The comparative study of rotating credit associations. *Journal of the Royal Anthropological Institute*, *94*(2), 201–229.

Armendariz, B., Labie, M., & Guérin, I. (2011). *The gender of finance and lessons for microfinance*. World Scientific.

Bauchet, J., & Larsen, V. (2017). ROSCA composition and repayment: Evidence from Taiwanese bidding ROSCAs. *The Journal of Development Studies*, *54*(9), 1483–1495.

Benda, C. (2013). Community rotating savings and credit associations as an agent of well-being: A case study from northern Rwanda. *Community Development Journal*, *48*(2), 232–247.

Besley, T., Coate, S., & Loury, G. (1993). The economics of rotating savings and credit associations. *The American Economic Review*, *83*(4), 792–810.

Besley, T., & Levenson, A. (1996). The role of informal finance in household capital accumulation. *The Economic Journal*, *106*(434), 39–59.

Bloommoney. (2023). *Names for money clubs around the world*. https://bloommoney.co/learning-hub/names-for-roscas-around-the-world

Bouman, F. J. (1979). *The RoSCA: Financial technology of an informal savings and credit institution in developing economies*.

Bousalam, I., & Hamzaoui, M. (2015, October 30). *Bank-based investing RoSCA for Islamic finance: A new alternative to drain households savings and reduce financial exclusion*. Munich Personal RePEc Archive. MPRA Paper 67510, University Library of Munich, Germany.

Busch, B., & Rhyne, E. (2006). *The growth of commercial microfinance 2004–2006*. Council of Microfinance Equity Funds.

Calomiris, C. W., & Rajaraman, I. (1998). The role of ROSCAs: Lumpy durables or event insurance? *Journal of Development Economics*, *56*(1), 207–216.

Canup, E. M. (2016). *Entrepreneurs and informal finance in Kenya* [Doctoral dissertation, Monterey, California: Naval Postgraduate School].

Chen, Y. (2016). *Rethinking of design excellence via building performance: With particular reference to the RIBA Award-winning schools in the UK* [PhD thesis]. University of Nottingham.

Dagnelie, O., & Lemay-Boucher, P. (2012). Rosca participation in Benin: A commitment issue. *Oxford Bulletin of Economics and Statistics*, *74*, 235–252. https://doi.org/10.1111/j.1468-0084.2011.00641.x

El-Gamal, M., El-Komi, M., Karlan, D., & Osman, A. (2014). Bank-insured RoSCA for microfinance: Experimental evidence in poor Egyptian villages. *Journal of Economic Behavior & Organization*, *103*, S56–S73.

Etang, A., Fielding, D., & Knowles, S. (2011). Trust and ROSCA membership in rural Cameroon. *Journal of International Development*, *23*(4), 461–475.

Fang, H., & Ke, R. (2006). *The insurance role of Rosca in the presence of credit markets*. Yale University.

Fang, H., Ke, R., & Zhou, L. A. (2015). *Rosca meets formal credit market*. National Bureau of Economic Research.

Francis, E. (2018). *Essays in the economics of development and behavior*. UC Santa Cruz.

Geertz, C. (1962). The rotating credit association: A "Middle Rung" in development. *Economic Development and Cultural Changes*, *10*(3), 241–273.

Gugerty, M. K. (2005). *You can't save alone: Testing theories of Rotating Savings and Credit Associations*. Evans School of Public Affairs, University of Washington.

Gugerty, M. K., Biscaye, P., Anderson, L., True, Z., & Clark, C. (2014). *Self-help groups in development: A review of evidence from South Asia and Sub-Saharan Africa* (EPAR Technical Report No. 283). Evans School Policy Analysis & Research Group. https://evans.uw.edu/policy-impact/epar/research/self-help-groups-development-review-evidence-south-asia-and-sub-saharan

Guha, S., & Gupta, G. (2005). Microcredit for income generation: The role of RoSCA. *Economic and Political Weekly*, *40*, 1470–1473.

Hamzaoui, M., & Bousalam, I. (2015). Bank-based investing rotating savings and credit associations for Islamic finance. A new alternative to drain households' savings and reduce financial exclusion. *Journal of Advanced Studies in Finance*, *6*(12), 57.

Handa, S., & Kirton, C. (1999). The economics of rotating savings and credit associations: Evidence from the Jamaican Partner. *Journal of Development Economics*, *60*(1), 173–164.

Hollis, A., & Sweetman, A. (1996). *The evolution of a microcredit institution: The Irish loan funds 1720–1920* [Working papers ecpap-96-01, University of Toronto, Department of Economics].

Hossein, C. S. (2015). Black women as co-operators: Rotating savings and credit associations (ROSCAs) in the Caribbean and Canada. *Journal of Co-operative Studies*, *48*(3), 6–17.

Hossein, C. S. (2020). Rotating savings and credit associations: Mutual aid financing. In J. K. Gibson-Graham & K. Dombroski (Eds.), *The handbook of diverse economies* (pp. 354–361). Edward Elgar Publishing.

Ibrahim, H. A. (2016). *Participation in rotating, savings, and credit associations and enhanced asset accumulation among African immigrants in the United States: An institutional approach*. Saint Louis University.

Ito, S. (2003). Microfinance and social capital: Does social capital help create good practice? *Development in Practice*, *13*(4), 322–332.

Jahangir, R., Bulut, M., & Dinc, Y. (2023). Evolvement of ROSCA to real property acquisition as a form of interest-free SBF model: A PRISMA-compliant systematic review. *Property Management*, *41*(1), 111–148.

Joshi, M. Y., Flacke, J., & Schwarz, N. (2020). Do microfinance institutes help slum-dwellers in coping with frequent disasters? An agent-based modelling study. *International Journal of Disaster Risk Reduction*, *49*, 101627.

Kabuya, F. I. (2015). The Rotating Savings and Credit Associations (ROSCAs): Unregistered sources of credit in local communities. *IOSR Journal of Humanities and Social Science (IOSR-JHSS)*, *20*(8), 95–98.

Karlan, D., & Morduch, J. (2010). Access to finance. In R. Dani & R. Mark (Eds.), *Handbook of development economics* (Vol. 5, pp. 4703–4784). Elsevier.

Kedir, A. M., & Ibrahim, G. (2011). ROSCAs in Urban Ethiopia: Are the characteristics of the institutions more important than those of members? *The Journal of Development Studies*, *47*(7), 998–1016.

Langley, A. (1999). Theorizing from process data. *The Academy of Management Review*, *24*(4), 691–710.

Levenson, A. R., & Besley, T. (1996). The anatomy of an informal financial market: Rosca participation in Taiwan. *Journal of Development Economics*, *51*(1), 45–68.

Lieberman, A., & Schroeder, J. (2020). Two social lives: How differences between online and offline interaction influence social outcomes. *Current Opinion in Psychology*, *31*, 16–21. https://doi.org/10.1016/j.copsyc.2019.06.022

Light, I. (1972). *Ethnic enterprise in America: Business and welfare among Chinese, Japanese, and Blacks*. University of CA Press.

Light, I. (2021). *Exiting poverty through self-employment: The Grameen model and rotating credit associations as alternative strategies*. World Scientific.

Light, I., & Dana, L. (2013). Boundaries of social capital in entrepreneurship. *Entrepreneurship, Theory and Practice*, *37*(3), 603–624.

Light, I., & Gold, S. (1999). *Ethnic economies*. Academic Press.

Light, I., & Zhong, D. (1995). *Gender differences in ROSCA participation within Korean business households in Los Angeles*. Routledge.

Misati, L. (2008). *Social capital and user-owned microfinance organizations: Savings, loans, and associational life in RoSCAs and ASCAs*. http://erepository.uonbi.ac.ke/handle/11295/15986

Mushuku, A., & Mayisa, J. (2014). Unlocking the door from poverty through rotating savings and credit associations: A study of group based savings in ward 14 of Gutu District, Zimbabwe. *Bangladesh e-Journal of Sociology*, *11*(2), 118–131.

Nwosu, O. B. (2008). *The GB-ROSCA hybrid microfinance model: A strategy for small-scale development projects in Nigeria*.

Ojukwu, N. C., Eke, C., Gombe, M., Achi, P. O., Efosa, S., & Olaleye, O. O. (2021). Impact of Rotating Savings and Credit Association (RoSCA) on the performance of MSMEs in Anambra State. *Journal of Economics and Allied Research*, *6*(4), 46–57.

Onda, M. (2021). Rotating savings and credit associations as traditional mutual help networks in East Asia. *International Journal of Asian Studies*, *18*(2), 271–287.

Rosca, E., Agarwal, N., & Brem, A. (2020). Women entrepreneurs as agents of change: A comparative analysis of social entrepreneurship processes in emerging markets. *Technological Forecasting and Social Change*, *157*, 120067.

Rugimbana, R., & Spring, A. (2009). Marketing micro-finance to women: Integrating global with local. *International Journal of Nonprofit and Voluntary Sector Marketing*, *14*(2), 149–154.

Satkunasingam, E. B., & Shanmugam, B. (2006). Underground banking in Malaysia: A case study of ROSCAs. *Journal of Money Laundering Control*, *9*(1), 99–111.

Schreiner, M. (2000). Formal RoSCAs in Argentina. *Development in Practice*, *10*(2), 229–232.

Seibel, H. D. (2003). *History matters in microfinance*. [Working Papers no 2003,5]. University of Cologne, Development Research Centre.

Shoaib, A., & Siddiqui, M. A. (2020). Why do people participate in ROSCA saving schemes? Findings from a qualitative empirical study. *Decision*, *47*(2), 177–189.

Smets, P. (1998). Money-go-rounds for women: Finance as instrument or as ultimate goal in lottery ROSCAs. *Anthropos*, *93*(3), 209–215.

Smets, P. (2000). ROSCAs as a source of housing finance for the urban poor: An analysis of self-help practices from Hyderabad. *Community Development Journal*, *35*(1), 16–30.

Srnec, K., & Hejkrlík, J. (2005). Microfinance institutions in Latin America, Africa and South Asia. *Agricultura Tropica et Subtropica*, 38.

Stewart, D. (2007). Collecting on their investments, one woman at a time: Economic partnerships among Caribbean immigrant women in the United States. *International Journal of African Renaissance Studies*, *2*(1), 35–57.

Tchuindjo, L. (1999). The evolution of an informal financial institution: The rotating savings and credit association in Cameroon. *African Review of Money Finance and Banking*, 5–20.

Thompson, L. M. S. (2016). Moving from rags-to-riches: Together or alone? In *Underground cooperative savings: An ethnography of workplace rotating savings & credit associations (ROSCAs)*. The New School.

Umuhire, P. G. (n.d.). *Articulation of informal financial practices and institutional microfinance: A case study with low income individuals* [Working paper Ucl-Cirtes-Cerisis].

Warnier, J. P. (1985). *Echanges, developpement et hierarchies dans le Bamenda precolonial*. Stuttgart.

Winston, G. (1980). Addiction and backsliding: A theory of compulsive. *Journal of Economic Behaviour and Organization*, *1*, 290–324.

Zainuddin, M., & Yasin, I. M. (2020). Resurgence of an ancient idea? A study on the history of microfinance. *FIIB Business Review*, *9*(2), 78–84.

Zambrano, A. F., Giraldo, L. F., Perdomo, M. T., Hernández, I. D., & Godoy, J. M. (2023). Rotating Savings and Credit Associations: A scoping review. *World Development Sustainability*, *3*, 100081.

Chapter 3

A Resource-based View on Microfinance in China: *Case Study of Rural Credit Cooperatives*

Abstract

In China, the government has embraced a trickle-down strategy to facilitate the financial inclusion of the agricultural community, aligning with the UN Sustainable Development Goals and demonstrating a steadfast commitment to fostering inclusive development. This approach stands out as a pioneering endeavour, particularly in contrast to the prevailing paradigm in many democratic nations elsewhere, where the 1990s witnessed a shift from donor and subsidy-based microfinance to sustainable finance amid the pursuit of liberalization goals. However, the rural credit cooperatives (RCCs) in China encountered a myriad of challenges, including non-performing loans, governance deficiencies, and inadequate risk management. In response, substantial reform initiatives were implemented to integrate and align these RCCs with the formal financial system in China. Despite these hurdles, the RCCs have fundamentally influenced the development of the rural sector in China, playing a pivotal role in its financial evolution. This chapter aims to furnish a comprehensive analysis of the RCCs and their profound impact on the financial development of the rural economy in China. By delving into the intricacies of the challenges faced, the collaborative efforts undertaken, and the ultimate contributions of the RCCs, this study endeavours to offer a nuanced understanding of their role in shaping the financial landscape of China's rural economy.

Keywords: Rural credit cooperatives; Sustainable Development Goals; financial inclusion; rural development; Guanxi

Global Perspectives on Financial Inclusion: Case Studies in Microfinance and Women's Empowerment, 43–59

Published under exclusive licence by Emerald Publishing Limited
doi:10.1108/978-1-83708-080-920251003

1. Introduction

In the process of rural development and poverty reduction, RCCs have an important role to play. China's rural financial markets comprise the formal lending institutions, informal financial institutions, and the money lenders. In China, a number of financial institutions are using the group guarantee, frequent loan repayments, and inclusion of the women to facilitate the access to finance for the people at the bottom of pyramid. The formal financial institutions provide access to finance and are regulated by the state and the government, whereas the informal financial institutions are provided the subsidy and donations to facilitate the access to finance to the people at the bottom of pyramid. The poor borrowers in the rural region do not have access to finance due to the credit rationing practised by the commercial banks. The credit from the RCCs has played an important role in increasing the agricultural output and production. Moreover, the group characteristics often impact the financial sustainability of RCCs in India. Various studies show that the group mechanism, homogeneity and relationship within the group, migrant income, and government or state affiliations have a large impact upon the financial sustainability and efficiency of the group lending in China. This chapter aims to delve into the history and objective of setting up of the RCCs to reduce rural poverty and promote livelihood. Through the financial system approach, which is aimed at promoting the financial sustainability and sustainable finance, instead of the donor and charity-based finance, this study aims to explore the impact of RCCs on the financial well-being, livelihood, and development of China. The various strands of literature highlight that there is an increasing demand for the rural finance in China and the RCCs play an extremely important role in the economic development of the nation. Li et al. (2011) in his research study highlight that the microcredit and microfinance access to rural households in China helps to improve the consumption and income of household in rural regions. This chapter uses the hermeneutical paradigm and symbolism to study the impact of the microcredit on the financial well-being and livelihood of the people at the bottom of pyramid.

2. Research Problem

Cooperatives or RCC societies have played an extremely important role in the financial system of China. Over the period of time, these credit cooperative societies have promoted the cause of financial inclusion of the marginalized and discriminated members of society in the financial system. RCCs play an extremely important role in the economy of China, and despite the relevance of these institutional designs in poverty reduction and women empowerment, there is no study that has explored the impact of the RCCs on the financial health and macroeconomic goals of Chinese economy. This study is the first of its kind to explore the impact of the cooperatives and collectives in achieving the goals of financial inclusion and capital formation. From a structuralist perspective, RCCs embody the values of Guanxi. However, besides the positive rhetoric, what are the other processes that lead to the success of RCCs in China. There is a research gap in terms of an exploratory study to gain an understanding of the various processes and phenomenon that lead to the achievement of the group goal of financial inclusion. Due to the exploratory design of the study, case study method has been used to study the impact of the RCCs on financial wellness of the collectives in reducing the poverty.

> *RQ*. What are the unique processes and phenomenon in an institutional design like Rural Credit Cooperatives based on Guanxi that lead to the success of the cooperatives in achievement of the financial inclusion?

3. Methodology

In the initial stage of the study, the case of Guaxin as format and institutional design was chosen to facilitate the access to financial services for the poor at the bottom of pyramid. In order to study the case, Guaxin as a cultural practice was chosen because the practice forms a rich heritage culture of the Chinese civilization and nobody else has earlier studied this research problem. Due to the exploratory nature of the research problem, the case study method has been used for the purpose of case study. In this study, a further hermeneutical research paradigm has been used to study the series of events that have led to the use of collaborative mechanisms such as the cooperative institutional designs for the purpose of generating enough social capital to facilitate the access to finance for the people at the bottom of pyramid. In order to study the issue of financial exclusion of the poor, the Guanxi basically aims to create a conceptual framework to study what are the characteristics of a group that enables the members to collaborate and share their resources and nurture leadership to ensure the achievement of the group goals. Resource-based view (RBV) basically refers to the resources available at the disposal of the unorganized and marginalized people for ensuring the access to finance for all. For example, in a Guanxi, the resources that are at the disposal such as the homogeneity of the members, the social relationships among the members are resources that are valuable, rare, imitable, and non-substitutable. Further, for the purpose of development of the conceptual framework, another theoretical lens of peer mechanism has been used for the purpose of development of the theory of collaborative mechanism among the members of the community of marginalized people in the rural setting.

4. Literature Review

Guanxi culture has its origin and roots in Confucianism, which enabled the development of Chinese economy into a society based on Guanxi and personal relationships (Luo et al., 2010). The Chinese business environment is based on a famous adage that *Whom you know is more important than what you know?* Thus, the personal connections and networks play an extremely important role in the development of business within the Chinese community. The strengthening of the existing personal relationships and networks within the Chinese economy leads to entrepreneurship. Guanxi in Chinese institutional design is embedded within the networks characterized by the interlinkages and transmission. Thus, Guanxi is the competitive advantage and the businesses with better personal relationships and connections are able to develop dynamic capability in terms of access to the resources, such as human resources and capital. One of the major benefits of the Guanxi networks is that it enables to reduce the relevant cost of setting the business and the transaction costs. Further Guanxi provides access to higher level of business relationships and better financial, physical, technology, and human capital. During the development of the business, the entrepreneurs use of Guanxi networks to solicit access to the resources and creating management and governance mechanism. During the operational phase, the firms and small businesses use Guanxi to access finance and human capital and develop a sustainable supply chain through vendor manages relationships with the suppliers. The circle of influence of a Guanxi-based social network is called *Guanxi Quan*. The trust and social capital that arise within a social network of Guanxi is called Xinyoung. The trust-based credit refers to the sharing of the capital resources among the members of the group. These relationships are based on mutual love and affection, which is also known as *Qing*. There are various classifications of the emotions among the members and they are further classified as *Ganqing*, *Qinqing*, and *Renqing*. The affections with the other individuals refer to the emotional relationships among the members within Guanxi networks. While *Qinqing* refers to the strong emotions with the family members. *Renqing* refers to the responses of the people to the challenges in the daily life guided by subjective norms and social norms. Generally, cultural differences lead to various challenges in conducting business with diverse people in different parts of the globe. *Renqing* refers to the adherence towards certain behaviour in response to certain situations and business challenges that are considered appropriate. While the trust and commitment are Western concepts to business relationships, the *Renqing* refers to the subjective norms such as the reciprocity, empathy, and long-term orientation. It is also referred to as business distance between the people of the social groups and it leads to higher commitment. It plays an important role in the success of business in China (Guo, 2001). *Jiaoqing* refers to the friendly relations and relationships that are not natural. It refers to the lowest level of affection and affinity between the members of the Chinese society. Thus, in the business relationships of the Chinese corporations Jiaoqing has come to play an important role in the ease of doing business. Similarly, the face refers to the public image of the individuals, which is recognized by the members of the society. Face and the public perception in the society are of increased relevance in promoting the business acumen among the members of the society. Qinren refers to the members of the family, which form part of the social network. In case of the poor and marginalized entrepreneurs, these attributes play an important role in promoting the business through the use of social capital. Besides this, Shouren refers to the people, both inside and outside of the business network that facilitate the interaction among the members of the group (Fan, 2002). Thus, as far as the microbusinesses are concerned, the Chinese concept Guanxi and its layers play an important role in promoting business generating livelihood among the members of the social group. Various studies indicate that cooperative banks have better capital adequacy and better capital structure than the banks under any other format (Wang et al., 2022). Nan et al. (2018) in their research study highlight that the RCCs have a great role to play in the creation of rural credit. Dong et al. (2012) in their study highlight that the credit constraint has a negative impact on the agricultural productivity of people in rural households. Li et al. (2024) in their study highlight that RCCs play an important role to promote market integration in rural areas. Ling (2002) in their research study highlight that RCCs enable the people at the bottom of pyramid to get access to finance. As per the study, the banks provide loans to only people that have collateral, but for the people without the collateral, it is not easy to get access to finance or capital. Lee et al. (2023) in his research study highlights that during the planned period, rural finance through the credit cooperatives has played an extremely important role in promoting resilience and economic growth in the rural regions. As per the research study by Clegg (2006), the reforms in the cooperative banking favour the large farmers while compromising on the interests of the small farmers. Wang et al. (2013) in their research study highlight that the borrower-level and the group-level characteristics determine the performance of the RCC lending groups. The main characteristics that enable better repayment include trustworthy relationship between microlenders and consumers. Dong and Featherstone (2006) in their research study highlight the need to understand the institutional and financial design behind the success of these cooperatives. Moreover, the rural cooperatives seem to be suffering from various challenges which include the lack of institutional sustainability. Due to excessive state intervention and the state control, these RCC societies are suffering from various issues and challenges. Also, the risk of failure of RCCs is extremely high due to the like of customer services, low quality employees, and high level of non-performing loans and assets. Jiang et al. (2024) in their research study highlight that the farmer cooperatives promote investment in the unorganized sectors, increase household investments, increase liquidity, and further improve the access to free credit for the people at the bottom of the pyramid. Ong (2009) in his research study highlights that the RCCs are not effective as an institution to meet the credit needs of the people at the bottom of pyramid. As per the various studies the model of RCCs has been a failure due to the increasing amount of bad loans and increasing non-performing loans. Ong (2009) in his research study again highlights the interference by the political parties and the states as the reason for the failure and deteriorating asset quality of banks, leading to higher rate of non-performing assets (NPAs). Zhao (2017) in his research study highlights that the main reason for the success of the RCCs is the social connectedness, local connectedness, and embeddedness, that is responsible for the success of group lending and achievement of financial sustainability. Yu et al. (2023) in their research study highlight that the social capital in a group increases the chances and likelihood of obtaining the access to credit and finance from a group. Clegg (2006) further highlights that the reforms in the banking and cooperative finance sector have been more entrepreneurial and not indeed helped the cause of the people at the bottom of pyramid. Peng et al. (2022) in their research study highlight that the cooperative formats of banking have a positive impact on the financial might of the people at the bottom of the pyramid. Ong (2009) in his research study highlights that there is a need for institutional reforms to facilitate the inclusion of the rural poor through RCCs. The interference by external forces and interplay of dynamic forces beyond the groups are the main reasons for the failure of RCCs in achieving their objective of financial inclusion. Turvey et al. (2011) in their research study highlight that the 7Cs – Credit, Character, Capacity, Capital, Condition, Capability, and Collateral – play an important impact on credit delivery and demand for the credit. The character refers to the cultural characteristics of the borrowers, capacity refers to the resource capability of the members in a group, and condition refers to the group guarantees and credit worthiness of the members. Collateral refers to the lack of physical asset that might facilitate access to finance for people at bottom of pyramid. Chen et al. (2022) in their research study highlight that formal credit has a positive impact on financial inclusion of rural households, while informal credit has a negative impact on financial well-being of rural households. Ping (2003) in his study highlights that the domain of microfinance is fraught with various challenges and the cooperative structure plays an extremely important role in the financial inclusion of the unorganized sector into the economy. Cheng (2006) in his study has highlighted that the unorganized members of society have to rely on the moneylenders and coercive lending practices. To financially include the excluded members of society, there is need for the market reforms. However, due to the large-scale poverty among the poor, there is need for a new institutional design with state intervention. Van Empel and Smit (2004) in their study highlight that it is extremely important to develop an effective rural banking system. The study also highlights the importance of consolidation of the fragmented small-scale institutions into network organizations to reap benefits of consolidation and economies of scale. Feng (2023) in his research study has highlighted that the RCCs were unable to comply with the requirements with principle of RCCs. The study highlights the importance of the state intervention and the need for new institutional design such as conversion of RCCs into rural commercial bank. Wang (2004) in his study highlights the main difference between the formal and informal cooperative societies as the supervisory regulatory framework and implementation process. The study highlights the need to put in place a detailed blueprint of the self-appraisal process to address the operational framework. Dong and Featherstone (2003) in their research study highlight that the small enterprises suffer from various challenges such as lack of credit. RCCs as an institutional design suffer from various challenges such as lack of institutional sustainability due to lack of formal adherence to governance norms and financial sustainability due to excessive dependence on the central bank, that is, Agricultural Bank of China (ABC) for state support and aid. Wang et al. (2022) in their research study highlight that restructuring the rural cooperatives, the rural cooperative banks have better capital adequacy that leads to higher financial sustainability. Clegg (2006) in his research study highlights that the reforms in the cooperative sector are favouring the entrepreneurial sector more than the poor farmers. The literature highlights the impact of the bottom-up approach in order to achieve equity and inclusion for all. Cheng (2014) in his study highlights the importance of simplification of the credit process such as removing the discriminatory policies against the female headed households, simplifying the loaning process as the panacea to the problem of social exclusion. Ong (2009) in his research study highlights that in a collective credit operative, where agent is responsible to report to the multiple principals, the collective principal will have a lower impact over agents. Wang et al. (2019) in their research study highlight that the asset growth has an impact on the profitability of regional credit cooperatives through the improvement in commercial performance. The studies highlight that the increase in asset growth increases the credit services for the lower income group. Zhao and Xu (2020) in their research study highlight that the cooperative model plays an important role. Zhao (2017) in his research study highlights that the mutual relationship among the peers, acquaintanceship among the members of the group, migrant income, and employment enable to improve the repayment rates of loans in the group. Peng et al. (2022) in their research highlight that the cooperatives enable to improve the credit access through social capital and reputation management. Dong and Featherstone (2006) in their research study highlight that the cooperatives enable the marginalized and discriminated to break the glass ceilings and the installations that prevent them from getting access to the credit. Van Empel and Smit (2004) in their research study highlight that rural banking and RCC societies enable in the development of the rural regions. Zhang and Chen (2023) in their study highlight that the inclusive finance can improve the risk-taking ability of the members in the group and increase the stability of these groups and cooperatives. Yu and Nilsson (2018) in their research study highlight that the social capital and relationship existing among the members enable the members to get access to finance, much more easily. Three dimensions of social capital are (1) relational, (2) external, and (3) cognitive. Existing relationship among the members and their knowledge, characterized by the relationship between members from same locality, same city, has a positive impact in providing access to loan to the marginalized and the discriminated. Nan et al. (2018) in their study RCCs highlight that RCCs help to increase the agricultural productivity and improve the managerial efficiency. Chen and Scott (2014) in their study highlight the importance of cooperatives can make important economic, social, and political contribution to the development of the villages. However, these entities also face various challenges such as massive loss of labour, weak internal management, and limited government support. Zachernuk and Liu (2014) in their study highlight that cooperatives play an extremely important role in poverty reduction. Zuo (2001) in his study highlights that the informal sector is yet not catered to by the financial institutions. The rural credit unions that exist in rural regions suffer from the lack of financial support, excessive bureaucratic interference, and control. Kurtenbach (1985) in his research study highlights that the collectives play an important role in development of rural regions and provide livelihood for the people at the bottom of pyramids. Hou (2011) in his research study highlights that community capitalism helps in removing the inequalities and poverty reduction and transformation of China. Hou (2011) in his study highlights the importance of villages as self-governing bodies that are responsible for the redistribution of the resources among the members of the group. However, Stiglitz (2012) in his study has highlighted the importance of state intervention in incomplete markets. Hayek (1968) in his study highlights the importance of the local knowledge in promoting financial inclusion and economic development. Liu (2008) in his book highlights that, for China, poor development of the agriculture sector is the main issue, referred to as San Nong, which implies san means 'three' and nong means 'agriculture', 'villages as nongcun and nongmin' implies 'farmers'. Jia and Guo (2008) in their research study highlight that rural and microfinance face various challenges in China, the most important being the financial sustainability of the microfinance firms in India. Zhou and Takeuchi (2010) in their research study highlight the importance of the informal sector in promoting the welfare of the rural financial system, in the rural regions where the financial system suffers from major challenges: (1) lack of collateral, (2) asymmetric information, (3) unique risks, and (4) non-productive uses of loans to name a few. Hayton et al. (2002) in his study highlights that in rural China, the informal sector plays an extremely important role in economic growth and development of the rural regions. However, the high cost of informal finance often possesses challenges for the rural areas. In his study, the author highlights that while ensuring the access to finance for the people at the bottom pyramid, the microfinance, within the neoliberal framework is a vehicle to deregulate the microfinance sector, without compromising the social and political legitimacy. He celebrates the Chinese model of microfinance that has enabled the access to finance through articulation of macro regulatory institutions: political and social milieu. The author highlights that in China the microfinance started to address the San Nong, the popular three issues (agriculture, village, and farmers). In China initially till 1994 all the microfinance programmes were never recognized and state never supported the non-government organization (NGO)-based microfinance programmes. However, in 1994, with a subsidized poverty alleviation programme was started by the government, which is more based on sustainable finance. However it also fell apart in 2000. In late 1990s, RCCs were on the verge of bankruptcy, and the state led microfinance programmes aimed to provide aid to these cooperatives to enhance their profitability and provide access to finance for the people at the bottom of pyramid. Due to thrust on sustainable finance, most of the small and marginalized farmers and rural households were excluded from the net of microfinance. The microfinance companies got a formal financial institution status only when Mohd Yunus visited China in 2006, and by 2007, there were 8,551 microfinance companies in India. Hu (2007) in his research study highlights that village trust, Rotated Savings and Credit Associations, Guanxi community, Integrating Village with Company governance plays an important role for facilitating modernization and social and economic development and serving the cause of poor through the integration of various values of group lending such as trust, reciprocity, responsibility, and obligation into the social exchange processes in a group that facilitates to reduce the transaction costs. Holz (2001) in his research study has discussed the history of the development of RCCs from the dissolution of rural credit funds (RCF) in India.

5. Temporal Strategy

Fig. 9 highlights the milestones in the formation of RCFs through the use of the temporal strategy (Langley, 1999). The culture of commune and group lending through collectives started in China after the institutional changes in 1950s. The Chinese economy witnessed high growth despite various challenges such as the Great Leap Forward (1958–1961) and the Cultural Revolution (1966–1976). In China, the separate agricultural banks were in existence for periods 1950s and 1960s. At most of the time, the financial services were provided by the rural credit system that comprised the RCCs. In China, during this decade, the formal banking was the responsibility of Agricultural Finance Division of People's Bank of China. In 1979, the Chinese Government established the ABC to contribute towards the effective execution of the Government's policy in China. ABC is responsible for providing the credit services, channelizing the saving funds to rural areas and providing financial leadership to the RCCs in China. RCC provides additional financial support to the people in the rural areas and regions. RCCs at the ground level help in mobilization of the savings to the individuals and providing them loans. The sources of funds include deposits from individuals, deposits of collectives, and loans from ABC. Through the lens of temporal and narrative strategy, in 1990, the local government began to promote the RCF. In 1991, the 13th central committee confirmed the legitimacy of RCFs. Also, in 1992, in Hebei province in China, the central committee told everybody to develop the RCFs. 1993 was the year in which the blueprint for financial reforms that RCFs are not financial institutions, and in 1994, the Chinese communist committee clarified that the RCFs to be transformed into the financial institutions. By 1995, all the townships were supposed to have RCFs, and in 1999, these RCFs are folded and formed into RCCs.

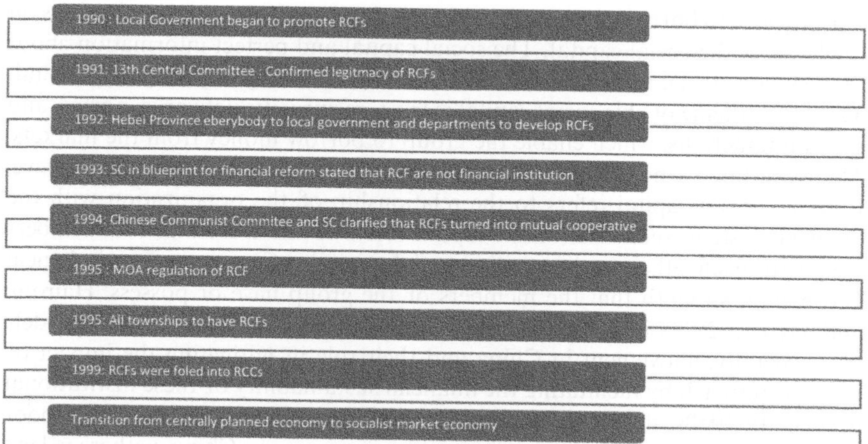

Fig. 9. Chronology of Events in the Formation of RCFs (Rural Credit Cooperatives). *Source*: Author's own work.

6. Discussion – Case Study – Guangxi, Rural Credit Cooperatives

Guanxi is one of the most important cultural concepts in China, reflecting the personal relationships built on shared connections and reciprocal exchanges of favours. Unlike general trust, which often relies on weaker interpersonal ties, Guanxi is characterized by strong bonds among individuals. These connections typically develop among people with common backgrounds, such as schoolmates, fellow villagers, and close friends. In the context of resource allocation, practices like group lending or cooperatives often leverage Guanxi to facilitate financial sustainability. By relying on these strong interpersonal ties, Guanxi helps mitigate issues like moral hazard and adverse selection that can arise from information asymmetry in business. Additionally, *lian* – or face value and reputation – plays a crucial role in motivating relationships within the business environment. The importance of *Renqing* – emotions such as cultural sensitivity and politeness – further enhances group dynamics by promoting social objectives. This sensitivity fosters social capital that empowers members of the business community to access financial resources and achieve their goals more effectively. From the various studies, it is established that the Guanxi leads to higher trust, cooperative intention, and responsibility. The perception or strength of ties in Guanxi depends on the duration of relationships, stability of relationships, importance of relationships, and intimation of the relationships. The number of farmer cooperatives in China have increased manifold to 1,373 million in April 2015. Within the group there are two categories of members: the core members and the common members. Both the types of members are based on Guanxi culture, which implies that the members within the social network provide social favours and support to each other. As dynamic incentive, the groups provide honours to the members of the group. The firms with honours are able to borrow more capital from the banks and financial institutions on the basis of the social capital. The social capital and perfect information about the riskiness of the members enable the members of the group to access capital. The major theme of this social capital is trust, reciprocity, networks, norms, and social interactions, which enable the group to borrow money from the markets. There are three kinds of social capital that a group or Guanxi generally have. External social capital refers to the relationship of the organization with the financial system, relational social capital refers to the trust that the members have with each other, and cognitive social capital refers to the psychological and mental strength that the members of the group have or possess. Hairong and Yiyuan (2016) in their research highlight the evolution of the new models of cooperative movement in China and their role in mitigating the impact of poverty outreach by facilitating the financial sustainability of these institutional designs. In 1950s, the RCCs were set up in the rural areas. Many of the poor people are still trapped in the vicious circle of poverty in China as there is lack of policy interventions despite their being allocation of resources through institutional designs. In China, CFIs in China had a very limited impact due to the lack of effect governance, low asset quality, out of date service, weak risk taking, and limited autonomy. Till 1980s, these institutional designs were not successful in combating the poverty, and in 1996, a series of reforms were launched with state intervention. In 1996, they started the cooperative bank of commercializing these RCCs. The year 2003 started the era of commercialization of these credit unions with the emergence of Village and township banks (VTBs), rural mutual cooperatives, and lending companies. The development in cooperatives can be thought of as a move in emancipation of women in phases. The first phase in 1919 was the phase of nationalism and national fervour. During the 1950s and 1959, the communes or the state emerged as a major body influencing the feminist movement. In the new era of opening up of economy, the phase is the era of new reforms that include emergence of institutional designs such as lending companies, VTBs, rural mutual cooperatives RCCs without state interventions, and more autonomy. Yu et al. (2023) in their study highlight that from transaction cost economics point of view, the cooperatives give more power to the members of the group as compared to individual members. And the social capital plays an extremely important role in the emancipation of the poor people at the bottom of pyramid. In another study, the author argues that RBV, allocation of the resources through policy interventions, cannot add soul to the mere structures of distribution of rare physical resources. And there is a need for more social intermediation and capacity building to facilitate change and reform. Guanxi culture is an important component of the Chinese behaviour. From the analysis of the literature, it is highlighted that emotional closeness has a positive impact on solidarity and cooperation among the members of the group. And the solidarity has a negative impact on the conflict among the members of the group. Hofstede (2011) highlights that in Chinese culture multiple people with diverse background living together in harmony with the each other, which further leads to cooperation and trust among each other. Various strands of literature highlight that Guanxi helps the member from diverse background to cooperate with each other and maximize the welfare of the members of the community. Guanxi, which is also called social capital, enables the entrepreneurs to leverage personal relationships to nurture business growth and development. Through localization and nurturing personal relationships and network with the people of the community, Guanxi enables to develop business relationships among the members of community.

6.1. Theoretical Lens

In this study, the theory of RBV and *dynamic capabilities approach* could have been used to study the unique phenomenon of Guanxi or collaboration among the members to facilitate the achievement of financial inclusion. But one of the major limitations of RBV is that it suffers from Kuhanian incommensurability. To overcome this challenge, in this study, the underlying premise of the argument that Guanxi through Renqing makes collaboration and thus financial inclusion feasible has been made very clear. Moreover, critical realism has been adopted as the research paradigm and agency theory have been taken as the theoretical lens to test whether monitoring efforts in a Guanxi lead to better shareholder welfare. The choice of the research paradigm was to make the research position very clear, that the objective is not to generalize that monitoring in a Guanxi leads to higher financial inclusion, but to critique the institutional design of Guanxi for financial inclusion and provide insights into other parameters such as Renqing, Mianzi, Lian that could be the reasons for the success of Guanxi through RCCs in China. In a collaborative context of group lending such as Guanxi, the members are homogenous, who already know each other and have perfect knowledge about each other's business and type of risks. The *collaboration* among the members, solidarity, cooperation, cohesion, and social control further lead to the achievement of the goal of financial inclusion. Further the peer mechanism leads to various dynamic capabilities such as agility and cost saving in terms of transaction and relevant costs. Group mechanism further leads to competitive advantage such as access to finance at the low costs. Thus, the group lending and cooperatives play an important role in the achievement of group goals. This *institutional design* leads to large amount of savings, as the group mainly relies on peer monitoring and supervision to coordinate the activities of the members in the group. This institutional design offers various advantages such as support of the financial intermediation such as the banks or NGO, self-governance, peer mechanism, social contract, Guanxi. *Guanxi* is the institutional design that generates positive rhetoric by virtue of *Mianzi*. *Lian* is the existence of the relationships among the members, which are leveraged to generate social capital. These obligations and relationships naturally exist in context of Guanxi. Yet for the corporate governance, *Renqing* plays an important role to facilitate equality and inclusion with fairness. Thus, the Renqing is extremely important to ensure corporate governance and regulation of these semi-formal financial institutions. Thus, a social bricolage like Guanxi turns into an institutional design that by virtue of positive rhetoric leads to effectuation in terms of achievement of goal of financial inclusion and wellness. Globally, Guanxi is serving as an institutional design for financial inclusion as part of adoptive or adaptive strategies. *Adoptive strategies* are perforce adopted by the members of a community without any social bond like subjective norms. While the *adaptive strategies* are more effective in achieving the objective of financial inclusion through localization and use of social norms. This *adaptability* leads to agility in terms of higher financial inclusion through dynamic capabilities such as lower cost of monitoring and setting up, lower cost of social intermediation, consensus, and solidarity due to higher localization. Thus, the institutional designs of the cooperative banks such as RCCs work on the principle of Guanxi that leads to the higher collaboration and success of the financial inclusion initiative and savings among the members of the group. Besides, that there are other factors such as the Renqing, Mianzi, Lian, and the processes of *peer mechanism* that enables the groups to be financially viable and sustainable. The positive rhetoric and the relationships that exist among the members of the group facilitate the achievement of the group objectives, such as *financial inclusion and financial sustainability*. The social capital within the group and the corporate governance mechanism lead to the achievement of the corporate objective.

Fig. 10 highlights the conceptual framework for the working of the apparatus of the RCCs to get to the heart of the issue of financial inclusion. Each of the cooperative or the collaborative mechanism functions through the functionalities of social capital, collaboration, leadership, and cohesion. This apparatus leads to the peer mechanism in a social contract that is made functional through the peer mechanism, solidarity, and cohesion. Though Guanxi, on its own is the driving force behind the success of the cooperatives and the RCCs. Institutional design of Guanxi facilitates the collaboration of the financial prowess of homogenous members. These members might be homogenous owing to their neighbourhood, qualifications or the professions. Renqing as part of the institutional design of cooperatives, characterized by Guanxi, further provides an institutional framework in the form of corporate governance rules pertaining to the disclosure. The group or the cooperative institution works towards the achievement of the Mianzi or the social capital or social face which further enables the businesses to access the financial capital. This mechanism further leads to various dynamic capabilities like low costs and higher financial sustainability and institutional sustainability.

There are various different theoretical lenses that can be used to measure the impact of the Guanxi or the group lending in a Chinese culture on the achievement of group goals. Guanxi plays an extremely important role in the control and mitigation of the costs. Guanxi, through the theoretical lens of the transaction cost theory, helps in the reduction of the cost of transaction and the relevant transaction costs relating to various environmental, coordinating, and communication activities. This type of institutional design also minimizes the cost

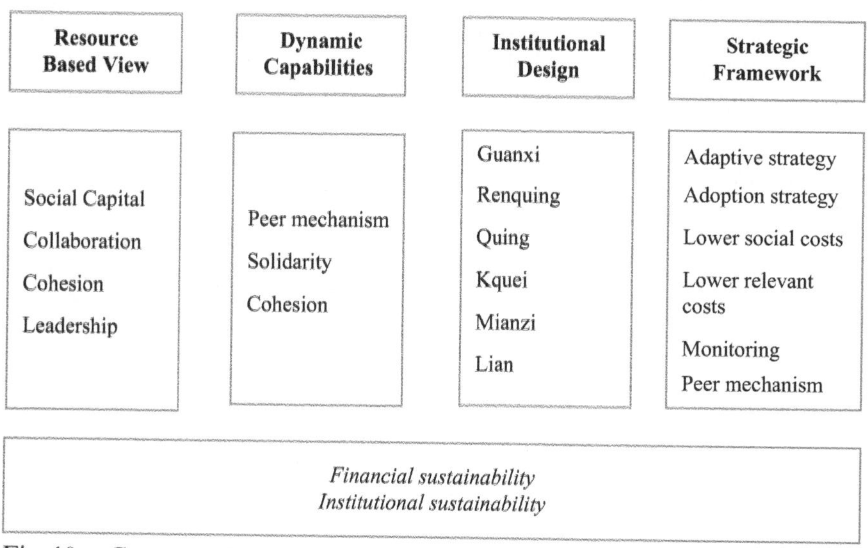

Fig. 10. Conceptual Framework (Strategic Framework for Rural Credit Cooperatives).

of social contracting and authentication. From the *peer mechanism* theory, the Guanxi plays an important role in the selection of the members by reducing the adverse selection. In a group the members know each other, and hence this homogeneity further helps in mitigating the adverse selection of the members. Further, *peer monitoring* is aimed at monitoring and observing the behaviour of the member. Once the members have joined the group, they share the joint liability and the social contract enables the members to monitor each other. This monitoring enables to reduce the moral hazard and the repayment of loans in time. Thus, peer monitoring has an important role to play in reducing the instances of non-repayment of loans. Further, in a cooperative institutional design, *peer enforcement* of the punitive measures in the form of punishment in the case of default helps in mitigating the bad loans. Thus, peer selection, peer monitoring, and peer enforcement in a cooperative enable the members of group to achieve financial sustainability and institutional sustainability. Thus, the theory of peer mechanism explains that the cooperatives through a social contract operationalize the phenomenon of peer mechanism that helps to reduce the instances of asset deterioration and NPAs in case of a cooperative. Guanxi also enables the members of the group to assess the financial resources through the existing social relations and relationships with the members of the group. Fig. 11 provides details of peer mechanism theory.

At the stage of formation of the group, peer selection plays an important role. The members of the group have perfect information about the other members of the group. Since, in a Guanxi, all the members have perfect information about each other, this homogeneity of the members enables the members to identify and deselect the risky member from the group of the risky member. Further, the members have the joint ability and thus they are motivated to monitor each other. This *peer monitoring* enables the members to supervise the working of the other members of the group, which facilitate the institutional sustainability and financial sustainability among the members of the group. In stage 1, which is the group

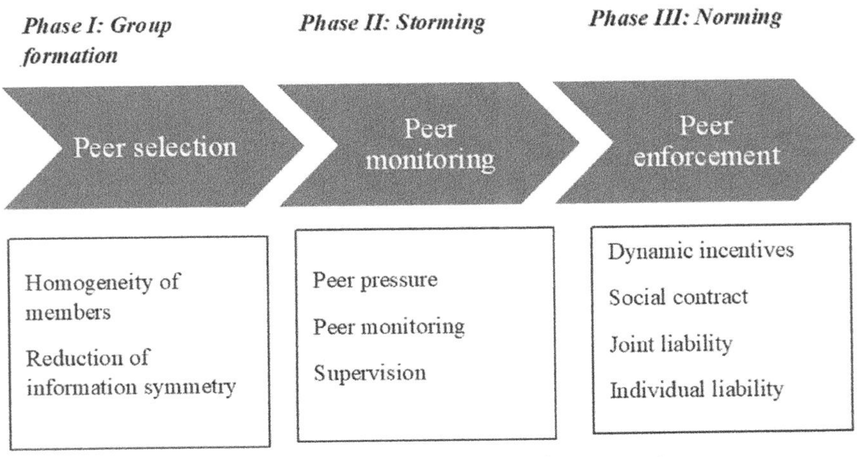

Fig. 11. Peer Mechanism Theory. *Source*: Author's own work.

formation stage, the homogenous members select each other by filtering the risky members from the group. Since the social contract in a cooperative involves pooling of the resources, the members peer-select each other to eliminate the risky members. Further, the members in a joint liability cooperative use the peer pressure, monitoring, and supervision to coerce the risky members to pay back the borrowings and loan. To create a disincentive for the members to default, the members enforce the social contract. The members of the cooperative who pay the loans in time are provided the additional capital and the members who default are penalized through bad mouthing.

7. Conclusion

The study highlights the importance of the institutional design such as RCCs in ensuring the inclusion of the poor people from the bottom of pyramid. Guanxi is an important characteristic of the collaborative and cooperative structures in China that facilitate the solidarity and cohesion for the achievement of the group objective. Further, characteristics such as Renqing, Quing, and Lian facilitate the financial inclusion of the poor members of the society. Moreover, the peer mechanism among the members of the group by virtue of social capital enables the poor and marginalized sections of society to access finance and capital. By virtue of solidarity, cohesion and cooperation members of cooperative groups come together to achieve the common goals and objectives such as local access to finance for people at the bottom of pyramid.

References

Chen, A., & Scott, S. (2014). Rural development strategies and government roles in the development of farmers' cooperatives in China. *Journal of Agriculture, Food Systems, and Community Development*, *4*(4), 35–55.

Chen, Z., Meng, Q., Xu, R., Guo, X., & Cai, C. (2022). How rural financial credit affects family farm operating performance: An empirical investigation from rural China. *Journal of Rural Studies*, *91*, 86–97.

Cheng, E. (2014). *The demand for credit, credit rationing and the role of microfinance: Evidence from poor rural counties of China*. China International Center for Poverty Alleviation.

Cheng, Y. S. (2006). China's reform of rural credit cooperatives: Progress and limitations. *Chinese Economy*, *39*(4), 25–40.

Clegg, J. (2006). Rural cooperatives in China: Policy and practice. *Journal of Small Business and Enterprise Development*, *2*, 219–234.

Dong, F., & Featherstone, A. (2003, February 1–5). *Scale economies and efficiencies for Chinese rural credit cooperatives* [Annual meeting]. *Southern Agricultural Economics Association annual meeting*, Alabama.

Dong, F., & Featherstone, A. M. (2006). Technical and scale efficiencies for Chinese rural credit cooperatives: A bootstrapping approach in data envelopment analysis. *Journal of Chinese Economic and Business Studies*, *4*(1), 57–75.

Dong, F., Lu, J., & Featherstone, A. M. (2012). Effects of credit constraints on household productivity in rural China. *Agricultural Finance Review*, *72*(3), 402–415.

Fan, Y. (2002). Questioning Guanxi: Definition, classification and implications. *International Business Review*, *11*(5), 543–561.
Feng, X. (2023). A study on customer satisfaction of economy hotels in the context of all-for-one tourism. *The World of Marketing*, *1*, 77–79.
Guo, X. (2001). Dimensions of Guanxi in Chinese elite politics. *The China Journal*, *46*(4), 69–90.
Hairong, Y., & Yiyuan, C. (2016). Debating the rural cooperative movement in China, the past and the present. In *Rural politics in Contemporary China* (pp. 49–75). Routledge.
Hayek, F. A. (1968). Wettbewerb als Entdeckungsverfahren. In *Kieler Vorträge, Neue Folge 56, Hrsg. E. Kiel*. Schneider.
Hayton, J. C., George, G., & Zahra, S. A. (2002). National culture and entrepreneurship: A review of behavioral research. *Entrepreneurship Theory and Practice*, *26*, 33–52. https://doi.org/10.1177/104225870202600403
Hofstede, G. (2011). Dimensionalizing cultures: The Hofstede model in context. *Online Readings in Psychology and Culture*, *2*, 8. http://dx.doi.org/10.9707/2307-0919.1014
Holz, C. A. (2001). China's monetary reform: The counterrevolution from the countryside. *Journal of Contemporary China*, *10*(27), 189–217.
Hou, X. (2011). From Mao to the market: Community capitalism in rural China. *Theory, Culture & Society*, *28*(2), 46–68. https://doi.org/10.1177/0263276410396917
Hu, B. (2007). *Informal institutions and rural development in China*. Routledge.
Jia, X., & Guo, P. (2008). Evolution of rural finance in China: Institutional 'lock in' or gradualism? *Savings and Development*, *32*(4), 279–299.
Jiang, M., Li, J., & Mi, Y. (2024). Farmers' cooperatives and smallholder farmers' access to credit: Evidence from China. *Journal of Asian Economics*, *92*, 101746.
Kurtenbach, E. (1985). *Role of specialized households and cooperative enterprises in China's rural economy*. University of Hawai'i at Manoa.
Langley, A. (1999). Strategies for theorizing from process data. *The Academy of Management Review*, *24*(4), 691–710.
Lee, C. C., Tang, M., & Lee, C. C. (2023). Reaping digital dividends: Digital inclusive finance and high-quality development of enterprises in China. *Telecommunications Policy*, *47*, 102484.
Li, W., Wang, L., Ren, Z., & Rehman, O. (2024). Farmer cooperatives in China: Diverse pathways to sustainable rural development. *Applied Soft Computing*, *159*, 111585.
Li, W. B., Chen, R., & Zhang, H. (2023). Enhancing stability and achieving high-quality development in rural credit cooperatives through inclusive finance: Evidence from Shaanxi Province, China. *Applied Economics*, *56*(45), 5412–5427.
Li, X., Gan, C., & Hu, B. (2011). The welfare impact of microcredit on rural households in China. *The Journal of Socio-Economics*, *40*(4), 404–411.
Ling, Z. (2002). Poverty alleviation during the transition in China. In A. Lu & M. F. Montes (Eds.), *Poverty, income distribution and well-being in Asia during the transition. Studies in development economics and policy*. Palgrave Macmillan. https://doi.org/10.1057/9780230503892_5
Liu, C. X. (2008). *Rural finance reform in China* [EconomiX Working paper 2008-43]. University of Paris Nanterre.
Luo, H., Tao, H., Ma, H., & Das, S. K. (2010). Data fusion with desired reliability in wireless sensor networks. *IEEE Transactions on Parallel and Distributed Systems*, *22*(3), 501–513.
Nan, Y., Gao, Y., & Zhou, Q. (2018). Rural credit cooperatives' contribution to agricultural growth: Evidence from China. *Agricultural Finance Review*, *79*(1), 119–135.
Ong, L. (2009). The Communist Party and financial institutions: Institutional design of China's post-reform rural credit cooperatives. *Pacific Affairs*, *82*(2), 251–278.
Peng, Y., Wang, H. H., & Zhou, Y. (2022). Can cooperatives help commercial farms to access credit in China? Evidence from Jiangsu Province. *Canadian Journal of Agricultural Economics*, *70*(4), 325–349.

Ping, X. (2003). Reforms of China's rural credit cooperatives and policy options. *China Economic Review*, *14*(4), 434–442.

Qinlan, Z., & Izumida, Y. (2013). Determinants of repayment performance of group lending in China: Evidence from rural credit cooperatives' program in Guizhou province. *China Agricultural Economic Review*, *5*(3), 328–341.

Stiglitz, J. (2012). *The price of inequality: How today's divided society endangers our future*. WW Norton & Company.

Turvey, C., He, G., Kong, R., & Ma, J. (2011). The 7 Cs of rural credit in China. *Journal of Agribusiness in Developing and Emerging Economies*, *1*(2), 100–133.

Van Empel, G., & Smit, L. (2004). Development of sustainable credit cooperatives in China. In *Rural finance and credit infrastructure in China* (Volume 97).

Wang, J., Chen, H., Zhang, H., Luo, J., Cheng, M., & Zhang, J. (2022). Property rights reform and capital adequacy ratios of rural credit cooperatives in China. *Economic Modelling*, *106*, 105707.

Wang, S.-Y., Luo, J., Murphy, R. W., Wu, S.-F., Zhu, C.-L., Gao, Y., & Zhang, Y.-P. (2013). Origin of Chinese goldfish and sequential loss of genetic diversity accompanies new breeds. *PLoS One*, *8*, e5957.

Wang, W. (2004). The regulatory framework for rural credit cooperatives: The role of Chinese supervisory authorities. In *Rural finance and credit infrastructure in China* (p. 129).

Wang, Y., Yang, Y., Zhou, Z., & Wu, H. (2019). Compatibility between commercial performance and agricultural services: Evidence from Anhui rural credit cooperatives. *Emerging Markets Finance and Trade*, *56*(13), 3060–3071.

Xiong, X., Tian, J., & Ruan, H. (2011). A DEA-model evaluation of the efficiency of peasant household credit investigation system in rural credit cooperatives: A positive research in Hubei Province, China. *China Agricultural Economic Review*, *3*(1), 54–66.

Yu, L., & Nilsson, J, 2018. Social capital and the financing performance of farmer cooperatives in Fujian Province, China. *Agribusiness*, *34*(4), 847–864.

Yu, L., Nilsson, J., Zhan, F., & Cheng, S. (2023). Social capital in cooperative memberships and farmers' access to bank credit–evidence from Fujian, China. *Agriculture*, *13*(2), 418.

Zhang, J., & Chen, Z. (2023). Exploring human resource management digital transformation in the digital age. *Journal of the Knowledge Economy*, *15*, 1482–1498. https://doi.org/10.1007/s13132-023-01214-y

Zachernuk, T., & Liu, G. (2014). Co-operatives and poverty reduction in China. In C. Gijselinckx, L. Zhao, & S. Novkovic (Eds.), *Co-operative innovations in China and the West*. Palgrave Macmillan. https://doi.org/10.1057/9781137277282_12

Zhao, L. (2017). Credit co-operatives and their role in poverty reduction in rural China. *Journal of Asian Rural Studies*, *1*(2), 97–108.

Zhao, L., & Xu, X. (2020). Credit co-operatives: A miracle solution for poverty reduction in rural China? *Emerging Markets Finance and Trade*, *56*(13), 3060–3071.

Zhou, L., & Takeuchi, H. (2010). Informal lenders and rural finance in China: A report from the field. *Modern China*, *36*(3), 302–328.

Zuo, X. (2001, September 11–13). *The development of credit unions in China: Past experiences and lessons for the future* [Paper presentation, pp. 11–13]. The conference on financial sector reform in China, Harvard University, Cambridge, MA.

Chapter 4

Bricolage Through Credit Cooperatives in Germany: A Historical Perspective

Abstract

Bricolage through microfinance provides a pathway for the financial inclusion of the people at the bottom of the pyramid. German credit cooperatives or collective associations signify the importance of the social capital in facilitating the access to the credit at their door steps. The exclusion of the migrant women is the major concern for the people at the bottom of the pyramid. Both Haas and Raiffeisen are the formats of cooperatives that ensure unlimited liability for the members of the group and limited liability for the members facilitate access to the physical capital for the people at the bottom of the pyramid. Through the case study, the chapter method highlights that the organizational innovation serves as mediator between the resource bricolage, financial performance, and competitive advantage of the members at the bottom of the pyramid. This study highlights that various mass movements started for the emancipation of the poor at the bottom of the pyramid. Two major mass movements that were started for the emancipation of the poor include Hermann Schulze-Delitzsch, a former judge, giving rise to the cooperative institutional structure of German Union of German Cooperatives (Schulze-Delitzsch) and People's bank based on the people's savings and credit. In the conclusion study highlights that the Schulze-Delitzsch, as an institutional format failed due to the economic cycles and reasons, Raiffeisen failed due to the unlimited liability and maturity mismatching, with small duration savings being used to fund long term loans.

Keywords: German cooperatives; bricolage; microfinance; social capital; financial inclusion

Global Perspectives on Financial Inclusion: Case Studies in Microfinance and Women's Empowerment, 61–78

Published under exclusive licence by Emerald Publishing Limited
doi:10.1108/978-1-83708-080-920251004

1. Introduction

The interplay between bricolage, culture, and historical heritage significantly shapes social and economic dynamics within rural economies, particularly in emerging economies with rich cultural legacies that foster sustainable practices such as savings and wealth creation. Germany's historical financial landscape is exemplified by the prominence of credit cooperatives, which originated in the 1850s as microfinance structures managed primarily by cooperative members. While initially successful, unforeseen exigencies and external shocks precipitated bankruptcy and liquidity challenges, underscoring the imperative of state regulation and oversight. However, traditional banking mechanisms exhibited reluctance to monitor these cooperatives due to perceived low financial returns and high costs. In response, the credit cooperatives innovatively aligned with credit audit associations, creating a unique mechanism that facilitated effective monitoring of these microfinance institutions (MFIs). The collaborative engagement with audit associations emerged as a vital catalyst in nurturing the sustainability of the cooperatives over an extended period. Despite the wealth of financial literature addressing the importance of monitoring, there is a notable absence of discourse on the significance of collective monitoring through associations of microfinance cooperatives. To address this gap, this chapter employs a case study approach to unravel how the bricolage of collective monitoring empowered the German credit cooperatives to persist and thrive, offering valuable insights into the dynamics of sustainable microfinance practices and the role of collective associations in ensuring enduring financial stability. By illuminating the pivotal role of collective monitoring in sustaining microfinance cooperatives, this chapter holds significant promise for advancing the understanding of effective monitoring mechanisms and fostering sustainable financial practices within the microfinance sector.

2. Research Paradigm

Social theory posits that society is shaped by the interactions among individuals and groups. This study utilizes a conceptual framework rooted in social theory and adopts an interpretivist stance to explore how individuals experience and make sense of their realities. By employing hermeneutics and analysing relevant texts, the study aims to develop a theoretical framework that examines the role of social change and norms in influencing financial sustainability, specifically within the context of cooperatives in Germany. Through a detailed discussion of discourse and literature, the study seeks to illuminate how these social dynamics contribute to shifts in financial sustainability.

3. Theoretical Lens

In this study, theoretical lens of social theory has been used to study the impact of the group mechanism, homogeneity of members, peer monitoring on the success of the cooperatives in Germany. Through the solidarity, cooperative behaviour, trust, and loyalty, the cooperative structures are able to achieve their objective of financial sustainability for the people at the bottom of the pyramid. Through the deep level cooperation, cohesion, and cooperation, trust, and reciprocity, augmented by the social norms, the groups can achieve financial and institutional sustainability.

4. Methodology

The cooperative model, grounded in trust, social cohesion, and reciprocity, has facilitated the financial and institutional sustainability of members in German cooperatives. This research study seeks to delve into the distinctive dynamics at play within these cooperatives through a case study approach. By analysing existing literature and relevant texts, the study aims to investigate and understand how group mechanisms, peer interactions, cohesion, and solidarity contribute to the financial and institutional sustainability of cooperative members in Germany.

5. Literature Review

Campos (2024) in his research study highlights that the local embeddedness and integration into the economic system. The study discusses the exclusion of the migrant women as a serious concern for the people at the bottom of the pyramid. According to the various studies, the migrant women have fewer job opportunities, with multiple obligations towards the family and the society. Various civil society-driven initiatives facilitate the inclusion of these women into the mainstream. Thus, the cooperatives have come to play an extremely important role in the functioning of the society. Korsgaard et al. (2021) in their research study highlight the importance of the spatial bricolage and maximizing the utility of whatever resources are available at the disposal of entrepreneur. Korsgaard et al. (2021) in their research study highlight the importance of the spatial bricolage and enable the entrepreneurs to overcome the resource constraint. The spatial context as per the study interacts with the various factors that are important for the allocation of the resources, and these factors include the availability of various factors of production. The spatial bricolage refers to the contextual agility, and knowledge of the entrepreneurs enables the members to access the resources, which further enables the members of the group to achieve financial sustainability and credibility. Seibel (2005) in the research study highlights that the microfinance started from a humble beginning in the 1990s and then made its foray into the commercial and private banking, and thus, the emergence of the group lending and microfinance emerged as the panacea to the woes of the people at the bottom of the pyramid. Kreuz (2006) in his research study highlights the importance of the German MFIs in establishment of the microlending institutions in Europe. Microfinance in Germany is highly subsidized and many driven through donations, charities, and government subsidies. Over the period of time with the enforcement of the social norms, the microlending model has helped to achieve the social profitability. In this regard, the savings clubs and the cooperative banks have emerged as the backbone of the German financial system. Further, there is sudden increase in the private–public partnerships and external financing through the capitalization of the markets that has facilitated the access to microloans for the financial institutions in Germany. Cozarenco and Szafarz (2019) in their study highlight that the microfinance and group lending play an important role in the penetration of the microfinance in the hinterlands. Agarwal (2010) in his research study highlights that the group lending suffers from various limitations such as inclusion and sustainability. Küpper (2016) in his report stated that it was extremely difficult for the small artisans and tradesman to avail the credit. Due to the lack of information and creditworthiness information, the lenders have to incur huge cost to screen the members. In this regard, the credit cooperatives had to rely on the availability of the local information to facilitate access to loans for the members of the credit cooperatives. Thus, the cooperative stipulated that in order to form the group, the members should be selected from the local area so that the lender has complete information about the borrower that will further help to reduce the problem of information asymmetry. German cooperative was formed by a few people with only limited liability, and with the increasing size of the German cooperative, the size of the groups declined. Microfinancing in Germany has evolved through two main phases: the informal phase and the community-based savings funds phase. The origins trace back to 1778 in Hamburg, where the first savings and thrift funds were established, followed by the establishment of community funds in 1801. Notably, the Prussian Savings Bank Decree of 1838 introduced new regulations that further shaped the landscape of microfinance. With the introduction of the regulations, the community groups were transformed into the saving banks and cooperative banks. In the mid-19th century, the ideas of microfinance were revitalized by figures like Friedrich Wilhelm Raiffeisen and Hermann Schulze-Delitzsch, who founded rural and credit cooperatives, now recognized as Raiffeisenbanken. Initially, these rural charity funds aimed to provide grain to those facing food shortages. The urban credit cooperative model arose in 1864 with Schulze-Delitzsch, leading to the formation of over 245 cooperatives across Germany within a decade. These cooperatives were later governed by the Cooperative Act of the German Reich, 1889, transitioning from joint liability structures to limited liability. As microfinance evolved, various factors contributed to its growth in Germany, including a focus on self-help initiatives, local outreach, and the development of a robust legal framework. At the present time, the German financial system is marked by approximately 39,000 branches, serving 75 million customers and holding 51.4% of all banking assets, while accounting for 64% of financial intermediation. German cooperative societies stand out due to their legal recognition of informal finance, the implementation of prudent regulatory measures, and effective supervision, distinguishing them from other cooperative models (Seibel, 2003). These financial institutions became extremely successful, paving the way for financial resilience and sustainability. Franzini and Lucciarini (2022) in their study highlight that the bricolage or any kind of social innovations provide social benefit, but they do have a social cost. Thus, microfinance though it provides social benefits such as inclusion of the poor, access to finance at low cost, but it does have a social cost, in the form of lower profits for the banks and financial institutions. Within the capitalist system, the loans and borrowings to the people at the bottom of the pyramid have a huge cost and it becomes extremely difficult for the banks to break even and financially include the poor. Without the collateral, the poor members of the society are unable to raise funds, as the banks are unwilling to provide loans to the poor people at the bottom of the pyramid (Iversen & Soskice, 2019). In their domain of legitimacy, the members of financial community and the borrowers make different financial arrangements, using the existing institutional vehicles such as bricolage, self-help groups, financial communities, Rotating Savings and Credit Associations enable the small artisans, entrepreneurs to access finance. Armano et al. (2022) in their book highlight the importance of the collective capabilities that enable the members with different sets of skills to come together and work for the attainment of the group goals. These members with the collective capabilities, thus come to exhibit collective solidarities and unity, which enables them to be the part of larger cohort. The collective organizations suffer from various forms of negative rhetorics, on the one hand, which include exploitation on pretext of peer pressure, micromanaging, and extreme individualization of the disadvantaged workers. On the other hand, positive rhetorics enable the workers to remain in solidarity and cohesion. However, overall negative rhetorics also play an extremely important role in exercising peer influence and monitoring to ensure the adherence to group norms and enabling the achievement of the group goals. Moreover, the solidarities and cohesion achieved among the group members play an important role in achievement of the goals. Huybrechts and Haugh (2018) in their research study highlight the importance of institutionalization through the use of various networks. Collectives and cooperatives are organizations that are formed on networks, which institutionalize various types of organizational formats. In this regard, the literature and text highlight the importance of the institutional pluralism that facilitates collective action through the integration of resources and capabilities, through a comprehensive process. In the first phase, the members of the collectives aim to diagnose the problems and failures of the existing institutional formats and organizations. The case in point is that banks and financial institutions are unable to provide loans to the poor, due to the lack of collateral and physical assets.

The collectives and the joint liability groups and cooperatives enable the members of the unorganized sector to access loans. In order to further the cause of financial inclusion, thus, there is a need for institutional pluralism. The cooperatives, the collectives, and the groups enable the members of the unorganized sector to get access to finance at the subsidized rates. The corporations as institutional formats exist for earning profits and face mission drift in catering to the social objectives. In this regard, the collectives and cooperatives are formed by advancing the community interests that are neglected by the corporations, and the environmental concerns that are neglected by the community. Cooperatives, self-help groups, and collectives play an extremely important in redefining the mission and the vision for the group objectives. After the enumeration of the vision and mission, the cooperatives need to document their agreement as a formal social contract among the members of the community. Moreover, the cooperatives and collectives highlight the importance of moral advocacy, which include the need for community development, improved community acceptance, and joint lobbying. Kalyanpur and Newman (2017) in their research study highlight that within the institutional bricolage, the paradigm of bricolage is based on making the best use of the resources that are at the disposal of the members. Kropp et al. (2022) in their research study highlight that how the social responsibilities and activities enable the members to prioritize the objectives of the business. Further studies highlight that mobilization of the resources by the social entrepreneurs plays an extremely important role and, as a bricolage helps to extend the social objectives of an enterprise. Moreover, the cultural affiliations and social affiliations play an extremely important role in the success of the cooperatives and collectives. Campos (2024) in his study highlights that in a resource constrained environment through simultaneous practices of imitation and bricolage and ethics of care, based on institutional, human, and cultural elements, in a foreign environment how bricolage of cooperative through ethics of care enable the women to combat their challenges, without any sort of mission drift. The literature highlights that in a resource constraint environment, the social entrepreneurship through institutional setups and bricolage and social networking activities enable bricoleurs to resolve the local problems. Though social initiatives aim to further the interest of community, these are constrained by the existing institutional setup. Bricolage in form of collective institutional structures aid to overcome the limitations of existing institutional and political settings and constraint of resources. Guinnane (1995) in his research study highlights the importance of the institutional design in combating the problem of the fraud and mismanagement of funds, often touted as the problem of informational asymmetry that comprises the moral hazard and adverse selection. According to the study, the cooperatives through a series of auditing associations and centrals, resolved to solve these issues without compromising the financial sustainability of these groups. In Germany, as per the study, in 1850s, the cooperatives played an extremely important role. By affiliating with the centrals and auditing associations, that helped these institutional structures called cooperative to verify information and credit behaviour about the members and the matching the supply of funds to demand for funds, helped to combat the issues of moral hazard and adverse selection. Cooperatives in Germany are as pristine as belonging to an era before 1849. The small traders, peasants, and artisans faced a lack of economic and financial resources, in raising the capital from the market. In this regard, the moneylenders played an important role in furthering the cause of these small peasants, through providing the loans based on the local information and by assuming the unlimited liability (Greve, 2002). During 1849, to meet the financial needs of the members of unorganized sector and people who lack physical collateral, three types of cooperatives, namely Schulze-Delitzsch credit cooperatives, Hermann Schulze-Delitzsch and Raiffeisen's credit cooperative, made their foray. Though Schulze-Delitzsch credit cooperatives was wary of the state intervention in functioning of the local cooperatives, Raiffeisen's credit cooperative was not opposed to the role of the state. Raiffeisen and Haas cooperatives made use of the cultural factors like belief in promoting the financial inclusion among the members of unorganized workers and artisans and other small enterprises. In their institutional design and structure, the cooperatives promoted the cause of supervision and monitoring through setting up committees. Both Haas and Raiffeisen were in favour of unlimited liability for the members of the groups, but where the wealth differences were large, the Haas cooperative furthered the cause of limited liability for the members. To mitigate the problem of adverse selection, Raiffeisen promoted the formation of the cooperatives among the members from the same geography and community. Weiss (2007) in his study highlights that credit cooperatives in Germany helped to overcome an extremely important problem of information asymmetry. Saunders (2016) in his research study highlights that Raiffeisen through the state-help and self-help helped to create a sustainable German cooperative movement. Guinnane (2011) in his research study highlights that microfinance deals with various sensitive issues such as lending policy, typical loan sizes, sources of finance, and role of larger social and infrastructure. Blondeau (2006) highlights that many non-governmental organizations, voluntary associations, friendly societies, savings and credit cooperatives, and private companies are the source. Otto and Ukpere's (2011) higher cooperative credits and thrift association are a source of capital formation. Holloh (2003) in his research study highlights that the microfinance organizations are extremely popular in providing access to credit to the people at the bottom of the pyramid. Pashkova et al. (2016) in their research study highlight that macroeconomic policy, institutional, and geographical factors play an extremely role in providing access to credit to people at the bottom of the pyramid. Meagher (2002) in his research study highlights that supervision and regulation of financial institutions are extremely important for the allocation of capital. According to the various studies, supervision and monitoring of the capital structure is extremely important for ensuring appropriate risk management and protect depositors. Seibel and Tam in their research study highlight that the cooperative self-help groups provide the opportunity for providing the access to finance for the people at the bottom of the pyramid. These cooperative groups are successful due to the regulatory framework, training, supervision, and prudential standards. Glenk et al. (2009) in their research study highlight that the lack of access to credit for the cooperatives, lack of marketing, and supply chain support to the people at the bottom of the pyramid are the major challenges and constraints faced by the cooperatives. Lack of trust among the cooperatives and information symmetry is another reason for the failure of the credit cooperatives. The only major constituent for the success of the cooperatives is the establishment of credit cooperatives. Christen and Rosenberg (2000) highlight that regulation plays an important role in success of cooperatives. Besides, that strict regulation plays an extremely important role in the emergence of sustainable MFIs in India. Fouillet et al. (2013) in their study highlight that microfinance interventions involve process of transformation of financially excluded people. Microfinance intervention plays an important role in the reduction of poverty. Kyazze et al. (2020) highlight that the cooperatives play an extremely important role in maintaining accountability, cooperative ownership, and advanced communication. Donaghue (2004) in his research study highlights that financial service usage has taken various forms which include the subsidized loans to the poor and demonstration effect. The emergence of positive rhetoric has played an important role in countries like Indonesia, Bolivia, and

Bangladesh, to name a few. Feather and Meme (2019) highlight that the savings and loan associations play an extremely important role in the development of financial sector. Meyer and Nagarajan (2006) in their study highlight that there are various important issues in microfinance such as outreach, sustainability, and impact among the members of cooperatives. Allain and Madariaga (2019) in their research study highlight the importance of recombination of the old and new ideas by policy entrepreneurs through the political manifestations and bricolage in the form of group lending. Frick-Trzebitzky et al. (2023) in their research study highlight that the engagement with the rules, people, and material through the adaptive governance increases the social impact. Desa (2012) in their research study highlight that the social entrepreneurs confronted with institutional engage in bricolage. Further, the study highlights that the regulatory, technological, and political factors impact the resource mobilization through the use of bricolage. Huybrechts and Haugh (2018) in their research study highlight that the institutional pluralism creates a hybrid institutional format leading to network becoming more formalized. Kesidou et al. (2024) highlight that according to various studies, bricolage leads to the emergence of symbolic knowledge innovation. Bricolage and actor's agency paves the path for knowledge innovation. Yang and Leppäaho (2023) in their study highlight that international entrepreneurs use various national international networks. Leišytė and Sigl (2018) in their study highlight that the trust in scientific leadership and entrepreneurship shapes the helix relationships in the form of bricolage and institutional entrepreneurship, paving the way for change. de Bruin et al. (2017) in their study highlight that the collaborative arrangements and partnerships are the lifeblood of social entrepreneurship. Lukat et al. (2023) in their study highlight that in certain cases, institutionally set targets conflict with pre-existing norms and rules. The informal aspects of governance influence interpretation of new rules. Abid et al. (2023) in their research study highlight that organizational innovation serves as a mediator in the relationship between resource bricolage, financial performance, and competitive advantage. Sarkar (2019) in his research study highlights that the people working at the bottom of the pyramid overcome resource constraints and are able to assemble resources and align the business strategy to create social value. Grivins et al. (2017) in his research study highlights that the bricolage refers to the free use of the resources that are at the disposal of the entrepreneurs. Altglas (2014) in his study highlights that the bricolage overestimates its personal nature and neglects the socio-cultural logics. Also, while critically analysing, bricolage fails to understand social significance of individualism. Hota et al. (2019) in their study highlight that various social enterprises create social value to generate benefits and reduce the cost for society. Korsgaard et al. (2021) highlight that there is an important difference in resource mobilization across activities for entrepreneurs due to various situational and dispositional factors. Ashta (2019) in his research study highlights that inequalities in the developed countries have worsened the level of aggregate consumption. The social enterprises are the means to reduce these inequalities. Correa (n.d.) highlights the use of venture capital and external finance based on socialization to access finance. In the existing scenario, the resources of these entities are less than utilized. The firms in possession of finance or venture capitalists enable the small entrepreneurs to get access to finance. The author highlights that in a market, general equilibrium is not possible, but the social force of social control and peer pressure enables the small businesses and entrepreneurs to get access to finance. The social capital and social finance facilitate the financial inclusion of the poor people at the bottom of the pyramid. Nyamathi et al. (2013) in their research study highlight that microfinance is a social innovation that through dynamic incentives leads to steep reductions in risk, transaction costs, and permits the small borrowers to be profitable customers. Harima et al. (2021) in their research study highlight that the refugee embeddedness interact to create value within the limited resources of the organization. Siti Nazariah et al. (2024) in his research study highlight the importance of the interaction of the social logic and the formal structure. The authors argue that the MFIs are based on the non-profit-making model. The transition of the MFI social strategy-based model to profit-making model is facilitated through the social awareness, linked to the informal structure and formal control practices that facilitate the commercial logic. This paved the way for the success of the financial innovations called the microfinance credit. Koehne et al. (2022) in their research study highlight that prosocial power acts as a double-edged sword that enables social entrepreneurs to attain success in their business. Hidayati et al. (2023) in their study highlight that microfinance provides various benefits to the borrowers on the basis of resource management that is based on relationship between institutions and policies. Ranabahu (2017) in his research study highlights that the effectuation through causation helps to financially include the people at the bottom of the pyramid. Entrepreneurs use the available resources, skills, and networks and the mean-driven thinking to facilitate access to finance for the people at the bottom pyramid. Through the social intermediation and repetitive actions the entrepreneurs enable the businesses access to finance for profit making. Sottini et al. (2022) highlight that the social enterprises build the business models for people at the bottom of the pyramid through symbiotic ecosystems. Through the symbiotic ecosystem, these enterprises deliver the value. Handayani et al. (2018) in their research study highlight that the access to microfinance for the people at the bottom of the pyramid is based on a dynamic of socio-political processes. Using Bourdieu's concept, the authors argue that the domain of Islamic finance is a separate *field* that is impacted by various socio-political factors. He defines that the field is the pattern of struggles and interests that shape the financial realities of the institutions and enterprises. Within *field*, the relational position of the agents and the principle determines the sustainability and viability of the financial institutions. This is further determined by the interaction of various economic, social, and cultural capitals. Instead of the coping strategies, the reconciliation enables the small, microfinance firms to get access to capital and finance. Kalyanpur and Newman (2017) in their research study highlight that the main actors in the process of financing the poor are mean-focussed. The conventional institutional structures, according to the study, suffer from various limitations, including extreme focus on means rather than the stock of tools available. The author highlights that the bricolage enables the actors to achieve dramatic impact and changes through creative uses of the resources at the disposal of the actors.

5.1. Institutional Pluralism

There are various kinds of management cultures and styles, which include fatalist culture, which includes internalizing risk. In a bureaucratic style of management, the rules determine the risk management in a public-sector institution. In an individualist style of management, the risk is the opportunity for the private owner. Besides that the institutional pluralism facilitates the pooling of the common resources and thus facilitates better risk management and risk sharing. Thus, the risk sharing through the institutional pluralism and pooling of the resources paves the way for the attainment of the corporate objectives such as financial sustainability and profit maximization. This institutional pluralism paves the way for the attainment of the group objectives.

5.2. German Cooperative Model

The literature has for the long term ignored the discussion regarding the successful German rural cooperatives and has concentrated only on rich capitalist model of industrialists like manufacturers of coal, iron, and steel to name a few. Moreover, within the tapestry of the German society, the literature concentrated mainly on the interests of the large capitalists, without any regard to the interest of the small and marginal farmers and traders. Thus, in order to counter the strong force of capitalists, the social historians and authors have always propagated the state intervention as the panacea for the emancipation of the plight of the small farmers and artisans. Thus, this study concludes that the institutional design plays an extremely important role in the emancipation of the interests of the poor and marginalized. The number of members who formed the part of cooperatives has increased rapidly.

The history of the cooperatives in Germany can be explored through the lens of the narrative strategy. During the period 1815–1850, it is the first phase of the formation of the German cooperative and the phase of peasant liberalization. It was the phase of falling of the iron wall of the feudal system, abolishment of the zamindari system, and integration of the cooperative structure with the markets. 'Bauernfreiung' in Prussia or peasant liberalization was essentially seen as top-down approach to emancipation of the poor. This approach further led to the revolt of 1848, where the 'Bauernfreiung' of the 16th century gave way to the **mass movement** to the urban and lower income groups. This revolution of 1848 paved the way for the long-term compromise between the upper-class bureaucrats and the ruling class. Thus, as discussed earlier, there was an institutional gap and lack of institutional format or design to ensure the inclusion of the lower classes. The revolt of 1848 extended this cause and led to the recognition of the cause of emancipation of the poor. As the top-down approach of 'Bauernfreiung' gave way to the mass movement, a bottom-up approach with a critical mass, the cause of poverty reduction, and emancipation of the peasants became much more recognized. This movement gave rise to the origination of new institutional design of cooperatives which was based on the paradigm of plurality. This plurality and critical mass served the cause of resource deficit lower classes. Moreover, spatial bricolage and effectuation of cooperative model led to more political and institutional integration. Cooperatives, through a unique institutional design, gave rise to positive rhetoric for the inclusion of the poor and their cause of financial emancipation within the field of the German financial system. Though, as per the studies, the first phase of this movement was mainly urban, with liberal political figures like Hermann Schulze-Delitzsch, a former judge, giving rise to the cooperative institutional structure of German Union of German Cooperatives (Schulze-Delitzsch) and People's Bank based on the people's savings and credit. Whereas Schulze-Delitzsch was an urban institutional cooperative, another cooperative institutional structure, the Imperial Union of German Rural Cooperatives, started by Wilhelm Haas, a liberal minded, social reformer, and excellent organizer. However, Wilhelm Haas and his social innovation were short-lived due to various reasons, whereas Germany's cooperative movement: the ascetic, Christian-motivated, stubborn, somewhat, odd figure of Friedrich-Wilhelm Raiffeisen had the most long-lasting impact upon the rural cooperation in Germany. The most probable cause for the demise of German Rural Cooperatives, started by Wilhelm Haas was economic events. However, the period from 1894 to 1914 is the period of boom, with demand for consumption goods rising. The post-World War I period, in Germany, the state intervention played an important role in the establishment of newer financial institutions such as Raiffeisen. The semi-formal agrarian structure like Landwirtschaftliches Vereinswesen played an important role in integrating the diffused mass movement by peasants into a national movement, in the form of Raiffeisen, which paved the way for the financial inclusion of the poor. This model of cooperative movement was based on homogeneity of the members to reduce the risk of adverse selection by selecting the members from the same locality and the same economic background and unlimited liability for the poor. The social contract of financial cooperatives that was based on solidarity and collaboration was furthered through the selection of the members, who are homogenous in terms of their geographic proximity and income. Raiffeisen, further in its financial contract, extended the cause of financial inclusion through cooperatives through long-term loans rather than short-term loans. This model of cooperative finance was replicated across the globe and in 1904, gave rise to the cooperative movement in India, with the passing of Cooperative Societies Act, 1904. Schulze-Delitzsch, as an institutional format, failed due to the economic cycles and reasons, Raiffeisen failed due to the unlimited liability and maturity mismatching, with small duration savings being used to fund long term loans. Despite all these analyses, the contribution of the German cooperative of Raiffeisen to microfinance and cause of financial inclusion through social contracting with rational are undisputable. The financial contract of Raiffeisen, emerged as an answer to the cause of mission drift and helped the economic systems to achieve financial sustainability.

Table 2 highlights the summary of the literature review of how the German cooperatives evolved in Germany.

According to the conceptual model as given in Fig. 12, marginalized women often face backlash and financial exclusion. However, spatial bricolage – such as cooperatives – can help these women access finance. This marginalized group

Table 2. Summary of Literature Review.

Findings	Author
Local integration and economic systems • Challenges faced by migrant women • Cooperatives as social innovation that integrate women into mainstream	Campos (2024)
Spatial bricolage and resource utilization • Leveraging available resources creatively to overcome constraints • Helps entrepreneurs utilize local resources effectively • Enhancing their financial sustainability and credibility • Bricolage involves optimizing available resources to achieve financial sustainability • Collectives and cooperatives use institutional design and bricolage to meet their objectives • Social responsibilities and activities help prioritize business objectives, extending social goals through resource mobilization and bricolage	Korsgaard et al. (2021) Kalyanpur and Newman (2017) Kropp et al. (2022)
Evolution and impact of microfinance • 1990s, transitioning into commercial and private banking sectors • Group lending has emerged as a key strategy for addressing the financial needs of those at the bottom • Role of German MFIs in developing micro-lending across Europe • In the 1850s, Germany cooperatives played a key role in addressing fraud and mismanagement through auditing and central associations, solving issues like moral hazard and adverse selection • Early cooperatives provided crucial support to small traders and artisans, using local information and assuming unlimited liability	Seibel (2005) Kreuz (2006) Guinnane (1995) Greve (2002) Schulze-Delitzsch and Raiffeisen model Weiss (2007)

• Established in the mid-19th century, these cooperatives addressed the needs of the unorganized sector with differing approaches to state intervention and liability • German credit cooperatives addressed information asymmetry, promoting trust and effective credit management	
Challenges and limitations in microfinance • Identify how microfinance and group lending are vital for reaching underserved areas, though challenges persist • Notes limitations in group lending, such as issues of inclusion and sustainability • Highlights difficulties faced by small artisans in accessing credit due to information asymmetry and high screening costs • Cooperatives face challenges like limited access to credit, marketing issues, and lack of trust. Success depends on effective credit cooperatives and regulatory frameworks • Microfinance interventions are crucial for transforming financially excluded populations and reducing poverty	Cozarenco et al. (2022) Agarwal (2010) Küpper (2016) Glenk et al. (2009) Fouillet et al. (2013)
Historical development of microfinance in Germany • Evolution of microfinance in Germany from the 18th century to modern times, including the establishment of savings banks, credit cooperatives, and the impact of regulatory changes like the Prussian Savings Bank Decree (1838)	
Social costs and benefits of microfinance Social benefits of microfinance, such as improved financial inclusion, while also acknowledging the associated social costs, including lower profits for banks and the challenge of providing loans without collateral In resource-constrained environments, cooperatives use bricolage and ethics of care to help women overcome challenges without mission drift, leveraging institutional, human, and cultural elements	Franzini and Lucciarini (2022) Campos (2024)

(*Continued*)

Table 2. (*Continued*)

Findings	Author
Collective capabilities and solidarity	Armano et al. (2022)
Highlight the importance of collective capabilities in achieving group goals	
Institutionalization and network formation	Huybrechts and Haugh (2018)
Explore the role of institutional pluralism and network formation in facilitating collective action	Saunders (2016)
Institutional pluralism is essential for achieving comprehensive financial inclusion	Blondeau (2006)
Cooperatives and collectives redefine mission and vision to align with community needs and formalize these goals through social contracts among members	
These institutions emphasize moral advocacy, community development, acceptance, and joint lobbying	
Raiffeisen's model, supported by state help and self-help, created a sustainable cooperative movement in Germany	
Highlight the efficiency of financial cooperatives compared to specialized MFIs	
Supervision, regulation, and innovation	Meagher (2002)
Emphasize the importance of supervision and regulation in managing capital and ensuring financial stability	Abid et al. (2023); Huybrechts and Haugh (2018)
Highlight the role of bricolage and institutional pluralism in fostering innovation and addressing resource constraints	

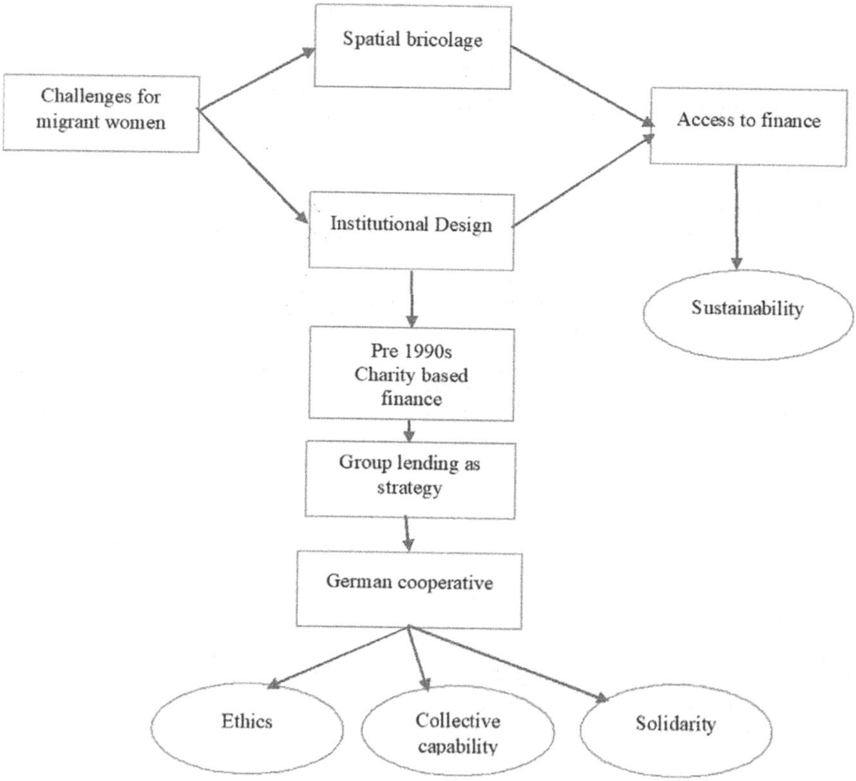

Fig. 12. Conceptual Model for German Cooperatives. *Source*: Author's work.

typically struggles with financial access due to a lack of physical collateral, which limits their ability to obtain credit or microfinance. In the 1990s, with the rise of privatization, the design and context of cooperatives and group lending mechanisms helped improve financial inclusion for the poor. Additionally, German cooperatives, as historical institutions, have facilitated access to finance through collective capability, solidarity, and mutual support.

6. Conclusion

The study highlights that mass movement in Germany gave rise to the social lending structure in the form of Hermann Schulze-Delitzsch and Raiffeisen. Schulze-Delitzsch credit cooperative is wary of state intervention and Raiffeisen's credit cooperative is not opposed to the role of the state in the functioning of the group lending for microfinance in Germany. These structures have played an important role in the microfinance and financial inclusion of the poor at the bottom of the pyramid. Further, these models have been replicated across different countries. Cooperatives have to play an important role in the rural economy of a nation. These microfinance models have to form a cornerstone of cooperatives finance model in the nation. These social practices have come to fill an important gap in microfinance of the nation.

References

Abid, N., Dowling, M., Ceci, F., & Aftab, J. (2023). Does resource bricolage foster SMEs' competitive advantage and financial performance? A resource-based perspective. *Business Strategy and the Environment*, *32*(8), 5833–5853.

Agarwal, A. (2010). Financial inclusion: Challenges & opportunities. *Skoch Summit*, *2*, 5–6.

Allain, M., & Madariaga, A. (2019). Understanding policy change through bricolage: The case of Chile's renewable energy policy. *An International Journal of Policy, Administration and Institutions*, *33*(3), 675–692.

Armano, E., Briziarelli, M., & Risi, E. (2022). *Digital platforms and algorithmic subjectivities*. University of Westminster Press.

Ashta, A. (2019). *A realistic theory of social entrepreneurship*. Palgrave Macmillan.

Altglas, V. (2014). Bricolage: Reclaiming a conceptual tool. *Culture and Religion*, *15*(4), 474–493.

Bina, A. (2010). Rethinking agricultural production collectivities. *Economic and Political Weekly*, *XLV*(9), 64–78.

Blondeau, N. (2006). *Microfinance an instrument of sustainable development* (9th ed.). Ètudes.

Bonus, H., & Schmidt, G. (1990). The cooperative banking group in the Federal Republic of Germany: Aspects of institutional change. *Journal of Institutional and Theoretical Economics*, *146*, 180–207.

de Bruin, A., Shaw, E., & Lewis, K. V. (2017). The collaborative dynamic in social entrepreneurship. *Entrepreneurship & Regional Development*, *29*(7–8), 575–585.

Campos, M. J. Z. (2024). The expansion of alternative forms of organizing integration: Imitation, bricolage, and an ethic of care in migrant women's cooperatives. *Journal of Business Ethics*, *194*, 1–16.

Christen, R., & Rosenberg, R. (2000). *The rush to regulate: Legal frameworks for microfinance* Occasional Paper, CGAP, Washington DC, CGAP.

Correa, A. (n.d.). Venture capital and microfinance: An instrumental approach Romar Correa. *Brazilian Keynesian Review*, *3*(2), 107.

Cozarenco, A., Hartarska, V., & Szafarz, A. (2022). Subsidies to microfinance institutions: How do they affect cost efficiency and mission drift? *Applied Economics*, *54*(44), 5099–5132. https://doi.org/10.1080/00036846.2022.2041176

Desa, G. (2012). Resource mobilization in international social entrepreneurship: Bricolage as a mechanism of institutional transformation. *Entrepreneurship Theory and Practice*, *36*(4), 727–751.

Donaghue, K. (2004). Microfinance in the Asia Pacific. *Asian Pacific Economic Literature*, *18*(1), 41–61.

Feather, C., & Meme, C. K. (2019). Strengthening housing finance in emerging markets: The savings and credit cooperative organisation (SACCO) model in Kenya. *Housing Studies*, *34*(9), 1485–1520.

Fouillet, C., Hudon, M., Harriss-White, B., & Copestake, J. (2013). Microfinance studies: Introduction and overview. *Oxford Development Studies*, *41*, S1–S16.

Franzini, M., & Lucciarini, S. (2022). The social costs of the gig economy and institutional responses: Forms of institutional bricolage in Italy, France and the Netherlands. *Digital Platforms and Algorithmic Subjectivities*, *24*, 225.

Frick-Trzebitzky, F., Alba, R., & Fehrs, K. (2023). Adaptive governance as bricolage. *Geographica Helvetica*, *78*, 397–407.
Glenk, K., Pavliashvili, J., & Profeta, A. (2009). Preferences for rural credit systems and their impact on the implementation of credit unions in Georgia. *Research in Agricultural and Applied Economics*, *37*(1), 1–16.
Greve, R. (2002). *The German cooperative banking group as a strategic network: Function and performance (No. 29)*. Arbeitspapiere des Instituts für Genossenschaftswesen der Westfälischen Wilhelms-Universität Münster.
Grivins, M., Keech, D., Kunda, I., &. Tisenkopfs, T. (2017). Bricolage for self-sufficiency: An analysis of alternative food networks. *Sociologia Ruralis*, *57*(3), 340–356.
Guinnane, T. W. (1995). *Diversification, liquidity, and supervision for small financial institutions: nineteenth-century German credit cooperatives* Papers 733, Yale – Economic Growth Center. https://ideas.repec.org/s/fth/yalegr.html.
Guinnane, T. W. (2011). The historical fertility transition: A guide for economists. *Journal of Economic Literature*, *49*(3), 589–614. http://www.jstor.org/stable/23071723
Handayani, W., Haniffa, R., & Hudaib, M. (2018). A Bourdieusian perspective in exploring the emergence and evolution of the field of Islamic microfinance in Indonesia. *Journal of Islamic Accounting and Business Research*, *9*(4), 482–497.
Harima, A., Periac, F., Murphy, T., & Picard, S. (2021). Entrepreneurial opportunities of refugees in Germany, France, and Ireland: Multiple embeddedness framework. *International Entrepreneurship and Management Journal*, *17*, 625–663.
Hidayati, E., Sofyan, A., Poernomo, D., & Supranoto. (2023, October 2). Building sustainable village-owned enterprises: The institutional change of microfinance in Banyuwangi Regency. *KnE Social Sciences*, *8*(17), 304–323.
Holloh, D. (2003). *Microfinance institutions study*. GTZ-ProFI.
Hota, P. K., Mitra, S., & Qureshi, I. (2019). Adopting bricolage to overcome resource constraints: The case of social enterprises in Rural India. *Management and Organization Review*, *15*(2), 371–402.
Huybrechts, B., & Haugh, H. (2018). The roles of networks in institutionalizing new hybrid organizational forms: Insights from the European Renewable Energy Cooperative Network. *Organization Studies*, *39*(8), 1085–1108.
Iversen, T., & Soskice, D. (2019). *Democracy and prosperity: Reinventing capitalism through a turbulent century*. Princeton University Press.
Kalyanpur, N., & Newman, A. (2017). Form over function in finance: International institutional design by bricolage. *Review of International Political Economy*, *24*(3), 363–392.
Kesidou, E., Plakoyiannaki, E., & Tardios, J. A. (2024). Symbolic knowledge innovation through bricolage in the periphery: The Bauhaus movement. *Journal of Economic Geography*, *24*(4), 567–594.
Koehne, F., Woodward, R., & Honig, B. (2022). The potentials and perils of prosocial power: Transnational social entrepreneurship dynamics in vulnerable places. *Journal of Business Venturing*, *37*(4), 106206.
Korsgaard, S., Müller, S., & Welter, F. (2021). It's right nearby: How entrepreneurs use spatial bricolage to overcome resource constraints. *Entrepreneurship & Regional Development*, *33*(1–2), 147–173.
Kreuz, C. (2006). *Microlending in Germany*. International Labor Organization.
Kropp, S., Klimovich, S., & Pape, U. (2022). Legitimation strategies of Russian companies: A bricolage of social responsibility. *East European Politics*, *39*(1), 15–38.
Küpper, S. (2016). *Efficiency and effectiveness of member-based microfinance institutions*.
Kyazze, L. M., Nsereko, I., & Nkote, I. (2020). Cooperative practices and non-financial performance of savings and credit cooperative societies. *International Journal of Ethics and Systems*, *36*(3), 411–425. https://doi.org/10.1108/IJOES-06-2020-0087
Leišytė, L., & Sigl, L. (2018). Academic institutional entrepreneurs in Germany: Navigating and shaping multilevel research commercialization governance. *Triple Helix*, *5*(1), 1–23.

Lukat, E. C., Schoderer, M., & Salvador, S. C. (2023). When international blueprints hit local realities: Bricolage processes in implementing IWRM in South Africa, Mongolia and Peru. *Water Alternatives*, *15*(2), 473–500.

Meagher, P. (2002). *Microfinance regulation in developing countries: A comparative review of current practice*. University of Maryland.

Meyer, R. L., & Nagarajan, G. (2006). Microfinance in developing countries: Accomplishments, debates, and future directions. *Agricultural Finance Review*, *66*(2), 167.

Nyamathi, A., Ekstrand, M., Salem, B. E., Sinha, S., Ganguly, K. K., & Leake, B. (2013). Impact of Asha intervention on stigma among rural Indian women With AIDS. *Western Journal of Nursing Research*, *35*(7), 867–883. https://doi.org/10.1177/0193945913482050

Otto, G., & Ukpere, W. (2011). Credit and thrift co-operatives in Nigeria: A potential source of capital formation and employment. *African Journal of Business Management*, *5*(14), 5675–5680.

Padilla-Meléndez, A., Del Aguila-Obra, A. R., Lockett, N., & Fuster, E. (2020). Entrepreneurial universities and sustainable development. The network bricolage process of academic entrepreneurs. *Sustainability*, *12*(4), 1403.

Pashkova, N., Trujillo-Barrera, A., Apostolakis, G., Van Dijk, G., Drakos, P. D., & Baourakis, G. (2016). *Business management models of microfinance institutions (MFIs) in Africa: A study into their enabling environments*. IGI Publisher.

Ranabahu, N. (2017). Entrepreneurial decision-making and expertise acquisition: A study among Sri Lankan microfinance borrowers. *Journal & Proceedings of the Royal Society of New South Wales*, *151*(1), 109–110.

Sarkar, S. (2019). *Grassroots entrepreneurs and social change at the bottom of the pyramid: The role of bricolage*. Routledge.

Saunders, T. J. (2016). Self-help and state rescue: The Raiffeisen bank and rationalization of the cooperative movement in Weimar Germany. *Canadian Journal of History*, *51*(2), 300–328.

Seibel, H. D. (2003). Taking stock: History matters in microfinance. *Small Enterprise Development – An International Journal of Microfinance and Business Development*, *14*(2), 10–12.

Seibel, H. D. (2005). *SHG banking in India: The evolution of rural financial innovation*. University of Cologne, Development Research Centre, Cologne.

Siti Nazariah, A. Z., Siti-Nabiha, A. K., & Azhar, Z. (2024). The commercialisation of microfinance: Deploying management control to address institutional complexity. *Journal of Accounting in Emerging Economies*, *14*(5), 1176–1193.

Sottini, A., Ciambotti, G., & Littlewood, D. (2022). Engaging symbiotic ecosystems to build community centred business models for the BoP: Evidence from small social enterprises in East Africa. *International Small Business Journal*, *40*(8), 935–965.

Weiss, D. S. (2007). *The impact of event scale: Revised. Cross-cultural assessment of psychological trauma and PTSD* (pp. 219–238). Springer Science + Business Media. https://psycnet.apa.org/doi/10.1007/978-0-387-70990-1_10

Yang, M., & Leppäaho, T. (2023). Network bricolage of international entrepreneurs for new market entry: A cross-national study of small biotech firms. *International Marketing Review*, *40*(7), 22–44.

Chapter 5

Power of Collectives in Combatting Resource Poverty: A Case Study of Grameen Bank in Bangladesh

Abstract

Grameen Bank in Bangladesh is a collective initiative that is aimed at providing the access to microfinance at the bottom of the pyramid. The people at the bottom of the pyramid do not have access to collateral and thus are unable to obtain finance. Mohammed Yunus in Bangladesh highlighted the importance of group lending through the social capital on the well-being of the people. Through Grameen Bank, the semi-formal financial institution emphasized the importance of promoting the financial welfare among the people at the bottom of the pyramid. The chapter highlights the importance of Village Pay for Phone (VPP) programme to facilitate access to finance through easy access. Through the VPP programme, the people at the bottom of the pyramid get access to alternate channel for banking through community banking. Grameen Bank provides a network structure of structural finance, which provide the benefit of community lending and access to finance for the people at the bottom of the pyramid. Comilla type of Grameen Bank institutional design helps to promote ensure competitive advantage in the form of stability and dynamic capabilities for the people at the bottom of the pyramid.

Keywords: Grameen Bank; microfinance; poor; financial inclusion; social capital

1. Introduction

Microfinance is an important tool for poverty reduction, and this is aptly visible in the Grameen Bank initiative taken by Nobel Peace Prize winner Mohammed Yunus in Bangladesh. Grameen Bank caters mainly to the extremely poor and

Global Perspectives on Financial Inclusion: Case Studies in Microfinance and Women's Empowerment, 79–95

Published under exclusive licence by Emerald Publishing Limited
doi:10.1108/978-1-83708-080-920251005

marginalized people who do not have their own savings and must depend upon the subsidy and charity for their financial needs. The Grameen Bank is a group-lending initiative that helps the poor people collect their money and then lend it among themselves for meeting their financial needs. This initiative became a landmark and a torchbearer for the microfinance sectors in the other parts of the world. This initiative also is involved in providing social aid and assistance for various charity-led initiatives in Bangladesh and world over. There are many studies that have looked at the working of this model and its replicability. But none of the studies have captured the modifications and changes in the working of this microfinance initiative. Though the model is highly successful, like any other financial initiative continuity of this model is also fraught with various difficulties including difficulty in adaptation to environment. Like most of group lending model this initiative is also on verge of discontinuance. And this chapter will provide a contemporary analysis of the challenges faced by the Grameen Bank Model in modern Bangladesh. Hermeneutical approach is used for collecting the data from existing repositories and literature. Semi-structured interviews are conducted with microfinance experts to capture their views regarding the feasibility of this model in the modern world. This chapter will be of interest to bankers and policymakers.

2. Research Problem

The financial inclusion of people at the bottom of the pyramid is a challenge for the governments all over the world. Most of the people who are discriminated do not have access to the financial resources, and they must rely on the informal sector that comprises of the unorganized money lenders and organizations like shops and relatives for the access to finance.

3. Literature Review

A Universal Declaration on Human Rights asserted that everyone has a right to the following:

A standard of living adequate for the health and well-being of himself and of his family, including food, clothing, housing and medical care, and necessary social services to security in the event of unemployment, sickness, disability, widowhood, old age, or other lack of livelihood in circumstances beyond his control. According to the author, the people at the bottom of the pyramid are unable to get access to finance due to the loss of social capital and collateral as the banks do not have any information about the credit worthiness of the poor. In this regard, the reduction in the information asymmetry is made possible through the selection of the homogenous members and also making available the telephone infrastructure in the villages to facilitate access to information and improve the financial literacy. Thus, the telephony for all has helped to improve the impact of the Grameen Banks on the financial plight of its members. However, despite all the efforts, the level of poverty in developing world is still very high. Yunus (1998) in his research study, highlights that the cause of poverty in Bangladesh is not lack of demand or the lack of skills among the labour and the poor but it is the lack of understanding about the human capabilities, poverty, and institutional designs that can address the abject poverty. The author of the study highlights the vagueness in definition of poverty and he cites the Gresham law. This Gresham law states that if the poor and non-poor are clubbed together in the same group then the non-poor will drive out the poors, and this will lead to inequities and further misery for the poor. Yunus (1999) in his research study has highlighted the grim realities of poverty, which force a family to migrate to Dhaka. And how the group lending through Grameen Bank has changed the economic realities for the family by providing the access to better financial resources. Khandker et al. (1995) in their research study highlight the importance of poverty reduction through group lending. According to the author, the peer monitoring has a far-reaching impact on the reduction of cost of lending, whereas the group formation and monitoring is a costly exercise. However, many authors in their paper discuss that the Grameen Bank has been able to overcome the issue of implementation of development programmes by upholding the good performance of the work force. Morduch (1999) in his research study highlights the new approach to poverty alleviation through market-based institutions that serve as the agents of opportunity creation for the poor people at the bottom of the pyramid. Various authors in their research study highlight that the Grameen Bank in Bangladesh has been the harbinger of rural development for the people at the bottom of the pyramid. The study further highlights the various disadvantages of the people at the bottom of the pyramid, in terms of reducing the risk for the poor people at the bottom of the pyramid. The authors in their research study highlight that the poor through the group lending institutions become the agent of change and development. Through skill building and capacity building they emerge as the partners in development and change. Hassan and Renteria-Guerrero (1997) in their study highlight the importance of the financial intermediation in promoting community development and development of group lending in India. Bernasek (2003) in his research study has highlighted that the Grameen Bank is the measure and vehicle of social change. However, the Grameen Bank does not help to reduce the poverty and indeed helps to bring about the social change. Rahman and Wahid (1992) in their study highlight that the Grameen Bank has been successful in providing the loans to people below the poverty line and people who own less than 1 acre land. This initiative has enabled the marginalized borrowers to earn their livelihood and also helped them build a financial attitude that has led to the recovery of more than 95% repayment rates. Rahman and Wahid (1992) in their research study highlight that the Grameen Bank has an impact upon the financial and macroeconomic growth of Bangladesh. Hulme (2009) further emphasize that the poor people are not passive spectator but active participants in the growth of the economy. Yunus (2003) in his study highlights the historical context of the Grameen Bank. It was a social innovation and a disruption that was initiated out of the urge to help the poor people in Bangladesh to fight poverty. Research studies further highlight that how the group lending leveraged the solidarity in diversity among the people from the different religions and beliefs but bound by one objective to cater to the needs of the people below the pyramid in their endeavour to access finance. The study highlights that despite the lack of collateral due to the adherence to group norms and consensus on goal and objective, the members feel united and work towards the achievement of the common goal of financial inclusion relentlessly. Karim (2008) in his research study highlights that the role of the gender in promoting modernization and financial inclusion among women from the bottom of the pyramid. Many research studies highlight that the Grameen Bank has played an important role to develop a model of self-reliance and sustainability among the members of the self-help groups. Many researchers in their research model highlight that the Grameen Bank in Bangladesh is an innovative microfinance model that through telecom-based infrastructure and VPP had extended the utility in the form of access to credit and finance for the people at the bottom of the pyramid. Hossain (2013) in his research study highlighted that the social capital has an important role to play in the welfare and social growth of the marginalized and the poverty-struck people. Rahman and Nie (2011) in their study highlight that the major microfinance approaches that exist in Bangladesh, which include the extending of the loans through social capital instead of the physical collateral. And the impact of the social networks in promoting the welfare and the financial sustainability of the members of the group at the bottom of the pyramid. Various authors in their research study highlight that the Grameen Banks play an extremely important role in further promoting the habit of savings among the members of the group. Many authors further corroborate that social capital and network enable the groups to achieve access to finance at the bottom of the pyramid. Pitt and Khandker (1996) in his study highlights the impact of the macroeconomic policies on the financial coverage and financial policies pursued by the Grameen Bank. According to the author, the macroeconomic policies have a major role to play in influencing the financial policies pursued by the microfinance institution. Further, the government highlights the importance of pursuing the social goals for inclusion while ensuring the financial sustainability. Auwal and Singhal (1992) in his study emphasize that the social innovation like Grameen Bank helps to further the interests of the people at the bottom of the pyramid. Develtere and Huybrechts (2005) in their research study highlight that the Grameen Bank and microfinance have a positive impact on the social and economic life of the people from the bottom of the pyramid. The social networks and peer mechanism play an important role in promoting the solidarity among the members of the group. This also helps the poor people get access to finance. Moreover, as per the members of the social groups, the Grameen Bank is based on the minimalist approach and decentralization, where by the members rely upon the borrowings from the other members of the group to get access to the loans at the bottom of the pyramid. Yet as per the author, critics highlight the inability of the microfinance to reach to the bottom of the pyramid. Besides, the social impact the microfinance initiative also helps to improve the economic well-being and the income of the people at the bottom of the pyramid. Rahman (2015) further highlights that the importance of the informant strategies in a group in generating information asymmetry and enabling the people at bottom of the pyramid to get access to finance. Fuglesang and Chandler (1986) in their study highlight that the challenge of financial inclusion is the problem of ensuring the participation of the disadvantaged women in the process of financial inclusion. This includes the creation of the proper social and economic environment to ensure the financial inclusion of all within the economic and financial system. Moreover, the literature highlights that the various institutional designs such as the Grameen Banks, Bangladesh Rural Advancement Committee (BRAC), and Association for Social Advancement (ASA) have been able to promote the participation of the poor in the credit creation and financialization. Hossain (2013) further highlights the importance of the various initiatives such as 'Sixteen principles' to train the members of the group to adhere to the group norms and principles of corporate governance. Bernasek (2003) in his research study highlights that if the Grameen Bank is in conjunction with the other programmes for the social change it will lead to higher impact in reducing the poverty for the people at the bottom of the pyramid. Various studies highlight that the Grameen Bank has been very successful in combating the financial indiscipline and changing the mindset of the people at the bottom of the pyramid. Bernasek (2003) in his study highlights that the Grameen Bank is a model of micro-credit and capital formation. Bhuiyan et al. (2017) in their research study highlight that the group lending through the Grameen Bank has a positive impact on reducing the poverty levels within the economy. Maskooki and Gunasekaran (2001) in their research study highlight that while adopting the institutional design of Grameen Bank, the various geographic regions should consider the economic, social, and political environment of the country. Mokhtar et al. (2012) in their research study highlight that the institutional designs for the cooperative and collaborative financial vehicles differ according to the geography. Khandker et al. (1994) in their research study highlight that the Grameen Banks as the institutional structured provide various benefits such as the decentralization and committed leadership that enable the members of the group to achieve financial inclusion and economic growth and development. Bernasek and Stanfield (1997) in their research study highlight that importance of the dynamic incentives in the form of excess loans and monitoring by the members in promoting the sustainability of the cooperative groups as financial vehicle. The study highlights that the women and females achieve a higher social change through the vehicle of social lending and group lending. The study highlights the importance of the cultural norms and the subjective norms such as existence of purdah and segregation of the men and women and the ritual of wearing the burqah in promoting the culture of group lending among the members of the group. The study highlights the importance of difference in gender roles and the existing discrimination in promoting the financial inclusion of through the group lending. Bhuiyan et al. (2017) highlight that the microcredit through the Grameen Bank has a greater impact on the various macroeconomic parameters that include the price, stability, and economic growth. Harper (2002) in his research study highlights that the cooperative lending takes place through the Grameen Bank of self-help groups. The Grameen Banks are the semi-formal groups that comprise various women members who are from the same profession, sect, or culture. These members they come together by collecting the savings to facilitate the financial intermediation and the rotation of the loans among the members of the group. On the contrary, the self-help group linkage programmes are cooperative financial inclusion plan that is run by the homogenous members with the aid of the banks and self-help promoting institutions. Various authors in their research study highlight that the Grameen Bank approach is an extremely innovative approach to provide the finance to the people at the bottom of the pyramid. According to study the women and marginalized need hand holding and support to be able to engage and pursue the business of group lending to ensure access to finance for all the bottom of the pyramid. The research studies highlight that the success of the Grameen Bank is driven by the great institutional designs and organizational formats that comprise of decentralized organizational systems. Unlike the commercial bank, the borrowers can borrow from the group free of interest and also earn an interest of 8.5% on the deposits. Compulsorily contributed 5% amount to the land fund the borrowers cannot be withdrawn. Despite the high cost of funds, the Grameen Bank has been able to cater to the financial needs of people at the bottom of the pyramid. Hassan and Renteria-Guerrero (1997) in their research study highlight that the financial intermediation through the Grameen Bank has helped the Government of Bangladesh to fight poverty.

4. Discussion and Analysis

4.1. Structural Approach – The Comilla Cooperative Model of Microfinance in Bangladesh

Existing literature highlights that microfinance suffers from various imperfections, including institutional and structural rigidities. Thus, over the period governments across the globe have been involved in adopting different formats and institutional designs that do away with the installation of rigid frameworks like banking based on the information regarding the creditworthiness available through the secondary sources. The cooperatives are institutions that are based on self-help and group mechanisms. The marginalized and poor who lack physical collateral are provided access to finance through the cooperatives. Cooperatives are formed by groups of marginalized women, who come together to provide access to finance to the people at the bottom of the pyramid. The world's first cooperative society was established in Aberdeen in the Shore Porter's Society (1498). The Shore Porter Society began as a group of porters or Pynours who worked at Aberdeen Harbour and formed the cooperative as a group of porters collectively for mutual existence. Several different cooperatives are formed subsequently, including the Lennox Town Friendly Victualling Society in 1812. Frnwick Weaver's Cooperative was the first evident cooperative society that was incorporated on 14 March 1761, in Fenwick, East Ayrshire. This cooperative society was started by accident when a local weaver manhandled a sack of oatmeal into John Walker's whitewashed front room. Robert Owen is considered to the pioneer of the cooperative society and his ideas influenced consumer cooperatives across the globe. He is accredited with having formed the villages of cooperation in Scotland and is also considered the father of cooperatives and microfinance in India. The Rochdale Society of Equitable Pioneers was established on the Rochdale principle based on the cooperatives. In 1892, Derrick Nicholson tried to find the means to establish institutions to support and help the agricultural sector. In 1904, the Cooperative Societies Act was passed as a recognition to the cooperative movement. In Bangladesh, the cooperative movement was given impetus with the initiatives of Dr Akhther Hamid Khan. The country celebrates National Cooperative Day on November 6 and the cooperative movement has become a truly mass movement in Bangladesh for the financial inclusion of the poor. The institutional approach to tackle the problem of financial inclusion of the poor in Bangladesh has existed since the 19th century when Bengali poet Rabindranath Tagore established Sriniketon in East Bengal in 1921. This institution has served more than 85 villages and during the pre-Independence era, many rural development societies developed in Bangladesh.

The problem of financial exclusion of the poor has existed in Asia Pacific as long as 1880. In 1880, the British Government recognized the importance of providing institutional credit to the peasants. In 1904, the Cooperative Societies Act was passed, which led to the cooperative movement. In the Asian subcontinent, the Cooperative movement officially received the consent of Lord Curzon in March 1904. Thus came into being the official system of cooperative societies started as a three-tier cooperative society, with primary societies at the bottom of the pyramids. In 1912, the movement gained new momentum with many credit cooperative societies being set up with limited liability, and the Apex Society known as Samabaya Bank was established in 1948. In Bangladesh, in 1971, the integrated rural development programme gave birth to the ***Comilla Two-Tier cooperative bank***, which gave further impetus to the movement for the inclusion of the people at the bottom of the pyramid. The Swanirbhar movement was further started in 1970s. Gradually, various non-government organizations started undertaking various initiatives such as Grameen Bank, BRAC, ASA, and Proshika. Grameen Bank started by Mohammed Yunus gave a new direction to microfinance through the decentralized organizational structure and core competencies in the form of social capital and financial leadership. The bank unravelled and dismantled the installations of rigid structures and centralized institutional designs such as commercial banks to empower the poor through microfinance. Two-tier institutional designs for microfinance in Bangladesh comprise (a) Bittaheen Samabaya Samity (b) Krishak Samabaya Samity, and (c) Mahila Bittaheen Samity, which were coordinated at the central cooperative bank level. Thus, these cooperatives, or the Samabaya samitis have made strides into the interior of Bangladesh to facilitate the inclusion of the poor. The conduct of the meetings and adherence to the shared norms have emerged as the major mode of governance of these Samabaya samitis (Sarker et al., 2019). In the recent past, the microfinance sector in Bangladesh has witnessed the coming up of the network structure, which are far more decentralized and are virtual organization. These organizations have helped the cooperatives to create core competencies and cost savings along with offering flexibility and adaptability. The Comilla-type cooperatives in Bangladesh have played an important role in giving the impetus to the rural development with self-reliance.

4.2. Strive for Stability

Microfinance industry is in nascent stage and not yet maturing. From 17th century when formally presidency Bank of Bengal and three other presidencies along with private banks started banking to current day emergence of myriad institution gap in terms of financial exclusion for poor has declined. Thanks to institutional designs like Grameen Bank and National Rural Livelihood Mission (NRLM) by Government of India under Hon'ble PM Modiji that paved the way for access to finance for poor despite mission drift faced by commercial banks. From the era of socialist and charity-based model of microbanking to sustainable finance, the initiatives like group lending have helped to improve the asset quality of banks, without tinkering with monetary policy or imposing fiscal burden on the state. Not only the Rotating Savings and Credit Association (ROSCAs), Guanxi have served as signposts and guideposts but initiatives like Grameen Bank have helped in creating best practices that are capable of replication and stand the test of multiple contexts and realities. Today the issue is not of innovation but achieving stability in NRLM. A decade later microfinance will see the wave of expansion with coming up of market institutions and digitalization but today there is a need for incremental growth and maintaining status quo. Unlearning and decimating of Microfinance can uproot the dream of financial inclusion for poor. The world is at an interesting juncture. The primary activities like marketing, service, follow-up, and disbursal are getting support through technology and digital channels. This is leading to the reduction of cost and emergence of profitable business models for SFBs and NBFCs or MFIs. A new sector of informal and semi-informal finance through regulation is emerging for the benefit of marginalized people globally. A true visionary and teacher who transformed the world of microfinance, Nobel laureate Sir Muhammad Yunus revolutionized the landscape with his ground-breaking concept of group lending through Grameen Bank, established in Jobran, Bangladesh. Not only he gave a model, but through collective learning and leveraging capabilities he enabled creation of core competencies in terms of microbanks run through peer mechanism. Yet another wave of digitalization can further give impetus to dynamic capabilities. Replication of the Grameen Banks as SHGs and microbanks has led to competitive advantage in microfinance. Today, his microfinance initiative has inspired millions of financial programmes worldwide. Sir Yunus has paved the way for financial inclusion for 1.7 billion people living in poverty, opening doors to new opportunities and hope. Beyond the goal of creating liquidity and providing access to liquidity for the poor, the self-help groups are paving the way for capital creation through savings and credit disbursal. This vehicle is not only leading to outflow and inflow of funds but also with livelihood programmes aimed at mindset change and social intermediation, it is adding to the country's gross domestic product through employment generation and growth.

4.3. Strategic View of Grameen Bank as an Organization

Grameen Bank is a group lending programme that enables the members at the bottom of the pyramid to get access to finance without collateral. The Grameen

Bank is based on the mission statement of helping the Grameen Bank to become the 'Bank of Poor'. The bank aims to achieve this objective by 'Providing comprehensive financial services to empower the poor to realize their potential and to break out of the vicious cycle of poverty'. This mission statement provides a direction to the group lending vehicle to enable the poor to get access to finance, without any collateral, through the access to the social capital. Both the mission and vision are part of the strategic intent of the Grameen Bank. Further, the strategic intent enables the bank to decide the measurable objectives that are the yardstick for measuring the financial performance of these group lending vehicles. As part of the strategic intent, the financial institution has laid down the explicit objectives that include the alleviation of the poverty, providing financial services, encouraging entrepreneurship, providing education, empowering the women, providing the peer support, and take banking to the people. Further, the primary activities such as sourcing the funds from the deposits, procurement of the funds, operations, marketing and sales, and after-sales services have played an important role in promoting the efficiency of the banks. Micheal Porter's analysis is an important technique that is used for studying, various factors that impact the competitive advantage of the banks through low cost and better efficiency. In addition, the primary activities such as procurement, human resource management, technological development, and infrastructure are intertwined with the primary activities, which further enable the organization to achieve its objectives and organizational goals. The value chain helps the organization to create value for the users in the form of lower costs for the products that are produced. The value chain also helps to create a competitive advantage for the organization through lower costs and niches among the premium segment to enable them to get access to credit and finance. Peer mechanisms and internal loan dynamics play an extremely important role in promoting the financial inclusion and sustainability of the members of the groups.

4.4. Case Study of VPP

The objective of this case study is to understand the role of VPP, in the development of the rural regions through (1) the sale of the services and (2) the buyer of the services. Digital transformation through a new channel of distribution of financial services plays an important role in delivering products and services at the lowest cost possible. The objective of the VPP programme is to provide access to financial services for the people at the bottom of the pyramid. The major mission of the Grameen Banks is to provide access to finance for the people in the interior of the hinterlands and the villages. Through the various non-financial incentives, phones offer various benefits such as easy access to finance which further helps to reduce the inequalities among the people. The financially excluded people and rural villagers are interested in getting access to information and also finance. Lack of information or informational asymmetry regarding the villagers and their creditworthiness is a major challenge for the people at the bottom of the pyramid. In this regard, VPP introduced by the Grameen Banks, acts as a conduit to provide the desired information for the people at the bottom of the pyramid.

Many of the programmes have far-reaching social impacts on well-being of rural people. This phone service and the current infrastructure are grossly inadequate to meet the information needs of the people at the bottom of the pyramid. Moreover, the telephone density in Bangladesh is as less as 0.26 lines per 100 people in the world, with a waiting time of more than 10 years. Thus, the current infrastructure of the nation is grossly inadequate to meet the needs. Despite all the shortcomings, the VPP model is an extremely innovative tool and channel to meet the needs of the people for finance and credit.

4.5. Theoretical Perspective of Dynamic Punctuated Equilibrium

On a temporal plane, initially, the Grameen Bank which started in 1970, served as the vehicle to serve the needs of the poor. Technological and digital transformation of any institution is often fraught with various challenges across the different phases. From the resistance from the general public to the digital transformation of the financial programme in the form of the need for constant communication, the ability to face and mitigate the resistance, implement the change gradually, and need for the training and assistance for the people at the bottom of the pyramid, this programme faces various challenges in the form of punctuation and hiatus. Punctuated equilibrium highlights the evolution in spurts rather than gradually and steadily. In this regard, the adoption of digital technology and the VPPs programme happens gradually. Within the purview of the communication theory, due to the bounded rationality, and lack of information processing, driven by the popular opinion punctuated equilibrium occurs in financial decision-making. This programme is a partnership between the Grameen Bank, Grameen Telecom, and Grameen Phone. The state or the government facilitates the appointment of the Village Phone service provider (Grameen Telecom) in rural villages who facilitate capacity building, which is a shared business model, where the phone services reach through a device provider. The past operators are selected to serve as the VPO (village phone service provider) based on their past credit records and credit scores. Moreover, the start-ups are interested in growth and expansion, while the established telecom service providers are interested in stability and stable growth. The people who are selected to manage the VPO (village phone service providers) are generally the people who are local to the area and meet regularly to meet the information needs of the people at the bottom of the pyramid.

5. Details of VPP

The goal of the Grameen Telecom is to provide the telecom phone services to the people or the members of the groups. Grameen Telecom is helping to connect the members and provide them the access to finance, based on a shared revenue model. The leadership or the village leaders who are nurtured as the women leaders are playing an extremely important role in providing the access to finance to the rural Bangladesh. The phone is bought from the loan that is sanctioned by the company and helps to identify the population which is having difficulty in accessing finance. As per the various studies, the connectivity provided by the state mobile connectivity provider BTTB is the single most player that provides the access to telecom services. But the connectivity of the villages is extremely poor, and this technology is the core installation that stalls the participation of rural people. Grameen Telecom first of all collects the information about the villages that have telecom connectivity from the existing Grameen Telecom network. The officers of the telecom company visit the villages to collect the information about the gram panchayat that have telecom connectivity. After the preliminary screening of the villages that have the mobile connectivity, the branch manager of Grameen Bank selects the women leaders to act as operators for each of the village. The criterion for the selection of the leaders is that they should have a good record of repayment, with a good business such as the grocery store. Further she should be literate and should have ability to read and write. The senior executive or the zonal manager finalizes the selection of the village operator and provides her the subscription to the Grameen telephone. In a period of two to three years, the Grameen operator has to return this amount back to the Grameen Bank. And periodically pay the usage charges, whereas the operator earns the difference between the charges levied by the operator to customer and the cost of operation. Grameen Phone is a commercial cellular service provider that operates both in urban and rural regions. Iqbal Quadir an investment analyst in partnership with the Mohd Yunus conceptualized and started the Grameen Phone with a funding of $125 million USD. Grameen Phone is a social innovation that provides an excellent solution through rural development and investment. This programme has drawn attention of the multiple public state agencies such as Canadian International Development Agency, the World Bank, the International Telecommunications Union, and the Food and Agriculture Organization of the United Nations. At the heart of any business model used by the Government is the issue of cost minimization to tap the opportunities to create a flow of funds to the people at the bottom of the pyramid. The liberalization of the banks in 1995 created a sea of opportunities for the Grameen Bank. The network structure enables to dismantle the installations of a physical structure and facilitate flexibility, adaptability, low cost, efficiency, and decentralized operations. However, the lack of participation by the users due to the lack of infrastructure and capability adds to the complexity of the problem. To select an operator to provide the telecom services to the people at the bottom of the pyramid Quadir US Company, Gonofone created a consortium with the Norway's Telenor, to bid for the licenses. A wholly owned non-profit organization Grameen Phone played an extremely important role in providing mobile services to the people at the bottom of the pyramid. Similar to the village-level entrepreneurs, the Grameen Telecom invites application from the villagers to select the most credit worthy village phone operators. The selected village entrepreneurs are provided the unsecured loan to procure a telephone. The revenue generated is further used to repay the loans. The operating model for the Grameen local phone is based on the shared access model to provide access to credit at affordable price to the poor villagers. Further, the peer mechanism in a joint liability set-up plays an extremely important role in providing access to finance to the people at the bottom of the pyramid. The VPP services were a result of integration of communication services and Grameen

Bank's expertise in mobile-based credit and fund services. Grameen Telecom a non-profit organization is responsible for the delivery of telecom services to rural people. Grameen Telecom a non-profit organization is a part of Grameen Bank and is responsible for the delivery of the Village phone services in rural villages of Bangladesh. Grameen Telecom purchases the telecom airtime in bulk from Grameen Telecom Ltd. Due to bulk purchase of the mobile services, Grameen Telecom is able to extend the economies of scale to the people at the bottom of the pyramid. In a group, a female leader, who is well versed with the use of technology and has history of creditworthiness is selected. She purchases the phone on lease finance basis and provides micro-credit and finance-based services to the people in the village. She is responsible for providing the financial services, collecting charges, remitting payments, and proper maintenance of the phone. Her income is the difference between the charges paid to the Grameen Telecom and service charges paid by the villagers.

M Commerce is different from information communication technology (ICT) in terms of different roles played by the users. The users of PC technology interact with the technology itself and the other users through the network. But in case of M Commerce, the users play the role of consumer of mobile technology, as network users and as technology users. The users of mobile technology have to subscribe to the mobile telephony services. The mobile users are the part of social network and they interact with each other including friends, peers, colleagues, alumni, and reference groups. With the advent of technology, the access to various citizen centric services is being provided at the door steps of the consumers. With the increasing thrust on development of digital villages, there is a creation of an independent self-sustaining system, in which the consumers can access all the citizen centric services online. It's an advanced version of a truly cashless economy and partnership between the state and the corporate. The financial viability of the Grameen VPP model has added extensively to the rural economy. The Grameen Phone model run by the Grameen Telecom enabled the rural women called as the phone ladies to render microcredit fund-based services to the rural people in villages. Through digital transformation this initiative has transformed the financial fate of millions of villagers. This initiative has not only changed the financial fate of the poor but has also led to a social revolution changing the social fabric of life in Bangladesh. Institutional design for the delivery of telephone-based banking services to poor comprises of creation of a group, with a woman leader who has access to the technology. At the heart of the issue of microfinance is objective of cost minimization and profit generation. At a particular instance, there are numerable opportunities chasing a given set of scarce resources. The process of entrepreneurship involves first the awareness of opportunities, second ability to acquire resources needed to exploit opportunity, and organizational ability to combine homogenous resources. There is always a dearth of resources and funds in an organization. The institutional design for delivering the citizen centric services to the villagers comprises the group of women, who appoint and select one leader capable of handling the technology. And this institution is further linked to the non-government organization Grameen Telecom, the telecom operator that provides the mobile services to the group, by providing access to a mobile phone procured through the unsecured loan given by Grameen Bank. One of the women leaders, who is literate and credit worthy, takes the responsibility to handle telecom. Grameen Telecom purchases the monthly bills and send them for collection to operators through the Grameen Bank. Grameen Telecom services have brought about an information revolution at the doorsteps of the villagers in Bangladesh and have explored new income generating sources for the villagers. It also helps to provide the easy access to telephone to people all over the Bangladesh.

As shown in Fig. 13, Grameen Telecom selects the village phone lady based on education and social capital. A rigorous selection process is used to appoint the village phone ladies, who are generally entrepreneurs. These village phone ladies purchase the phone handset from unsecured loan money. The village phone lady pays regular service charges and the bills. The revenue earned by the entrepreneurs comprises the excess of the service charges over and above the cost of providing these loans. Generally, the village phone ladies are entrepreneurs, who are in the early stage of their business. These are generally the start-ups and enterprises like the grocery stores that are run through borrowed money. Digitization further provides impetus and agility to the working of start-up enterprises. Organizational agility, through the implementation of the technology, gives rise to various core competencies and creates value in the form of service levels that cannot be easily imitated by the competitors or substituted by the competitor's product and service levels. This initiative has helped to increase the livelihood and income levels of the people at the bottom of the pyramid.

As far as Grameen Telecom is concerned, three distinct sources of resources and capabilities of non-profits. First, are the 'structural resources and capabilities', such as the human capital of volunteers, and employees. Second, are the 'institutional resources and capabilities', that are a by-product of the confluence of social, political, and economic relationships and the complex set of historical

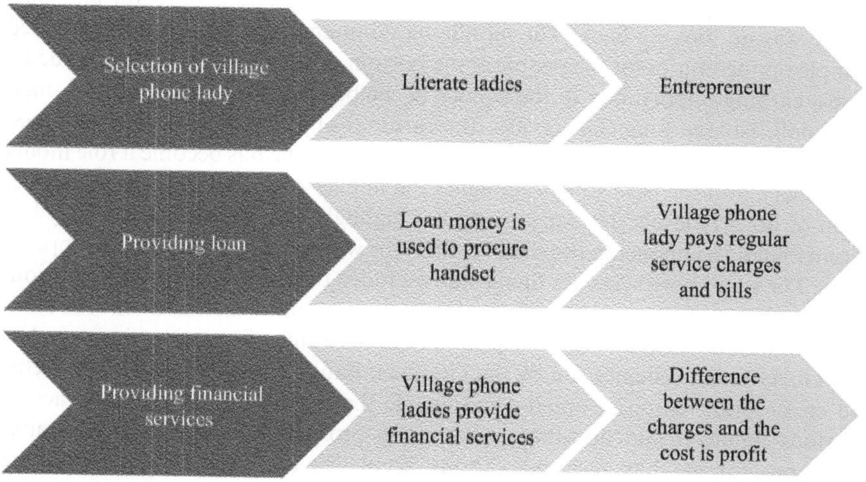

Fig. 13. Operational Model for Village Phone.

forces that give rise to non-profits. Through social interactions, non-profit like Grameen Bank acquires, develops, and deploys competencies, social networks, and tangible assets to gain a competitive advantage. A key component of institutional resources is social capital, defined as the character and value of relationships within and outside the organization. Entrepreneurship in the group works through opportunity refinement competency; leveraging competency; and, championing competency. In the groups, which endorse to the VPP, the social capital helps through uniting people in group and carrying activities, including saving and credit, norms, and trusts and behaviour and cooperation. Collective Bank Organization emphasizes the importance of frequent meeting and implementation of joint activities for collective benefits. The last but not the least the innovation or technology is the biggest disruptor that has helped Grameen Bank to bring down the cost of banking drastically paving the way for the inclusion of the poor and generating consumer surplus and benefits for the people at the bottom of the pyramid. The case study of VPP programme highlights the importance of the durable network. Though the membership in a community provides help when needed, it demands conformity restricting individual freedoms. And downwards levelling pressures in strong groups deter innovation and acquisition of human capita. Structural social capital are roles, rules, procedures and precedents as well as networks facilitate mutually beneficial collective action.

5.1. Case Study of Laily Begum from Bangladesh

Source: Zamin (2024).

Laily Begum and her husband were trapped in poverty and did not have access to the basic necessities of life like food, shelter. They lived in a tiny house in Patira in Dakshin Khan, Dhaka city. In order to get financially included and improve their livelihood, Laily and her husband took a loan from the Grameen Bank to start a milk diary by buying a cow. This loan was to the tune of 4,500. In 1997, she applied for a license to become a mobile phone operator and then there was no looking back. The mobile-based financial services model provided ample opportunities for the people at the bottom of the pyramid. This provided a great earning opportunity to the women at the bottom of the pyramid. Through the mobile-based financial services, the earnings of Laily Begum have increased manifold. With the transformation in her livelihood, she has become a role model in society, and the case study highlights the impact of technology on the reduction of poverty levels. The various studies highlight that modern technology has contributed to enhancing the social capital for women leaders and mobile operators. The small borrowers are financially excluded due to the lack of information. The banks and financial institutions do not have any information about the creditworthiness of the poor. And the poor do not have any information about the latest Government schemes run by the Grameen Bank. The VPP programme helps to create information symmetry and enable the marginalized women to access various financial and non-financial services provided by the Grameen Bank. This programme has received various accolades and rewards including the CAPAM Bronze Award for the Public (1998), GSM Community services in 1998,

Petersburg prize for use of IT, and recognition with National Museum located in Scotland. The glory of this programme is embedded in its ability to provide agility to start-ups and ideation of development and growth.

6. Strategic Model for VPP

VPP is aimed at achieving the objective of financial inclusion through digital transformation. The use of ICT in the form of mobile phones is playing an extremely important role in promoting financial inclusion and developing entrepreneurship. Technology plays an important role in the decentralization of the operations. Through the use of mobile technology, financial services like banking can be provided at a much lower cost, without the burden of visiting the bank branches which are located at a distance of 7–8 km from the main village. Further, the village phone services provide flexibility and adaptability as the villagers can easily approach the phone lady, and despite not having any prior mobile literacy they can, they can take the help of the phone ladies to access financial services. It helps to increase the efficiency of the business operations. Thus, digital transformation is playing an extremely important role in financially including the people at the bottom of the pyramid. Through the theoretical lens of the community-based lending model, the VPP model creates synergies, by percolating the benefits to the people at the bottom of the pyramid. Moreover, this initiative is based on collective advocacy as the village phone lady, is generally chosen based on their social capital and popularity among the villagers or the community. This initiative is based on the reduction of information asymmetry and the creation of a flow of information to ensure equity and financial inclusion. One of the major reasons for the financial exclusion of the poor is their lack of information on the latest financial schemes and financial services. Mobile technology enables borrowers to get important information about their creditworthiness at their doorstep. However, despite all claims, the VPP programme was fraught with various challenges such as a lack of telecom infrastructure, mobile illiteracy, and resistance to change. The first phase of introduction of the mobile telephony was under punctuation with many people not using the technology despite the thrust on use of this technology, due to the resistance from the people at large. In this regard, the strategic digital implementation through gradual implementation, partnership with Grameen Telecom a non-profit organization, and continuous training and social intermediation for the users. Thus, the durable network of the village phone ladies has led to the emergence of an alternate banking channel that enables the financially excluded people to bank and provide financial inclusion to the people at the bottom of the pyramid.

7. Conclusion

Grameen Bank is the brainchild of Nobel laureate Mohammed Yunus, and this initiative has played an important role in promoting financial inclusion among the poor and marginalized sections of society. By providing loans to the people at the bottom of the pyramid through the decimation and de-installation of the structures of power that defy the poor the rights to the bank. Further, the initiative has played an extremely important role in taking the bank to the poor through the use of technology such as Village Phone for Pay. This revolutionary financial inclusion programme has seen evolution and reform through various stages and it has been replicated across the globe in several countries and nations.

References

Auwal, M. A., & Singhal, A. (1992). The diffusion of Grameen Bank in Bangladesh: Lessons learned about alleviating rural poverty. *Knowledge*, *14*(1), 7–28. https://doi.org/10.1177/107554709201400102

Bernasek, A. (2003). Banking on social change: Grameen Bank lending to women. *International Journal of Politics Culture and Society*, *16*, 369–385. https://doi.org/10.1023/A:1022304311671

Bernasek, A., & Stanfield, J. R. (1997). The Grameen Bank as progressive institutional adjustment. *Journal of Economic Issues*, *31*(2), 359–366.

Bhuiyan, A. B., Chamhuri, S., Ismail, A. G., & Omar, N. B. (2017). The experiences of the Grameen and Islami Bank microfinance on the poverty alleviation in Bangladesh. *Journal of Islamic Economics, Banking and Finance*, *13*(3), 64–81.

Develtere, P., & Huybrechts, A. (2005). The impact of microcredit on the poor in Bangladesh. *Alternatives*, *30*(2), 165–189. https://doi.org/10.1177/030437540503000203

Fuglesang, A., & Chandler, D. (1986). *Participation as process: What we can learn from Grameen Bank, Bangladesh*. Norwegian Ministry of Development Cooperation.

Harper, D. (2002). Talking about pictures: A case for photo elicitation. *Visual Studies*, *17*(1), 13–26. https://doi.org/10.1080/14725860220137345

Hassan, M. K., & Renteria-Guerrero, L. (1997). The experience of the Grameen Bank of Bangladesh in community development. *International Journal of Social Economics*, *24*(12), 1488–1523.

Hossain, S. (2013). Migration, urbanization and poverty in Dhaka, Bangladesh. *Journal of the Asiatic Society of Bangladesh*, *58*, 369–382. https://www.asiaticsociety.org.bd/journal/10ShahadatHossain.pdf

Hulme, M. (2009). *Why we disagree about climate change: Understanding controversy, inaction and opportunity*. Cambridge University Press. https://psycnet.apa.org/doi/10.1017/CBO9780511841200

Islam, R., Karim, M. A., Ahmad, R., & Nittoli, A. (2018). Loan repayment pressure in the practice of microfinance in Bangladesh: An empirical study on Grameen Bank, BRAC and ASA. *Journal of Rural Development*, *37*(4), 697–718. https://doi.org/10.25175/jrd/2018/v37/i4/112814

Karim, L. (2008). Demystifying micro-credit: The Grameen Bank, NGOs, and neoliberalism in Bangladesh. *Cultural Dynamics*, *20*(1), 5–29. https://doi.org/10.1177/0921374007088053

Khandker, S., Khaily, B. K., & Hossain, Z. (1994). *Is Grameen bank sustainable?* [Working papers no. HRO 23]. Human Resources Development and Operations Policy, World Bank Group. http://documents.worldbank.org/curated/en/658601468768006874

Khandker, S., Khalily, B., & Khan, Z. (1995). *Grameen Bank: Performance and sustainability* [Discussion paper]. World Bank, Discussion Papers 306, World Bank.

Maskooki, K., & Gunasekaran, A. (2001). Implications of Grameen banking system in Europe: Prospects and prosperity. *European Business Review*, *13*, 26–42. https://doi.org/10.1108/09555340110366462

Mokhtar, S. H., Nartea, G., & Gan, C. (2012). Determinants of microcredit loans repayment problem among microfinance borrowers in Malaysia. *International Journal of Business and Social Research, 2*(7), 33–45.

Morduch, J. (1999). The microfinance promises. *Journal of Economic Literature, 37*(4), 1569–1614.

Pitt, M., & Khandaker, S. (1996). *Household and intrahousehold impact of the Grameen bank and similar targeted credit programs in Bangladesh*. World Bank Discussion Papers, World Bank. https://econpapers.repec.org/paper/fthwobadi/320.htm

Rahman, A., & Wahid, A. N. M. (1992). The Grameen Bank and the changing patron–client relationship in Bangladesh. *Journal of Contemporary Asia, 22*(3), 303–321. https://doi.org/10.1080/00472339280000221

Rahman and Nie. (2011). Loan repayment pressure in the practice of microfinance in Bangladesh: An empirical study on Grameen bank, BRAC and ASA. *Journal of Rural Development, 37*(4), 697–718. https://doi.org/10.25175/jrd/2018/v37/i4/112814

Rahman, M. W. (2015). An empirical investigation in the state-designated poor counties of Shaanxi, China. *Journal of International Development, 27*, 1012–1026.

Sarker, F. H., Islam, M. S., & Islam, M. K. (2019). Use of e-learning at higher educational institutions in Bangladesh: Opportunities and challenges. *Journal of Applied Research in Higher Education, 11*(2), 210–223.

Yunus, M. (1999). *Banker to the poor*. Public Affairs.

Yunus, M., & A. Jolis (1998). *Banker to the poor, the story of Grameen Bank* (p. 313). Aurum Press Ltd.

Zamin, M. (2024). http://www.kiwanja.net/database/project/project_GTC_villagephone.pdf, 2024

Chapter 6

Harnessing Peer Mechanism to Ensure Financial Inclusion in India: A Case Study of Joint Liability Groups in India

Abstract

This study aims to see how peer monitoring, selection, and enforcement might help formal financial institutions overcome moral hazards and adverse selection issues in working with disadvantaged borrowers in an agency relationship. This study aims to generate a grounded theory of how peer mechanism leads to the sustainability of self-help groups. According to the study, adverse selection in a joint liability group is mitigated by peer selection which is motivated by social ties and borrower risk type matching, and moral hazard is mitigated by peer monitoring and enforcement. A theory of peer mechanism is formulated using the three-staged grounded theory method of qualitative research. The data for the study are collected through semi-structured interviews with 68 leaders of handicraft-based self-help groups, members of state-level banking committees, and directors of self-help group promotion institutions across India. Through open, focussed, and theoretical coding, peer selection, peer monitoring, and peer enforcement emerge as the significant theoretical code that facilitates peer mechanism facilitates. The data for the study were collected and analysed simultaneously. The study deploys strategies of constant comparison, theoretical saturation, theoretical sampling, and theoretical sensitivity through literature to facilitate the research study. At each stage, the data were transcribed manually, and memos were prepared to capture the essence of the interviews. Until the development of theoretical coding, the coding and constant comparison process was carried out iteratively. This study indicates that in a joint liability group, people monitor each other due to homogeneity and information about other members.

Keywords: Agency theory; moral hazard; information asymmetry; self-help group bank linkage; financial inclusion

Global Perspectives on Financial Inclusion: Case Studies in Microfinance and Women's Empowerment, 97–193

Published under exclusive licence by Emerald Publishing Limited
doi:10.1108/978-1-83708-080-920251006

1. Introduction

Muhammed Yunus, the person who revolutionized microfinance with the Grameen Bank model, once said:

> I founded Grameen Bank to provide loans to those considered traditionally unbankable. Grameen Bank works with the poorest and often illiterate, providing uncollateralized micro-loans for tiny business enterprises by which they can lift themselves and their families out of poverty. (Bateman, 2014)

1.7 billion are financially excluded globally (Demirguc-Kunt et al., 2017), and these people lack physical collateral. Formal institutions suffer from information asymmetry due to a lack of information on the creditworthiness of poor clients (Ray, 1997). Because of information asymmetry, formal financial institutions are hesitant to lend to these marginalized poor, as monitoring and screening costs are high, leading to asset quality deterioration. This credit market failure leads to the under-allocation of finance to the poor. This is crucial for money lenders' success in rural areas (Stiglitz, 1990). Only low-quality lenders thrive in the market (Akerlof, 1970), as formal institutions do not find it viable to lend to the poor. Social finance is envisioned as a component of a long-term financial policy framework (Ledgerwood, 1997; Weber & Ahmad, 2014). It aims to impact society and the environment through microfinancing (Brundtland, 1987).

Within Emily, Durkheim's Social Theory theoretical lens is embedded in the concept of social solidarity and cohesion, which leverages social capital to achieve the common good. In joint liability groups, social capital refers to institutionalized relationships. This social capital exists among poor people due to social ties, trust, and norms (Sanae, 2003). Self-help groups meet the needs of microborrowers by providing loans to those lacking collateral and creditworthiness by substituting social collateral for physical collateral and reducing transaction costs. Group lending and peer monitoring ensure access to local information and banking for the unbanked (Thorsten et al., 2004). According to existing research, information asymmetry can lead to adverse selection, that is, selecting the wrong person for credit distribution (Jensen & Meckling, 1976). External lenders know less about members, and groups are repositories of information about financially disadvantaged members (Harriss & Renzio, 1997). Peer selection by members is an excellent technique to resolve the issue of adverse selection. Under social contracts, members act as agents for the group and have joint liability. Individual members have limited liability and joint liability for the group. This social contract harnesses the benefits of peer pressure and enforces peer sanctions to drive greater debt collection, savings, and cost reduction (Angelucci & Karlan, 2015; Basu & Srivastava, 2005). Also, social capital through social collateral allows financial inclusion by substituting physical collateral (Pitt & Khandekar, 1998). Existing studies highlight 'What' the financial outcomes of a group mechanism are in promoting saving (Gugerty, 2007), increased credit (Deininger & Liu, 2009), income (Puhazhendi & Satyasai, 2000; Puhazhendi, 2006), and asset ownership (Greaney et al., 2016), recovery performance, and reduced transaction costs (Puhazhendi & Badatya, 2002). Given the lack of physical collateral and knowledge asymmetry among the needy members of joint liability groups, there is a shortage of research on 'how' the group mechanism promotes financial discipline and sustainability (BIRD, 2019). Very few studies directly address the issues of information asymmetry, that is, moral hazard and adverse selection, in the context of group lending.

Furthermore, there has been minimal research on how the peer mechanism affects the group's financial sustainability (Bastelaer, 1999). Besides that Timberg and Aiyar (1984) argue that within informal lending mechanisms, such as moneylenders, the lenders personally interact with the borrowers and have perfect information about the borrowers (Coleman, 1988). This study will most likely be the first to examine how asymmetric information and agency affect joint liability group efficiency and effectiveness in the context of self-help group bank linkage programmes. This study will investigate how social capital and peer mechanisms affect microfinance institutions' long-term viability. The research study seeks to evaluate the data collected from the ground and literature regarding 'how' peer monitoring influences the success of group lending. The study uses the grounded theory method. It will provide academic discussion on the role of social capital in supporting microfinance via effective peer monitoring and enforcement and create a process view of peer mechanism in group lending.

2. Problem Statement

> Good ... members seem to be getting new loans even if someone with the same group defaults. Why, then, do they bother to exert Peer pressure on defaulters? That is because otherwise, there would be a huge problem for all members at the center.

Existing studies highlight 'what' the financial outcomes of a group mechanism are in promoting saving (Gugerty, 2007), increased credit (Deininger & Liu, 2009), income, and asset ownership (Greaney et al., 2016), recovery performance, and reduced transaction costs (Puhazhendi & Badatya, 2002). But there is a shortage of research on 'how' the group mechanism promotes financial discipline and sustainability in the context of the self-help group linkage programme.

This study will most likely be the first to examine how asymmetric information and agency affect joint liability group efficiency and effectiveness. This study will investigate how social capital and peer mechanisms affect microfinance institutions' long-term viability. The research study seeks to give a rigorous evaluation of qualitative data collected regarding 'how' peer monitoring influences the success of group lending. It will provide academic discussion on the role of social capital in supporting microfinance via effective peer monitoring and enforcement and create a process view of peer mechanism in group lending through the theoretical lens of agency theory.

RQ1. The broad research question is, 'How peer mechanism works in the self-help group bank linkage programme context?'

RQ2. How the process of the peer mechanism affects the financial outcomes of the members of the self-help group linkage?

RQ3. What are the various stages and factors in the process of peer mechanism in the context of the self-help group bank linkage programme?

3. Objective of Research

This work will contribute to the literature on behavioural finance by studying multiple dimensions of information asymmetry, including moral hazard and adverse selection. There is no literature on peer monitoring in the self-help group bank linkage context. The study seeks to answer the following questions:

1. How do peer mechanisms, such as peer selection, monitoring, and enforcement, help reduce moral hazard and adverse selection?
2. What is the peer selection, monitoring, and enforcement process in the self-help group linkage programme?
3. To contribute to the literature on peer mechanisms in the self-help group bank linkage programme context.

4. Literature Review

The Agency theory (Jensen & Meckling, 1976) intends to investigate the relationship between borrowers and lenders who borrow credit from formal financial institutions. The principal is the lender in an agency framework, and the agent is the borrower. This is a multiagent perspective, in which all the borrowers are the agents. The group members make decisions cooperatively regarding monitoring, but regarding production, they act non-cooperatively in our study. This theory highlights how the agent has more information than the principal regarding production and monitoring activities. Also, the agent can use this information to fulfil his selfish motives. Below are mentioned the significant themes in peer monitoring in an agency framework. The borrower is an agent with limited liability in group lending, while the lender is the principal. Information asymmetry is a significant barrier to financial inclusion for the poor. Borrowers face moral hazards, and lenders face adverse selection. The literature analysis suggests that in a joint liability group lending scenario, the borrowers act as the agents, and the lenders act as the principals. The moral hazard pertains to the choice of monitoring, project riskiness, and information about project output and production. Fig. 14 depicts the agency theory framework.

4.1. Information Asymmetry

4.1.1. Background on Joint Liability Lending

Robinson (2001) argued that microfinance is a social revolution that holds promise in poverty reduction and initiating social change (Baruah, 2012). Due to mission drift, the subsidized banking model became unviable for large commercial

Fig. 14. Agency Theory Framework *Source*: By the authors.

banks. Despite all efforts, formal financial institutions in developing nations could not uphold the promise of affordable finance for the rural poor until the 1980s (Bhaduri, 2006). Basu and Pradeep (1997, 2005) argued that banks had no information about the creditworthiness of the clients. Pischke (1996) argued that millions of impoverished rural people need financial literacy training. Sanae (2003) has proposed that social capital (Quidt et al., 2016) and peer pressure play an essential role in ensuring the sustainability of the group lending model through higher repayment rates and lower transaction costs (Armendariz & Morduch, 2010).

4.1.2. Agency, Information Asymmetry, and Joint Liability Groups

One of the most critical concerns in finance is allocating resources to the most worthwhile projects. The funds in a capital market with perfect knowledge are allocated so that the marginal return of capital equals the marginal cost. However, there are other inefficiencies in the microfinance business, including information asymmetry and lack of physical collateral. According to the literature, a joint liability group and, in this case, the self-help group is a type of social contract in which the primary source of the problem is lenders' incomplete information about borrowers. Spence and Zeckhauser (1971) state that the output and income of the members are exogenous and unobservable by the lender but observable by the members. Harris and Raviv (1979) argue that verifying the output by the lenders is costly and depends on various factors, including the probability distribution of production. According to extensive literature, if even a single member defaults, the banks would sanction the entire group. The joint liability leads to a peer mechanism and better repayment. And peer pressure, monitoring, sanction, and enforcement are three stages of the peer mechanism. Fig. 15 summarizes the research in this domain. The topics covered in existing research are group dynamics, credit linkages, and market linkages. The peer mechanism is a three-step process composed of peer selection, monitoring, and sanctioning. The main issues in group lending are moral hazard and adverse selection. Market linkages refer to capital markets and are the least studied area.

Peer monitoring begins with a simple mechanism in a heterogeneous population of risky and safe borrowers. Safe borrowers are reluctant to cross-subsidize risky borrowers due to limited responsibility. The model further evolved into peer selection and enforcement. Banerjee et al. (1994) highlighted the importance of

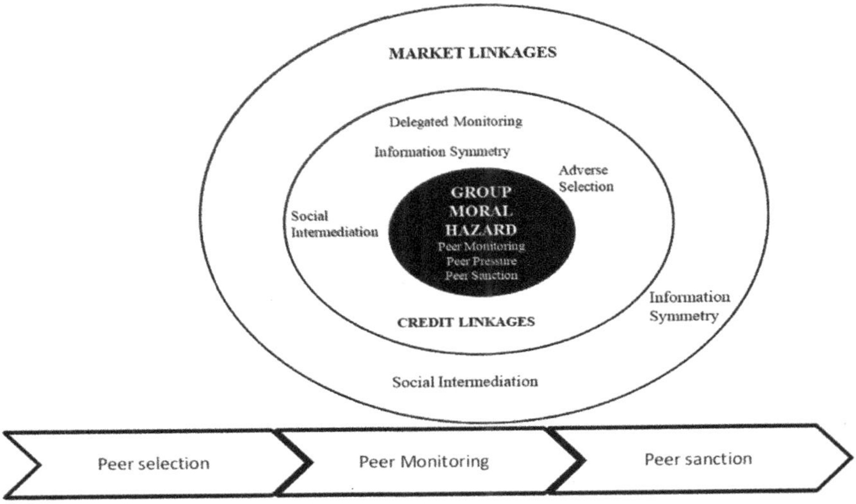

Fig. 15. Themes in Peer Mechanism. *Source*: By the authors.

peer selection by risk matching to address adverse selection problems, and Besley and Coate (1995) highlighted the importance of peer sanction. The findings supported formal financial institutions' reluctance to invest in delegated monitoring, social intermediation, and screening of the micro-poor at the credit linkage level. Various studies highlight that group lending contracts help extract rents when collaboration is feasible. These findings should hold for variable-sized loans, endogenous grouping, and other adverse selection formulations of the bank's agency problem. Ahlin and Townsend (2007) examine the role of screening, monitoring, group pressure, self-selection, and social ties on a group's repayment behaviour. Stiglitz and Weiss (1981) emphasize the importance of interest rates, endogenous peer selection through random or assortative matching, heterogeneity or homogeneity of members, the riskiness of the borrowers, correlation of project outcomes, and group size as screening devices for distinguishing between good and bad risks that impact the adverse selection at the group formation stage. Che (2002) argues that a free-rider problem arises in a joint liability group in a repeated game scenario, resulting in peer sanction enforcement. Besanko and Thakor (1987) argue that no one knows about payoff-relevant borrower traits.

4.1.3. Recent Developments in Social Contracts with Heterogenous Risk Types

Ghatak (2000) highlights that homogenous groups with the same risks are formed under joint liability, which cannot be greater than an individual liability. Gangopadhyay et al. (2005), on the other hand, this argument counters that ex post optimal separating equilibrium can achieve higher welfare and repayment rates, even if the joint liability penalty is greater than the individual liability, particularly for risky borrowers. The study assumes a co-signer since debtors have no choice but to accept a specific debt arrangement with a co-signer. However, though Ghatak (2000) argued that joint liability does not exceed the amount of individual liability, in the recency version, the author highlights that joint liability can be greater than an individual liability. Banks profit from risky borrowers and have zero profits with safe borrowers. Guttman (2008) argues that positive assortative matching, in which safe borrowers prefer to join with other safe borrowers rather than risky borrowers since dangerous borrowers have a larger risk of default, does not hold in the case of dynamic incentives, according to their study article. The author of the research describes dynamic incentives as a refinancing threat. The likelihood of members not receiving a loan in the future is equal to the product of future failure probabilities in a group. Furthermore, the marginal effect of a safe member on the probability of default is lower than that of a hazardous borrower on the likelihood of default. This is known as negative assortative, meaning that a safe borrower will pay less to have a risky borrower, and a risky borrower will pay more to have a safe borrower. Katzur and Lensink (2012) contribute to the body of knowledge by investigating the impact of group loans on project outcomes. Several studies have found that group loan contracts are less practical when project outcomes are positively related or in the case of high covariance of outcomes. In an adverse selection problem with underinvestment, group loans can provide a greater welfare outcome when relatively secure projects are positively correlated (Ahlin & Jiang, 2008).

5. Research Methodology

This section describes how the data were collected and analysed and how codes, concepts, and patterns evolved. It depicts the conceptual development process related to a theory's development. The data collection and analysis to develop grounded theory are repeated iteratively. This is done to make the development of patterns, themes, and multidimensional correlations easier so that the collected data may be compared, categorized, abstracted, and conceptualized more easily. Theoretical sampling and coding are used to collect and analyse data until theoretical saturation is reached and a dense theory emerges. The abductive theory-building method was used to understand the phenomenon of peer monitoring in a group lending scenario. The data were collected and analysed simultaneously to understand the group's real-life problems. The exploratory research is undertaken through the grounded theory approach to generate a theoretical framework. This study is based on the grounded theory method. In this study, the data are central to the model, and theory is allowed to emerge from the data, using constant comparison, conceptual categories, and patterns to derive the core category of peer mechanism. In this stage, each slice of data is compared to existing categories and concepts until theoretical saturation.

Contrary to the Straussian model that emphasizes theoretical sensitivity from the beginning, in this study, theoretical sensitivity is built only in a later stage. The data coding stages in this study are open – focussed – theoretical, as suggested by Charmaz (2006). In this method, the problem is allowed to emerge from the data. Initially, three sensitizing concepts of peer selection, peer monitoring, and peer enforcement were used to examine the impact of network ties, social capital, and social intermediation on the success of self-help groups. The researcher's previous preconceived conceptions are set aside to facilitate the systematic analysis of data and allow the formation of ideas and concepts from the research field. The semi-structured interviews were conducted to generate the data. Data from the interviews and observations are used to discover emerging concepts and relationships. Further, the emerging codes are compared with the earlier codes and categories to ensure theoretical sensitivity in the data. The historical documents were referred to for theoretical verification. This analysis provided a direction and helped in theoretical sampling. While doing the research, efforts are made to ensure an enabling environment conducive to research for the participants.

5.1. Research Strategies

The primary objective of the research is to contribute to the theory through theory building. This study aims to investigate the effect of peer processes on the repayment rates and financial sustainability of self-help organizations in India (Saunders et al., 2009). In this study, the abductive approach, which refers to how researchers move between the inductive and deductive while practising the constant comparative method, has been used (Creswell, 2012a, 2012b; Eisenhardt, 1989). This study's major purpose was to examine how microentrepreneurs, which lack physical collateral and creditworthiness, join together to gain access to financial resources. This abduction approach attacks Bacon's 'naïve empiricism' and provides a solution to Hume's 'problem of induction' and Kant's critique of naturally perceived causal relations. Lakota Sian's paradigm propagates that most of the observation is theoretically informed. Despite cursory references, this research question is not a well-investigated problem, and this research design is appropriate to investigate the poorly investigated phenomena (Glaser, 1978; Yin, 2003). This will be the first study in this domain to comprehensively explore the role of peer mechanisms in the joint liability group lending scenario (Eisenhardt & Graebner, 2007). Instead of a priori articulation, the research problem emerges from analysing the data through abstract wonderment and starting with a broad research field of group lending.

This study uses a mix of observation, interviews, and references to the existing research material to ensure theoretical sensitivity (Bogdan & Biklen, 2006). Until data saturation, interviews are conducted to create a theoretical account of the observations made. Within the constructivist grounded theory framework, data are coded using three stages: open, focussed, and theoretical coding (Charmaz, 2006). In the initial phase of open coding, data are analysed by comparing and identifying categories, attributes, and dimensions. In the selective or focussed coding stage of data analysis, the codes developed are grouped based on specific relationships using the abduction processes. The core category is developed in the final stage of theoretical coding. Theoretical coding aims to identify and use the appropriate codes to create a consolidated theoretical framework for grounded theory.

5.2. Philosophical Stance for the Research Study

Because this study is exploratory, the various research strategies recommended by Saunders et al. (2009) have been used to conduct grounded theory research. The researcher's philosophical stance or worldview assumptions regarding the nature of reality impact the methodology adopted for research and the interpretation of results (Creswell, 1994). This comprises a set of beliefs that guide action (Guba, 1990), which have been referred to as research paradigms (Lincoln & Guba, 2000). The research paradigm is referred to as ontologies and epistemologies (Crotty, 1998). In this study, the philosophical stance is pragmatism, which is derived from the works of American pragmatic researchers like Dewey et al. (concept of looking glass self; Cherryholmes, 1992). 'Methodology' refers to theoretical assumptions, and 'methods' refer to the technique. The study emphasizes the research problem and uses both qualitative and quantitative methods. It uses a pluralistic approach to derive the solution to the problem (Morgan, 2007; Patton, 2005). Sequential mixed methods have been used, and the method used for the first part of the essay is grounded theory (Lincoln & Guba, 1985; Tashakkori & Teddlie, 2003).

The research is undertaken across the rural regions and villages in India. The method of coding suggested by Charmaz (2006) is followed for this study. The grounded theory is ideal for probing social issues in rural India's natural settings and exploring the basic social process of group lending through understanding the multiplicity of social interactions. Despite using the Glaserian and Charmaz data coding method, the study builds theoretical sensitivity by referring to literature in the second stage. The emerging codes were continuously analysed to determine how they fit the theory.

In the first part of the study, social constructivism as an epistemology is an interpretive approach focussing on how people make sense of the world, primarily through sharing their experiences with others (Smith et al., 2002). Instead of being independent of facts and maintaining an objective position, the social constructivist approach holds that the observer is part of what is observed and that reality is not correct but is instead interpreted by people. According to Saunders et al. (2009), the sample size is determined initially through purposive sampling. And as the codes emerged, sampling was done using theoretical sampling. The codes were generated based on the constant comparison till theoretical saturation was achieved (Corbin & Strauss, 2015; Thomson, 2011). It was done to take care of the theoretical sensitivity.

5.3. Data Collection

This study used broad, open-ended questions, narrative semi-structured interviews, and the historical document appraisal approach to collect the data and understand the events (Walshe et al., 2012). A constructivist approach was adopted to collect data. For example, the first question is, 'Tell something about the group formation?'

While conducting the exploratory interviews, due consideration was given to the principled sensitivity to the rights of others (Blumer, 1969). Before collecting the data, the access was negotiated, and consent taken was informed consent to avoid deception and provide protection to the privacy of the members; human subjects are the primary data source in this study, and the sensitivity towards informants' rights and ethics (Chen, et al., 2002; Hammersley & Traianou, 2012) has been taken care off.

Memoing was done simultaneously with data collection through observation (Phillippi & Lauderdale, 2018). Interviews help collect the data in Grounded Theory (Burgess, 1982). Despite assertions by Saunders et al. (2009) that interviews can be structured or semi-structured, in this study, the semi-structured interview, and open-ended interview approaches have been adopted (Leavy, 2014; Shazia, 2014; Silverman, 2010; Starks & Trinidad, 2007). In addition to interviews, archival records, internal reports, and news articles were used to obtain data (Rennie, 2000). This study has followed the rigorous memoing that involves taking field notes throughout data collection and analysis (Birks et al., 2008).

As per Douglas (2003), the data collected through the semi-structured interview were followed by recording and transcribing the interviews manually (Glaser & Strauss 1967). This transcription and recording enable revisiting of the data. Charmaz (2000) has suggested the newer version of the grounded theory, where theory must be grounded in the data to produce an integrated theory. Our analysis method transcends the abstract conceptualization of the data to ensure that the grounded theory, though grounded in empirical data, transcends it to produce an integrated theory. In certain cases, the interview summaries were prepared. Fig. 16 provides details of the stages of interviews taken.

5.4. Data Sampling

This study began with purposive sampling (Edmondson & McManus, 2007) to select participants from self-help groups across India. As the theoretical ideas developed, the concepts generated from the process guided the collection of additional data to create theoretical categories to address the emerging gaps in the literature. This data collection is carried out till the stage of data saturation (Charmaz, 2006; Hunter et al., 2011; Strauss & Corbin, 1998; Walker & Myrick, 2006).

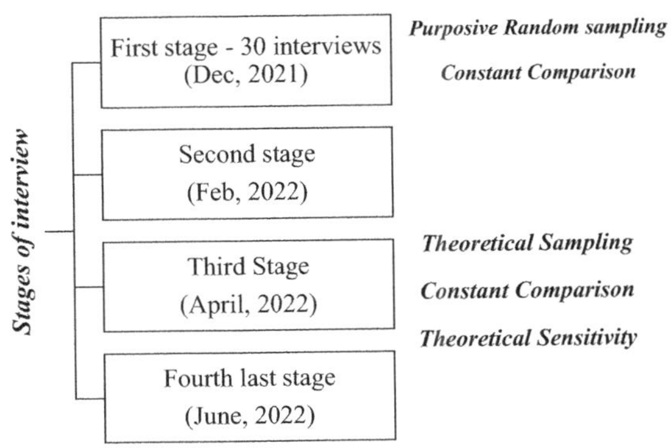

Fig. 16. Stages of Interviews.

Later, the members were selected from the self-help group promoting institutions (SHPIs) and the state-level banking committees (SLBC). The theoretical sampling was used to select only participants most representative of the population as the research moved from open to focussed coding (Glaser, 1998). Additional data were gathered based on the concepts derived during the data analysis to maximize variations among concepts and densify the categories. The dimensions and properties of the most popular concepts were sampled to maximize variation. This sampling further helped develop a theory and ensured that it was based on collected data. The study also considers theoretical sensitivity, or the ability of the researcher to understand the data. Also, the data were constantly compared, code with code, and category with category to identify commonalities and differences in the data (Charmaz, 2006). Initially, the theory built from the data is substantive. It comprises a set of hypotheses that provide explanatory power for the phenomenon of the study by delimiting the phenomenon. And then, the formal theory is generalized from the substantive theory, encompassing a broader level of abstraction with wider applicability (Charmaz, 2014; Morse, 2001; Streubert & Carpenter, 2011).

A purposive sampling method was used to select 25 SHGs founded by women and 43 self-help promotion institutes (SHPIs) across India and covered by the Ajeevika and DAY NRLM programmes. Ajeevika and DAY NRLM support all self-help groups and informal women-owned businesses across India. Twenty-five self-help groups from Ajeevika and DAY NRLM databases were chosen based on theoretical criteria of women run and covered by Ajeevika or DAY NRLM. These 25 self-help groups provided a solid foundation for inductive theorizing (Nelson & Baker, 2005; Zott & Huy, 2007). From December 2021 to June 2022, key informants were interviewed through semi-structured interviews. The interviews were conducted democratically with elected group leaders, co-founders, and directors or presidents of self-help group promotion agencies. As data analysis progressed, the respondents were theoretically sampled for repeat interviews. A total of 68 interviews are conducted, each lasting 20–35 min. The follow-up interviews are undertaken one to two months later to increase the data validity by gaining real-time insights into resource mobilization (McDonald & Eisenhardt, 2020).

Every interview is done via zoom video or phone in the local language. The data triangulation approach has been used (Campbell & Fiske, 1959) to validate the data. Multiple secondary sources were used to better comprehend the study issue in the context of self-help groups in India (Eisenhardt, 1989). Other sources included government websites (Ministry of Textile, Ajeevika programme, and Ministry of Commerce), news (IFC, World Bank, BBC, and high-quality local news), and other organizations mentioned in interviews. The primary sources of data have been used to cross-validate our data. This allowed me to validate information, gain insight, and adapt interview questions. Fig. 17 gives the data collection process.

The process of data collection and analysis is iterative. The codes and categories were generated simultaneously. The data were collected in four stages. The ethical requirements were completed in the first round before data collection. Due importance was given to the principle of sensitivity to the rights of others. And the consent of the members was taken before the interview. After purposeful

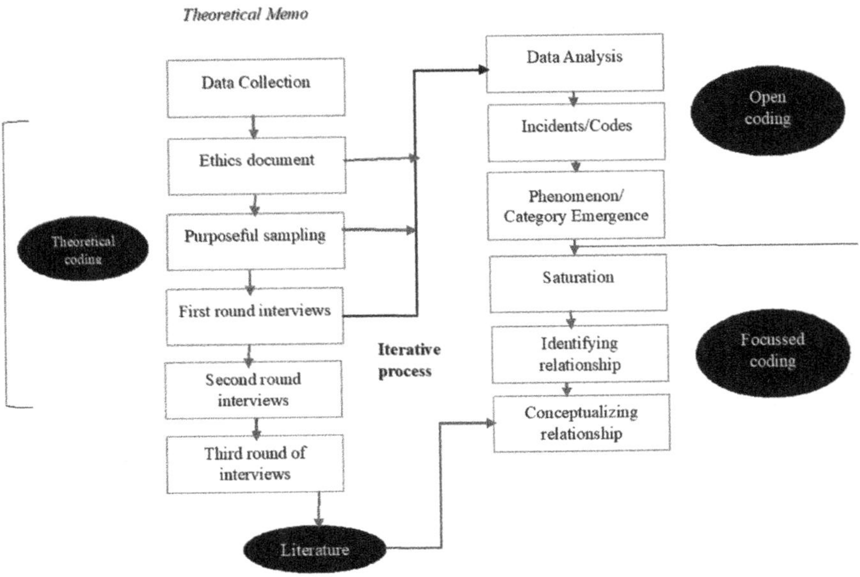

Fig. 17. Data Collection and Analysis Process.

sampling, the first round of interviews was conducted to generate open codes. This process was repeated till theoretical saturation and is called open coding. After 50 open codings, focussed coding was done to generate a core category. Theoretical sensitivity was taken care of during focussed coding, and constant comparison was made to generate a theory.

5.5. Data Analysis

The constructivist grounded theory drives the study (Charmaz, 2006). The problem is explored using the constructivist grounded theory three-stage method composed of open coding, focussed coding, and theoretical coding (Glaser, 1978). As a result of the grounded theory methodology, this study aimed to collect information on how the peer mechanism functions within the context of self-help group bank linkage programmes in India to ensure the achievement of the group's revenue enhancement and social welfare objectives.

5.5.1. Within Case Analysis

Interviews and publicly available data are used for analysis (Eisenhardt, 1989; Santos & Eisenhardt, 2009). The codes are derived from the data using intensive abductive grounded theory coding (Strauss & Corbin, 1998). The interviews were transcribed, triangulated, and then supplemented with secondary data. Coding revealed various themes and constructs. The primary focus was on how the groups obtained formal credit without physical collateral or creditworthiness. The initial case analysis phase focussed on financial resources and how these organizations accessed and used them (Eisenhardt, 1989). Within the case analysis researchers were familiarized with data and paved the way for cross-case research.

5.5.2. Cross-case Analysis

The cross-case analysis was performed after the first two rounds of data collection (Santos & Eisenhardt, 2009). This ensures case replication reliability (Eisenhardt, 1989). A cross-case analysis is done using pairwise case comparisons. Initially, the patterns in the paired cases were explored in the group. The stakeholders and groups were selected based on the within-case analysis. The self-help groups are compared and contrasted based on linkages, that is, (1) those that have taken loans through the self-help group bank and those that rely solely on internal loans or loans from other formal or informal sources, (2) groups formed and mediated by SHPIs or NGOs, and (3) clustered groups. This method helped to identify patterns across self-help groups funded by formal sources like banks and internal sources like savings. The findings suggest that more successful women entrepreneurs who form collectives use group mechanisms more extensively than those who don't. Some of the most successful female entrepreneurs run small businesses with limited resources.

5.5.3. Identification of Categories and Peripheral Concepts

The classification of the groups based on the network relationships enabled to develop relevant follow-up questions and recruit new participants for replication logic (Santos & Eisenhardt, 2009). Five major themes emerged from a small group during the comparison process, that is, *information sharing*, *influencing & control*, *solidarity*, *sustainability*, and *social change*. This helped to identify groups based on 'Network relations', that is, high within-group relationships or horizontal relationships, that is, 'Bonding', groups with high relationships with formal financial institutions, that is, 'Linking' relationships with banks and 'Bridging' relationships with other self-help groups through a federation. These structured and diverse lenses go beyond the apparent group dynamics. The tabular analysis compares and contrasts possible emerging constructs (Miles et al., 2014). The stark differences between groups helped to generate categories (open coding) and peripheral concepts (selective coding). This study uses the constant comparison method by comparing groups based on network relations, that is, whether groups have bank linkages. Different groups with different network relations have varied information flow capabilities. The other significant difference was in the source of motivation. Whether the group is promoted through the self-help group promotion institution or not? Then each case was reviewed to confirm the relationship between the various emerging constructs and themes from the cross-case analysis (Eisenhardt, 1989). This improved the accuracy and reliability of the theory by improving the theory data fit. As discussed in the findings section, this aided the researcher in capturing the findings from the data.

6. Discussion and Analysis

Our findings suggest that collectives and self-help groups use three main strategies to overcome resource constraints in fragile contexts. These strategies include, that is, 'network relations', 'social capital in the form of shared norms, relationships', and 'peer mechanism in the form of peer selection, peer monitoring, and peer enforcement or sanction'. This outcome resulted from the open and focussed coding of the data collected.

6.1. Coding

Coding is an interactive process (Charmaz, 2006). This study uses coding to delimit the research, as suggested by Charmaz (2014) Gehman et al. (2018). This study collected and analysed data simultaneously (Spradley, 1979). Despite the literature review, a mix of inductive and deductive coding or abduction has been used (Peirce, 1958) to develop the codes. These codes go through a second coding cycle for higher categories or themes. After generating the significant categories, the existing literature is used to create the theory. The data were arranged before analysing it. Memos are prepared for each interview and interaction to summarize the main points. The data's theoretical sensitivity was considered when interviewing self-help group members (Strauss & Corbin, 1998). Glaser (1978) warns against excessive prior knowledge engagement to avoid data bias. However, Kelle (2007) argues that the researcher can use existing theoretical knowledge to interpret the observed phenomenon. Theoretical sensitivity is the ability to see with analytical depth. This study is based on memoing, line-to-line data analysis, and recording thoughts and feelings during the data collection. Further, the existing literature has been used to build theoretical sensitivity, but with caution.

6.1.1. Open Coding

The data for the study was collected using the exploratory interview approach. These were open-ended interviews. In the first phase, the data were analysed using the open coding technique (Glaser, 1998). Coding was done in two cycles. In the first cycle of open coding, codes were small words that captured the essence or attribute of verbal data (Oxford, 2021; Saldaña, 2009). The second coding cycle through memoing provided a conceptual framework for the codes. The data are coded and analysed sentence by sentence, asking the following questions:

(1) What is happening in the data, and what is this observation sentence a study of?
(2) What is the primary concern in the data?
(3) What is the category that is emerging from the data?
(4) What actions are people taking for granted in the data?
(5) What are the common problems that people face?

The emerging data were analysed using gerund coding (focussing on human interactions) to generate the open codes; these open codes represent the incident, idea, or process and are the foundation of all theory building (Strauss & Corbin,

1998). These were generally reflections of the action going on in the field. We asked a few questions to develop open codes: (a) What is the action or speak? (b) Why does this seem significant?

The data were collected for open coding, and a summary of the data was prepared as interview transcripts. The first step in the open coding was transcribing the interview and then using *line-by-line coding*. These initial open codes help the data to be transformed into *categories*. The open codes were prepared from the summary of the data. From the first interview onwards, the process was repeated iteratively until theoretical saturation or sufficiency was achieved. The data were collected and analysed simultaneously using the Memos (Corbin & Strauss, 2015).

The scholarly literature is not consulted in the initial stages. But the categories started emerging after the open coding of 10–15 first interviews. Initial codes

Table 3. Interviews.

Interview Excerpt (First-stage Interview)
Interviewer: Tell something about your group and members
Respondent: These members are from the same village. We ensure that the member has the Aadhaar card, utility certificate, and bank account. This ensures that the pension cannot be provided to the member if he does not have a bank account. In the group, the NGO facilitates the member to form the group. Under Ajeevika, support is provided to the member. The Central Bank loan did not pose any difficulty. We made an application, visited the bank, and sanctioned the loan. Thus, for the Central Bank, there was no difficulty
Interviewer: The loan is to be disbursed as per the Government mandate; how do you ensure that the payment is made in time?
Participant: We use the loan for investment and the group members' use. For the supervision of the loan, regular monitoring and stock-taking of the commodity manufactured are done. We make Agarbatti, and money is not utilized for personal purposes. In a group, we have a leader, and members come from NRLM and Ajeevika, and there is no support provided during the lockdown. The members get an opportunity to exhibit their products in the exhibition. Agarbatti making is our traditional profession. In our group, we have disabled members, and we help them. After joining the group, there was a drastic improvement in people's standard of living. Improvement in standard of living is because the members do not have to depend on anybody. It has helped us to be financially self-reliant. The group maintains registers for savings and loans and conducts monthly meetings. Adhyaksh is a metric pass, but the Kosha Adhyaksh is under graduation. And all the members have undertaken BCA computer courses. My best friend is blind. We help them, take the Agarbatti and deliver him on the bike, and he in his home arranges for the sale of the Agarbatti. Impaired people should be provided more capital, and this group's strength is derived from determination. If the group decides that tomorrow's raw material is needed, then we do not get bogged down by how the money will be arranged

Source: Author's own work.

were created, and substantive codes were derived as categories. At this stage, the scholarly literature was consulted and coded to generate theoretical sensitivity. Theoretical sampling was used to generate the concepts, maximize the variations in the concepts, and densify the categories.

Table 3 presents an example of how data were transcribed as an interview and descriptive codes were generated. From these interviews, memos were generated, capturing the insights and researcher's reflections through contemplation. In the open coding stage, memos were prepared (Table 4).

After preparing the memos, each interview was analysed line by line, and in vivo codes were extracted. In vivo codes are meant to preserve the meaning of what the participant says. These in vivo codes were upscaled to descriptive and analytical codes, as shown in Table 5.

The in vivo and descriptive code formation process continued until some concepts and patterns emerged from the data. To develop codes, a constant comparison was made between groups promoted through the SHPI and not promoted through the SHPI.

6.1.1.1. The Conceptual Framework The research started with the broad question: What is the mechanism through which the group operates? How do the groups operate and maintain financial sustainability? Who are the various stakeholders in the process?

Initially, no psychological or conceptual framework was adopted. The initial phase of open coding continued over two to three months. We have used

Table 4. Memos.

Memo
In this interview, the main focus is the formation of a group and selection of the members in the group of impaired people by the SHPIs. The participant strongly asserts that members should be from the same village and have identity proof. The 'formation of group based on common ground' is the central theme. The participant appreciates the group's control through monitoring, supervision, bookkeeping, and leadership. Regular monitoring and supervision of the activities of the members are done. Further, the interview highlights that the members regularly maintain the book of accounts and registers. There is an Adhyaksh and Kosha Adhyaksh, who help monitor the activities of the group members. Overall, the interview highlights the presence of network relations and risk matching among members of the group. It highlights the importance of bonding and horizontal relationship among the group members. It also highlights the presence of shared norms, trust, and rules that facilitate achieving the goal of poverty reduction through financial inclusion. Besides network relations and social structures the interview also highlights the importance of leadership and solidarity and cohesiveness among the members to facilitate the achievement of objectives of financial inclusion

Source: Author's own work.

Table 5. In Vivo and Descriptive Codes.

Line-by-Line Analysis	In Vivo Coding	Descriptive Coding	Analytical Coding
SHG is linked to Ajeevika NRLM and is involved in manufacturing the Madhubani paintings. There are 15 members in my group, and all do Madhubani painting. There are more than 40 members who are part of the Kala Kriti SHG. And all of us are involved in Madhubani painting, and we do an exhibition in various states such as Kerala, Mumbai, Karnataka, and Patna	Forming a homogenous group based on profession Clustering members through SHG federation	The criterion for selection in the group is a homogenous profession Groups are bridged through the formation of SHG federations	Peer selection based on homogeneity Bridging of members through clustering in SHG federation
And all of us are involved in Madhubani painting, and we do an exhibition in various states such as Kerala, Mumbai, Karnataka, and Patna. Not all but a few women members are selected who can talk to the people outside the SHG. We make paintings, and this style commands an excellent price and involves a lot of hard work and labour	Exploring international markets and getting recognition Creating products of high quality that have market Selecting members based on extrovert personality	Collective benefits through representation on international forum Economic benefits through income increase and selection of good members	Collective benefits Economic benefits Market expansion Group selection and group benefits

(*Continued*)

Table 5. (*Continued*)

Line-by-Line Analysis	In Vivo Coding	Descriptive Coding	Analytical Coding
The Government of India has started the Ajeevika programme, under which the members initially join the group to earn a livelihood. Then the members from the Ajeevika group, who are self-selected, join the self-help group. We have not taken the bank loan, but we have taken the loan under the CLF Ajeevika programme. We do not face any difficulties in making payments or savings amounts	Linking through Government scheme Ajeevika	Government schemes provide easy access to a loan	Network relations – bridging
	Financial inclusion through Government scheme	The hassle-free loan disbursement process	Financial inclusion
	Getting access to financial services		
Our members are aligned to households and are not part of any organization. Our members are versatile in Madhubani painting, a traditional art form. It is a heritage art and is passed on from generation to generation. My mother, grandmother, and great-grandmother used to pursue this art form, and we have become proficient in this. Ajeevika has given a push to this, and our group deposits Rs 10 per member per month, and then we became eligible for the loan	Homogenous groups of Karigars from the community pursuing Madhubani art	Local Artisan community organized in the form of groups	Homogenous groups of the Madhubani community
	Regular savings and bonding	Members of the group save regularly under Ajeevika	Bonding through regular savings
	Linking with Ajeevika	Ajeevika loans are based on social capital and savings	Linking with Ajeevika
			Social collateral

And our women members are very proactive. In our group, the CM or the Chief (Kosh Adhyaksh) maintains the books of accounts. Members of the group are not literate and are made aware by the Kosh Adhyaksh. All the members are not literate and illiterate members are apprised of their savings and outstanding loan amount by the chief accountant	Appreciating group control through books preparation, leadership and peer monitoring	Members prepare regular books of accounts	Shared norms – book keeping and meetings
	Leadership and collaborative effort	Supervision and control of the Kosha Adhyaksh	Leadership
		Regular savings by members	Bonding – regular savings
		Information sharing by the accountant	Linking on the basis of social capital
Our group members are hard-working and collectively work extremely hard from 11 p.m. to 4 a.m. None of the members have received any help from any of the members. Ajeevika NRLM block officers come and assist the members in making the loan repayment	Access to loan based on social capital	Members receive loans and assistance in repayment based on social capital	Collective benefits of solidarity in the form of access to a loan
	Delegated monitoring by members	Delegated monitoring through NRLM	Delegated monitoring

Source: Author's own work.

an inductive approach to open coding through analysis of stories and narratives from the self-help group leaders, heads of self-help group promotion institutions, and the members of the state-level banking committee. In total, 68 interviews were conducted. And we let the data speak for us. The interviews were transcribed to initiate the conceptualization of the data. A line-to-line analysis was performed at this stage to develop codes.

Further, the associated memos were prepared to capture the reflections of the discussion of the interview excerpt. In the first phase of open coding, it was discovered that self-help groups or collectives use influence and control, information, and solidarity to achieve group sustainability and social welfare in the context of the agency of self-help groups. The findings suggest that successful collectives use their networks and relationships (discussed later as peripheral concepts) to gain access to information and achieve trust and solidarity among members through social control. After the initial stage of memo writing, data analysis became simple, allowing for a broader view of the data.

6.1.2. Narratives from the Ground Realities

> Microfinance is much more than simply an income generation tool. Directly empowering poor people, particularly women, has become one of the key driving mechanisms toward meeting the Millennium Development Goals(Mark Malloch Brown, Chef de Cabinet, Office of the Secretary-General to the United Nations)

This part of the study mainly explores how the unique social innovation of group lending enables poor people to attain economic well-being. It aims to analyse whether lack of financial access is a social problem or a challenge to achieving the sustainable development goal of financial inclusion and poverty reduction. There are existing studies that address the question of 'why' poor people are not able to access financial services. But there is a lack of studies on 'how' social innovation, or the self-help group, enables the members to access financial services. This part of the study mainly aims to get insights into the local realities of the communities called the self-help groups and create a skeletal theoretical structure of how groups help poor individuals achieve access to financial services. This part of the study provides a glimpse into the detailed lives of the microborrowers linked to the self-help groups.

6.1.2.1. A Glimpse into the Routines of Three Self-Help Groups. The first group is pursuing Sikki Artwork in Madhubani village. The leader of this self-help group asserts that the members of the group peer learn from each other. She recalls how their group solicited a loan and utilized it to set up a workshop by buying furniture and raw materials. Moreover, the group is linked to three other self-help groups through the federation. Her federation has four self-help groups: Bhairav, Bhagwati, Ganesh, and Jawala. According to the group's leader, Jawala and Bhagwati form a Tulla Mohalla, as these groups are closer to each other. While the other two groups, Bhairav and Ganesh, are far from each other. The leader emphasizes that the members of the group peer monitor each other due to the joint liability. The group members work under the leadership of Adhyaksh and follow the group's rules and regulations. The group strongly believes that self-help groups are based on social cohesion and social capital. As per the respondent, 'Our group is like a family which comprises of 4 different households, and there have been instances of counselling and difference of opinion, but it helps us to ensure better repayment of loans'.

The next respondent is the head of the SHPI (Self-help group promotion institution), promoting self-help groups involved in Dhokra handicrafts. He is himself involved in promoting the Dhokra self-help groups. He feels that the groups should be provided the tool kits and should be helped in product verification. He takes only those members in the group who are from the same profession and are homogenous in terms of work. He highlighted the difficulties faced by the self-help groups in accessing financial services. He feels that many of the members of the self-help groups waste the money allocated to them in wasteful activities and divert the money from product generation to consumption purposes. Many members divert the money for the purchase of assets for personal use. Though these members conduct the meetings regularly, he feels that there is a need for more effort to adhere to group rules. According to the author, these members stay extremely close to each other. For better repayments and financial sustainability, as per the respondent, there is a need for better training and financial intermediation. He asserts that there is a need for more monitoring within the group. The members of his group maintain regular books of accounts. In one of the groups, there was a member called *Rammare*; this group member was already a loan defaulter. He contends that if the bank gets to know that one member has defaulted and they will deny a further loan to the group. In his opinion, members do not take adequate interest in the training and are more interested in stipend. He contends that there is a need for strong motivation to enable the financial inclusion of the poor. When the group is formed, members must know each other. According to him, the defaulting members should not be in the group. Some of the groups are extremely good. He emphasizes that there are at least 55 good self-help groups out of the total 120 self-help groups. Members are given the Karigar cards. He laments that though these Dhokra artists are given ID Cards, not all have Karigar cards. They go to the exhibition, and the Government gives them a stipend based on the Karigar ID card. The groups must monitor and follow up on the members' performance.

> In another group, the leader is a middle-aged gentleman handling 13 women making textiles and bedsheets. He highlights that his group has taken loans from the bank and has an extremely high rate of loan repayments. In his opinion, the members are from the same profession, so the members stay together. He is incredibly proud that the group members have very high repayment rates, due to which the banks are ready to lend money to the members. He says there are few instances when anybody has defaulted on the group loan. And according to him, the members regularly pay the

amount. He exhorted that the members have been pursuing this art since they came from Pakistan. And most of the groups are engaged in artwork in Bapu Bazaar and City Palace in Jaipur. He lauds the women for using the peer mechanism and peer pressurize to enable them to repay the defaulting loan of other members.

SHPI Head of another NGO is a middle-aged gentleman handling self-help groups of around 11–15 men. He mainly deals with women's self-help groups in solid waste management. He is extremely passionate about how self-help groups have progressed and how it has led to incremental change in the well-being of the group members. Every month, in the beginning, his SHPI contributes to members. He has been instrumental in enabling the members of the self-help groups to sell recycled plastic waste in the markets worth Rs. 200–300 per day. This amount is then directly credited to the member's account at the end of the month. His SHPI takes only homogenous members, and then they help form a group with institutional governance and rules. He allows the members to form the group, and the bank enables the members to earn interest from money deposited. Similar to the Amul cooperative, this SHPI allows the member to market recycled waste and handicrafts. In his view, all the members live in the same locality and are taken by each other's reference. Thus, he thinks that members can easily monitor each other. He emphasized that they have to conduct meetings at a gap of 15 days. The SHPI, according to the Head, is where the members can relax and unwind. They are served *tea* and *karah* during the break by the SHPI. Leaders are the lynchpin, and according to the SHPI head, the leader helps the members to maintain the books of accounts. According to him, the primary source of stress for the members of SHPI is the misutilization of loans. The members take the money and misuse this money for personal purposes. In a group, the members counsel the defaulting members in case of default, and at times there is a big fight. Only the strongest member in the group is made the group leader. This helps in reducing the tension in the group. He calls it a small get-together and party in the slum, where poor people come together. He proudly says that the members also get delicacies and refreshments for the meetings. Gradually, the members started saving bit and bit, and now they can buy Pizza for the refreshment party and gift wall clocks to celebrate International Women's Day. He is happy to see so many poor people enter the prosperous world of higher savings and income. Some people have escaped the vicious circle of poverty, such that even if they do not get a salary for two months, they assume that money will be paid. This has helped to improve the social bonding among the member of the group. The groups work relentlessly and very efficiently. They can finish the

> work in significantly less time. He shares that the SHPI addicts these people to have tea, enabling them to celebrate Holi Milan, teach them to recite the national anthem on the 15th of August and celebrate Yoga Day. And all this gives them enjoyment, as they get a social platform to express themselves. Now, everything is getting ok. They have started wearing good clothes. He says all the members are from the same *kunba,* but one or two might be from different communities. According to the SHPI head, the members are like pearls, and the thread keeps them together. The agency or the SHPI is the thread that keeps the members together. Thus, initial hand-holding protects them from getting disengaged.

This process took several months due to a large amount of data. Many diagrams were created to link the open codes.

6.1.2.2. Codes to Categories. Identifying in vivo codes led to more descriptive codes and higher abstraction of analytical codes through open coding. These codes form the foundation for theory development. After the initial stages, we began collecting data to develop categories and properties using theoretical sampling. Table 6 further provides detail of categories generated in the open coding stage. Theoretical literature was referred to at this stage multiple times to facilitate memoing and coding. The data were rigorously coded line by line to facilitate theoretical linkages.

6.1.3. Patterns and Concept Governance

During data analysis, the concepts grew, and a series of open and tentative coding emerged. The excerpts from the interviews are given in Table 3. The categories are identified to provide conceptual information. It became apparent from the data analysis the core categories of the peer mechanism process in the Indian self-help group are *social exchange*, *social control*, *social cohesion*, *sustainability*, and *social welfare*. These five categories describe the phenomena regarding what is taking place in the data in the Agency relationship between the agent (borrowers) and the principal (lender). After the development of the core categories, theoretical memoing was done to identify the concepts and patterns in the data. It describes what people are doing and how people act. These five codes label the phenomena in the context of the research. The voice of the self-help groups was captured using the triangulation approach. It took several months to map the relationships across the different contexts (self-help groups, perspectives of banks, and SHPIs) and geographic boundaries. Table 7 represents the open codes for the study. Fig. 18 highlights the main categories that have emerged through various phases of data analysis.

6.1.4. Identification of Categories

The categories were identified using the questioning technique: who, where, when, how? It also involved questions about spatial and temporal context. The first category

Table 6. Categories Generated.

Social Exchange	Social Control	Social Cohesion	Sustainability	Social Welfare
Respondent 1: People with similar characteristics form these groups, that is, go to the wells to fetch water or spend time together. This affinity helps the members come together	**Respondent 1:** The members stay together because they belong to the same group. A late payer should return the loan in time. Otherwise, he is socially sanctioned	**Respondent 1**: If there is a group in which members make terracotta pottery. We make pots from mud and bake them in the fire. On baking, it gets converted into terracotta. And lets if a member is making Ganesh Murti and they cannot make the seat for the lord, then the other members help him. This improves the solidarity of the group.	**Respondent 1**: Let's assume the member has taken a loan for Rs 2 lakh, and they have not generated the work; the loan must be returned to the bank. In this case, pressure is used, but it is essential to take deliberation and meeting. There is a need for monitoring by the SHPI. These NGOs help the groups to become financially sustainable	**Respondent 1:** We make small, big ideas, a lamp made of mud, and it becomes terracotta when baked in the fire. The group members get letters from Patan vihbaag, NRLM exhibition, and NRLM vihbaag, and if we do not get funds, we get loans from these agencies. Even the honourable Chief Minister has visited our facility to see our work. Since joining the group, the self-efficacy group has improved
Respondent 2: In this group, members know each other even before joining the group. They all pursue handicrafts and have the same professional interests	**Respondent 2**: The members of the group peer monitor each other by conducting the regular meeting and through regular record keeping through the maintenance of the books of accounts. This leads to better financial control and reporting	**Respondent 2:** In our cluster, groups make bamboo handicrafts, Zari Zardozi. The group remains strong if they maintain the proper books of the account	**Respondent 2:** On a personal level, the members maintain the relationship. There is also a bookkeeper. They work voluntarily to audit the members' workings, savings, and borrowings. This leads to the better repayment of the loans	**Respondent 2:** Since joining the group, the big officials have started coming, and our group is near Khajuraho, and foreigners have also been coming to Khajuraho. This has boosted our sales

Respondent 3: We take people only from our village. Since they are from the same village, the members already know each other. This group has very high repayment rates	**Respondent 3**: In the group, we have Adhyaksh and Kosha Adhyaksh. They counsel the defaulter that you have taken a loan and other members in the group need a loan. The defaulter agrees and promises to pay back the loan. We have regular bookkeeping monthly	**Respondent 3:** In 2010, we formed a self-help group of members pursuing Madhubani paintings. We are from Madhubani, and if the new member cannot work, they observe senior didi. By attending, she learns leading to solidarity	**Respondent 3:** All the members make bedsheets on the handloom. Due to this, the members can monitor each other, and we members stay together. There is transparency in our operations, leading to social capital	**Respondent 3:** Group lending has far reached social impacts, including better living and income. Common vocation and all women make bedsheets on a common khadi and handloom; the members can better peer monitor each other
Respondent 4: Members meet four to five times a month to apprise each other of the group's financial condition. They discuss and report savings, repayment of internal loans, and rotation of funds	**Respondent 4**: These women have pursued the vocation of making handicrafts since independence. In many of the Karkhanas in markets, Karigars pursue handicrafts as an ancestral art form. We make leather products. If some women members cannot pay the loan, all the members get together and visit the home of the said member	**Respondent 4:** Dhokra artists form a self-help group. They live on the outskirts of town. These artists pursue an ancestral art form. This town is known for its unique art. The artisans use metal casting to create diyas, pots, and animal figurines. These members have world-famous hand skills due to their profession and art. Community members feel connected because of this	**Respondent 4**: In the case of handicrafts, we have groups of six and seven members. We receive the loan requirement only from the Master artisans. Masters' artisans or group heads will be responsible for the distribution and repayment of loans	**Respondent 4:** In one area, if the work is done on a large scale, for example, in Saharanpur, the artisans do Pittal work; in Hathras, in metal Zari work, glass work, stone work, then in those places, if people work in the closure, they automatically get buyers. After production, market planning is extremely important. Groups help members achieve scale

(*Continued*)

Table 6. (*Continued*)

Social Exchange	Social Control	Social Cohesion	Sustainability	Social Welfare
Respondent 5: SHPI classifies the members who approach joining the group based on their vocation. Some people are interested in block printing; some are interested in dye painting, and so on. We form groups of members from the same profession or are homogenous in terms of profession	**Respondent 5:** These groups comprise around 10–20 members. They make leather Jutties. This is their ancestral art. All the members are from the same profession. These members save regularly, and they do not take external loans, but they do internal lending. The educated women counsel the other members and maintain the books of accounts. This leads to the success of the group	**Respondent 5:** There are 12–13 ladies and 7–8 men. They all work in their home and make items from silver. Since all the members make silver jewellery, they are experts and train new members	**Respondent 5:** There are 12–13 ladies and 7–8 men. They all work in their home and make items from silver. Since all the members make silver jewellery, they are experts and train new members. If the product is not sold, we give back the amount. Sonar community work only on making jewellery, and Adivasi designs are fantastic and are known as khatwah, bhongiri, and phechwa. These designs are unique to us. And nobody else can do that. All these are handmade. The melas for the Adivasi design are very high in demand. These products are available on the web under the Adivasi brand, and the Government has launched this	**Respondent 5:** Through the self-help group, there is a tremendous change in the lifestyle of the members of the group. There is an enormous change in the status of the members as we have taken the women to meet CM Anandibai Patel. The members in a group learn to get together and greet the members. This leads to an increase in social status. In Vrindavan, in Chaatikraha village, there is a Tulsimala cluster formed by the bankers. And HOD of Mechanical IIT has been to the village, and he went to the village. He developed the method of making the mala from Tulsimala from the seeds, and the work which used to be done in eight hours gets done in a few hours. This has highly impressed the members, and this has helped them, members. This is a social innovation that helps in social change

Source: Author's own work.

Table 7. Categories.

Social Exchange	Social Control	Social Cohesion	Sustainability	Social Welfare
Grouping with other members to access credit	Selecting a team leader from the group	Assuming joint liability	Institutionalizing group norms Enforcing joint liability	Promoting financial inclusion
Selecting members from the same village	Noticing other members of the group	Seeking group financial access	Peer monitoring and sanctioning Saving regularly	Promoting higher repayment
Seeking like-mindedness in other members	Reporting the financial behaviour of the other members of the group	Institutionalizing common goals	Paying loans regularly	Seeking autonomy
Wanting to work together for mutual benefit	Discussing the problem with other members of the group	Sharing common cultural beliefs	Regular record keeping	Seeking women upliftment
Carving economic and social gains	Paying on behalf of other members of the group	Generating social capital in the group	Conducting regular meeting	Eliminating moneylender
Seeking access to financial services	Assuming joint liability with other members of groups	Bonding and bridging with members	Seeking access to financial services	Promoting social welfare
Seeking less risk and high rewards	Sanctioning the bad credit behaviour of other members	Social contracting with members of the group	Group norming	Exploring ways to reduce poverty
Rationalizing the selection of same-risk members	Exercising peer pressures to ensure repayment	Exhibiting solidarity in the group	Seeking profitability in the group	Saving regularly
Bonding with members already known	Seeking intermediation from SHPI	Seeking cooperation through social ties	Striving for financial sustainability in the group	Promoting credit creation
Grouping with members from a common background	Peer selecting members of the group	Seeking motivation through adherence to group norms	Soliciting intermediation by SHPI	Seeking empowerment

(*Continued*)

Table 7. (*Continued*)

Social Exchange	**Social Control**	**Social Cohesion**	**Sustainability**	**Social Welfare**
Grouping with members with the same profession	Enforcing sanctions to ensure contract performance	Working together to seek higher repayment of loans	Undertaking financial literacy training	Reducing inequalities
Collaborating with members with the same skills	Record keeping to control the financial behaviour of a group	Leveraging cultural affinities to seek cooperation	Adhering to group norms	Promoting equity in the group
Avoiding grouping with unknown members	Selecting leaders who can control financial behaviour	Leveraging business correlations to seek cooperation		Financially including women
Working together in a known environment	Conducting regular meeting	Peer monitoring to seek higher repayment of loans		
Wanting prior information about other members	Institutionalizing Panchsutras for social control	Peer selection to seek higher repayment of loans		
Grouping to access bank loans	Groups seek monitoring by banks	Feeling connected due to the business correlations		
Social contracting to access joint liability loans	Norming in a group to achieve social control	Reciprocating through social contract		
Grouping to rotate savings as internal loans	Paying on behalf of each other	Exhibiting collective efficacy through group		
Working together in groups	Institutionalizing obligations	Emotionally supporting other members of the group		

Source: Author's own work.

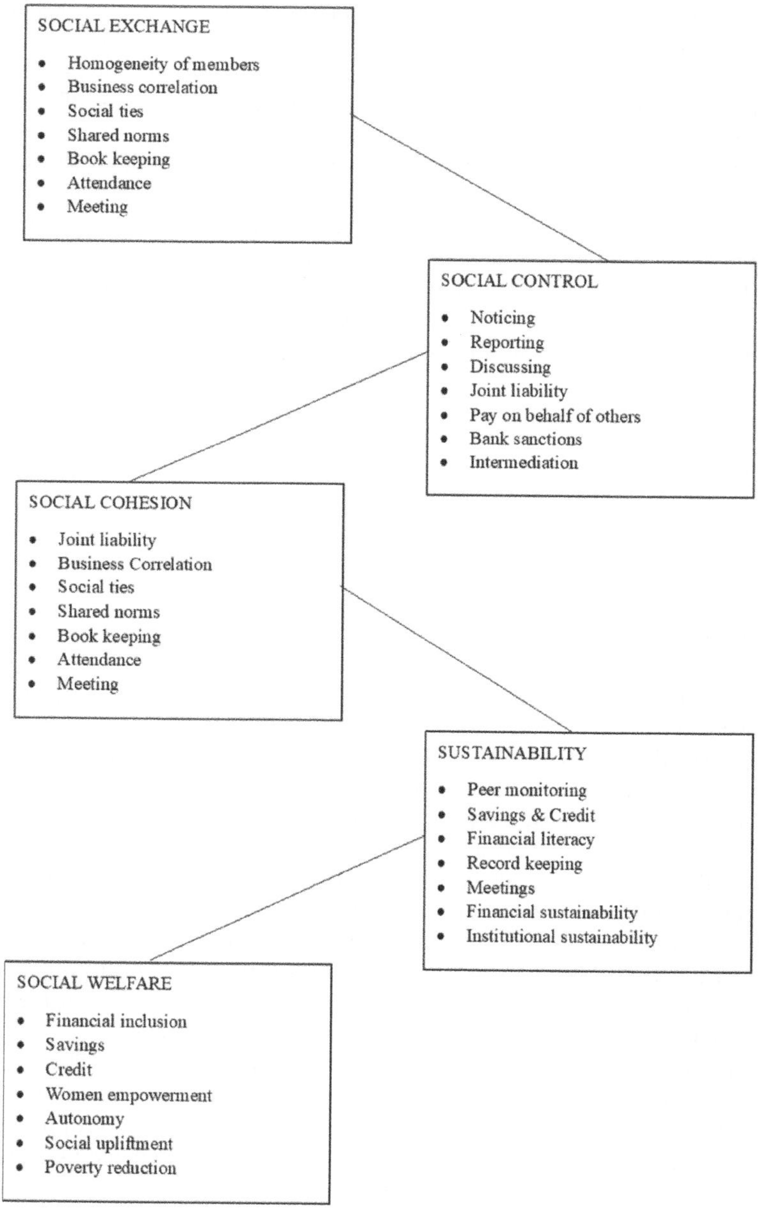

Fig. 18. Categories for the Grounded Theory. *Source*: By the authors.

emerging from the data are social exchange facilitated through the web of interactions. The data analysis analysed who shares information with whom, how much, and what the result is. In this case, the borrowers do not share information about creditworthiness with the bank. They share information with peers. They 'socialize', which leads to perfect information symmetry that generate social capital and finance access. They share information in the neighbourhood and the workplace.

Similarly, regarding social control, the borrowers are influencing their peers. They influence each other through social networks, monitoring, and social sanctions. They again exercise control or influence in social settings such as meetings, workplaces, or neighbourhoods. Banks and promoting institutions influence the members through monitoring and meetings. The groups exhibit social cohesion with peers in social settings during sessions by paying on behalf of the defaulters. The group promotes social welfare in social settings by improving people's standard of living. SHPIs intermediate the relationship between the group members, the bank, and the members. The intermediate and handhold the group for a year. This results in the social welfare of the group, sustainability, and welfare of society. These categories are defined in the context of an agency relationship. The borrowers are the *agents*, and the lenders are the *principal*.

6.1.4.1. Emerging Categories

We now have five categories:

(1) Social exchange
(2) Social control
(3) Social cohesion
(4) Sustainability
(5) Social welfare.

Regarding social control, the common ground of domicile and profession homogeneity emerged as essential criteria. The data analysis yields a new insight that 'intermediation by SHPI' impacts sustainability. Intermediation also helps form groups and motivates them to follow the semi-formal contract's terms. The data analysis revealed a tentative relationship between the codes. It became clear that intermediation is vital in motivating related group members to exercise control. The financial intermediary, the SHPI, or contract terms like joint liability, keep them together to achieve financial sustainability. The intermediary, the SHPI, trains the group members and hand-holds them during the initial period. SHPI motivates the members to follow the group norms. Also, leadership became vital to a group's financial stability. A group's legitimacy emerges after the designated NGO or SHPI intercedes. So, the pattern is given in Fig. 19.

Initial codes help sort the data into categories (Charmaz, 2006). The scholarly literature was consulted to build theoretical sensitivity into the data at this stage. Interviews were conducted with stakeholders, including self-help group promoting agencies, banks, and state-level banking committees. Initial coding identified five major categories and focussed codes. Social exchange, social control, social cohesion, sustainability, and social welfare. Peripheral concepts identified include 'network relations', 'trust', 'shared norms', and 'peer mechanism'.

6.1.5. Categories and Properties

The theory has two parts: categories and properties. A category is a theoretical element. The property is the dimension of the conceptual element of the theory.

Fig. 19. Codes. *Source*: By the authors.

For example, five categories for microfinancing are 'social exchange', 'social control & contingency planning', 'social cohesion', 'sustainability', and 'social welfare'. The interview excerpts and verbatim highlight the process of identification of the categories. The categories were identified and developed across the properties and dimensions. For example, 'interacting', 'discussing', and 'reporting' were labelled as events that share the characteristics of social exchange through communication because each involves the exchange of ideas. Each category was derived from the open codes generated from the interview verbatim, given the context/subject of discussion.

As each event was compared with another, it was noted that these objects have a trait in common, that is, the exchange of ideas. These categories were developed to give them specificity along specific dimensions. This implies that individuals can communicate formally and informally with higher and low intensity. The group members can interact at higher intensity through informal and formal channels. Social exchange refers to the general category, with properties such as formal and informal, and dimension refers to the location of property over a range, that is, higher intensity of communication among peers in a group and lower intensity of communication between the members and the bank officials. With limited communication with banks and others, it was theorized that a group or community members are an excluded population that does not communicate with others except through their social connections. This leads to a pattern of communication among microborrowers. Microborrowers communicate more within social groups or communities and less outside the community. Initially, the members come together due to a common ground or like-mindedness. They formalize a social contract to save and rotate saving with joint liability for the group. This becomes the basis for social exchange. On this basis, the members can get a loan from banks and financial institutions.

Similarly, social control can be higher intensity or lower intensity. Peers can exert more control due to frequent interactions, social ties, and joint liability. At the same time, the banks and federations exercise limited power due to a lack of social relations and motivation. Social cohesion due to homogeneity is high among the group members from an ordinary background and is low among the members from a non-homogenous experience. The details of the categories are given below:

(1) *Social exchange*: Social exchange highlights how the group members leverage the group affinity and social capital to derive financial benefits in terms of access to loans greater than the individual capability to raise loans. The exchange of social capital for access to loans leads to the social contract to leverage internal savings and access external loans. Members endorse a 'Social contract' with joint liability that leads to 'generalized reciprocity'. Besides that, 'Strategic communication' through the enforcement of group norms leads to the development of the targeted mission to achieve the group's purpose of financial inclusion. Every group has a particular purpose; they exist for a goal that must be communicated and fulfilled. Trust also leads to 'group identity', 'social capital', 'adherence to norms', and 'repayment of loans'. Thus, the 'collaborative and collective power' ensures access to credit and financial sustainability through regular repayments.

Within this category, 'information asymmetry' refers to the lack of information about the group members' creditworthiness to formal financial institutions. It concludes that information sharing occurs in 'closed networks' or 'bonding' among members. This category highlights how the group generates and shares information about its members, facilitating finance access. This category explains how the banks, through groups, get the right to access information about the creditworthiness of the group members, who individually lack physical collateral. The social structure of groups facilitates institutional discourse that has its 'credibility'. So, the group becomes the media through which the 'legitimacy' of the member's claim to credit is established. 'People with similar characteristics form these groups, i.e., go to the wells to fetch water or spend time together. This affinity helps the members come together'.

The data analysis revealed that the group members engage in frequent social interactions. Groups are formed based on 'homogeneity', which means that members share a 'common ground' that leads to 'collective power', 'group affinity', and 'trust', which leads to 'generalized relationships'. They share a profession and ethnicity, making them a 'source of information'. In a group, the 'exchange of information' about financial goals through socialization depends on 'information flow capability'. Information flow capability depends on community connectedness, homogeneity of groups, and relational network. In a group, the information flow capability is very high. Sharing information and intermediation leads to consensus and reciprocity. This communication facilitates social contract and social exchange.

Once in the social contract, the members develop an economic goal. Knowing that in case of a single member default, the bank will not extend the loan to the group, the members 'cooperate'. This human behaviour is rationalized due to 'incentive compatibility constraint' by banks in the form of 'progressive loans' to groups that pay all their loans in time and penalize the 'defaulting group'. The fundamental basis of social exchange is the 'commitment' of the members to perform their 'group duties', 'repay loans', and 'exchange information'. 'Generalized reciprocity' is the basis of social exchange in this self-help group linkage programme.

Groups consent to a 'common goal' to resolve their economic woes. Thus, the group members must communicate two plans: economic and social goals or objectives. Members conduct meetings to discuss the books of accounts and the group's financial position. They frequently 'socialize' and exchange information. The comparative flip-flop technique was used to derive the category. The dimension of ease and difficulty in communication was analysed using the flip-flop technique. What if the members do not interact or communicate? Will financial access be difficult? The answer is yes due to lack of information; the members will be financially excluded as the banks will not lend to them. And the members will not trust each other to come together for a common cause. What if the members do not reciprocate? Will financial access for the other members be difficult? The answer is yes, and the 'homogeneity of members', 'collective identity', 'group norms', and 'joint liability' in 'social contract' facilitate reciprocity and social exchange in the groups. Thus, the category of social exchange based on incentive compatibility in the form of access to low-cost credit emerged as significant. It shows the classification based on homogeneity. Communication impacts relational governance development depending on the network's information flow capability. During an interaction, it became clear that the group's 'size' and 'capacity' influenced the outcome.

The group's members' 'skill' was another major characteristic. 'Community connectedness' is critical to group success. Sharing information among members builds networks and improves 'self-efficacy'. 'Joint liability' through social contract leads to 'generalized reciprocity' in a group. Through data analysis, it was found that information sharing through a 'web of interactions' based on 'social ties' such as network relations in the form of 'bonding' or 'social ties' among the group, 'linking' with banks, and 'bridging' with network relations ensures that the groups remain sustainable. And formally, a group adheres to a social contract through enforceable norms to ensure reciprocity that leads to social exchange, which makes the group sustainable. In one of the interviews, the member said, 'Members meet 4 to 5 times a month to apprise each other of the group's financial condition. They discuss and report savings, repayment of internal loans, and rotation of funds'. Fig. 20 represents the category of social exchange.

(2) *Social/control*:

> It is the social process of group life that creates and upholds the rules, not the rules that create and uphold group life. (Blumer, 1969)

This category shows how a group with homogeneous members uses peer influence and sanctions to monitor and control. In a group, members are bound by a social contract, and the social control is operationalized through reinforcement. The dynamic incentive of the progressive loan in case of loan repayment and sanction in case of default by even one group member works as a stimulus. This contract

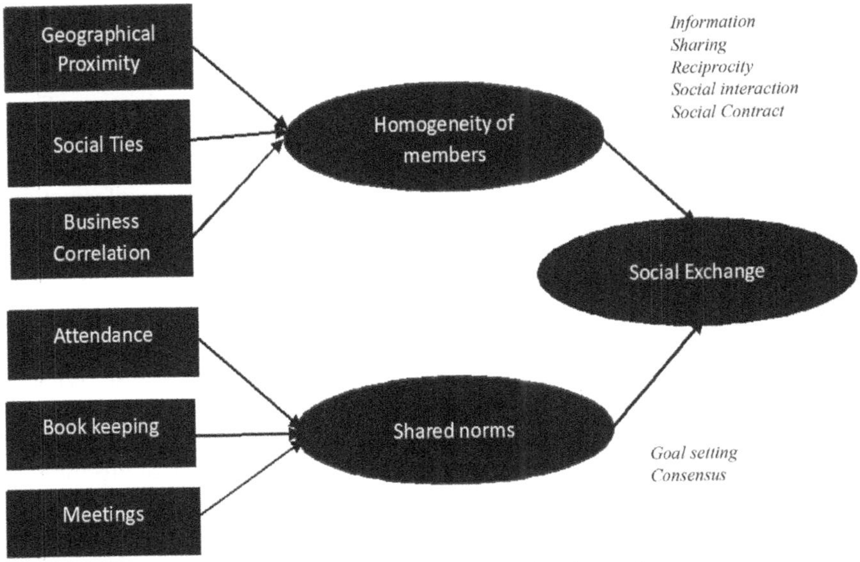

Fig. 20. Category 1 – Social Exchange. *Source*: By the authors.

provides joint liability for the group and limited liability for the individual. In case of default by one member, all other members have to repay the loan. Influence and control are rooted in the cognitive and cultural norms of the social contract. Social norms facilitate the enforcement of the social contract. The cultural component refers to social norms and sanctions. And the cognitive elements of the social contract, that is, refer to the group norms such as maintaining minutes of meetings and books of account. In one of the interviews, the member cited:

> These women have pursued the vocation of making handicrafts since independence. In many of the Karkhanas in markets, Karigars pursue handicrafts as an ancestral art form. We make leather products. If some women members cannot pay the loan, all the members get together and visit the home of the said member.

The cognitive norms in a group become operational through the social contract and bank sanctions. Peer monitoring by the joint liability of the group and limited individual liability also leads to social control in a group. In a group, social norms facilitate the enforcement of the social contract. In a group, the community's norms to save and repay loans facilitate control through reinforcement. Social contracts and joint liability play an essential role in social control. Further, the measurement of outcomes through meetings and accounting facilitates control.

In another interview, the group members cited:

> If there is a group in which members make terracotta pottery. We make pots from mud and bake them in the fire. On baking, it

> gets converted into terracotta. And lets say if a member is making Ganesh Murti and they cannot make the seat for the lord, then the other members help him. This improves the solidarity of the group.

Fig. 21 highlights the category of social control. The social norms in the form of noticing, discussing, reporting, social contracts, and bank sanctions lead to open code social control.

(3) *Social cohesion*: Solidarity in a group promotes cohesion and camaraderie. It helps them build relationships, trust, and cohesion, which drives financial sustainability. Geographic proximity and shared vocation unite a group. Puritan values unanimously bind group members based on some higher consciousness. These values bind members together and create a common bond in the form of social capital. Task dependencies and business correlations and cultural affiliations lead to like-mindedness. Social ties, cultural affiliations, and task dependencies lead to cooperation. Cooperation and like-mindedness lead to solidarity. Solidarity leads to motivation for peer learning and adherence to norms. Adherence to group norms leads to higher loan repayments.

One example of solidarity and cohesion is the art groups like Dhokra. Dhokra art is pre-Mohenjo-Daro and Harrapan art from Bastar, Chhattisgarh, India. This art depicts Eastern Indian heritage. Interview excerpt:

> Dhokra artists form a self-help group. They live on the outskirts of town. These artists pursue an ancestral art form. This town is known for its unique art. The artisans use metal casting to create diyas, pots, and animal figurines. These members have world-famous hand skills due to their profession and art. Community members feel connected because of this.

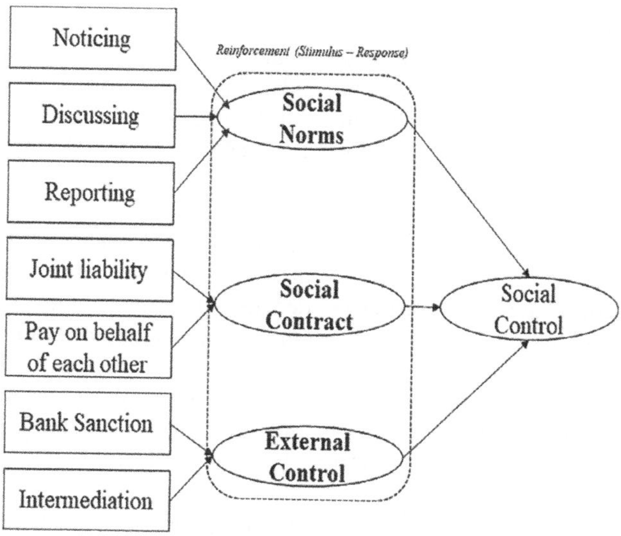

Fig. 21. Category 2 – Social Control. *Source*: By the authors.

In another interview, the member stated, 'Poor women are bunker and do thread kattai, and their husbands weave Resham. Women who worked elsewhere buy cocoons and threads from her, which is helpful. Homogeneity, like-mindedness, and common ground motivate economic collaboration'. The SHG Leader cited professional homogeneity as a source of solidarity. This story shows how ethnicity and heritage unite a community. Repayment of loans is determined by trust. The member said the group might not eat but will repay the loan. Honesty promotes group cohesion.

Further, in an interview, the member said,

> We make green Ganesh Ji. From March to September, we'll make and sell mud-made Ganpati when mud comes from the mountains to the banks. Pach is our ancestral art form. When community groups face the same financial goals and lender sanctions, it promotes unity.

Thus, social norms in the form of shared beliefs, attitudes, culture, and values promote social cohesion among the members. An interview discusses how homogeneity fosters unity. 'Members of our group only pursue Madhubani paintings and Sujani art', said another interviewee. This shows how cultural repertoire can encourage unity. Group solidarity is also attributed to government programmes like Ajeevika or DAY NRLM. Norms promote unity. It shows how self-help group members leverage existing social relationships (cognition and cultural affiliations) to create new network relations (bonding and bridging), leading to economic resources. Moreover, the shared norms regarding bookkeeping lead to higher repayment of loans in a group.

To sum up, two kinds of norms, that is, cognitive and social norms in a group, lead to solidarity. In a group, members institutionalize the common goal through a social contract. Members use shared bookkeeping norms to embed *cognition.* They also use shared *cultural beliefs* to build community. Group membership forms horizontal bonds. Common culture and heritage lead to group solidarity and cohesion. Lower borrowing costs and reliance on informal networks have increased group solidarity. According to a member of a silver jewellery SHG, 'SHG helps reduce reliance on informal moneylenders or Mahajan'. Culture influences group solidarity. Respondent:

> 'If a member can't pay, we all do'. Next comes repayment. Trust requires mutual dependence. Social ties and trust result from work-related, bilateral, and task dependencies. Also, 'leadership' affects group cohesion. The group members are not that literate, and the group selects Adhyaksh and Kosha Adhyaksh for the group. These leaders guide the group members in preparing books of accounts, minutes of meetings, and conducting the meetings. This also promotes solidarity among members.

Thus, there are two sources of solidarity, that is, cognitive and affective embeddedness of norms. Fig. 22 represents the category of social cohesion.

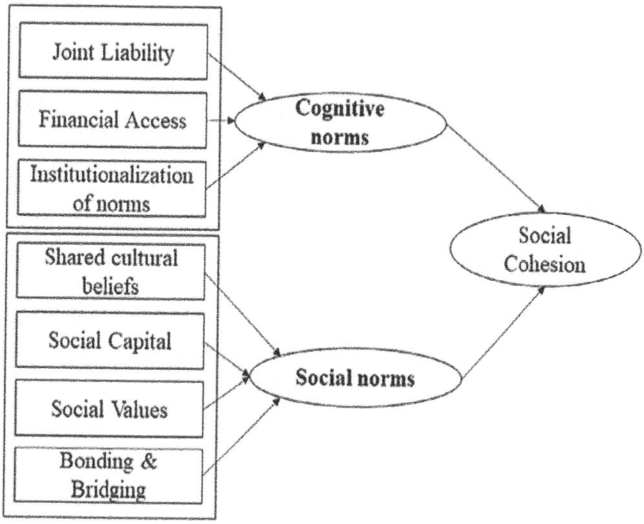

Fig. 22. Category 3 – Synergy Perspective to Integrate Networks for Generation of Social Cohesion in Groups. *Source*: By the authors.

(4) *Sustainability*: The future productivity of existing systems is called sustainability. The central issue in finance is whether the existing financial processes and structures are sustainable. The process of sustainability was defined initially as structure and process stability. This concept now includes financial and institutional sustainability. Sustainability is the system's future production ability to repeat the performance. During the group's functioning, concerns about the group's financial and institutional sustainability emerge.

The financial viability of a self-help group depends on access to savings, thrifts, loans, credit rotation, and loan repayment. In one interview, a respondent said:

> We meet weekly and closely monitor the group. We use WhatsApp to reach our members. In a group, peer sanction and monitoring also promote financial sustainability. The Adhyaksh is in charge of records, and a defaulter is expelled from the group. We ask the state banking committee and SHPI to investigate the defaulters. The members exercise peer sanctions to ensure the financial sustainability of groups. Intermediation with Self-help promoting institutions is pivotal in promoting financial sustainability.

The sustainability of the group is ensured through literacy and capacity-building. The respondent says that 'they train their members to maintain books'. NABARD also provides training to strengthen its *capacity*. 'When they join, we teach them the importance of maintaining the books of account. Self-Help Group training has a direct impact on the success of the group. The self-help groups meet monthly and keep tabs on the group's functioning. The members of a group also use the tally application. The members also maintain regular books of account and attend meetings. SHG meetings are held regularly, and Kosha Adhyaksh oversees the financial matters. The members in a group pay on time because Khajanchi keeps the books of account ready. The bank and NRLM monitoring help manage the group's finances. This has helped make the group sustainable', said one respondent. Thus, intermediation leads to adherence to group norms. And adherence to group norms leads to the institutional sustainability of groups. In yet another interview, we discovered that the group's sustainability is impacted by the 'Financial literacy' of the members. In interaction, the member highlighted, 'Few members are literate, but the Kosha Adhyaksh and Secretary help prepare the books of account'.

Fig. 23 highlights the category of sustainability. Intermediation leads to better savings and credit. Peer monitoring and sanction improve the financial performance of the groups and lead to financial sustainability. Moreover, the financial literacy of members leads to better record-keeping and meetings. Through accepted group norms, the group can achieve institutional sustainability. Thus, financial and institutional sustainability leads to sustainability in the group.

(5) *Social welfare*: The study confirms that the self-help group members benefit significantly from the self-help groups. According to the procedural utility theory, these groups are instrumental in promoting the group's welfare. These groups lead to the instant gratification of the individual's needs. The members achieve positive well-being through microcredit, including positive affect (better financial well-being, financial achievement, better community standing, social *welfare*, and *better family relations*).

Individuals' welfare can be further classified as (1) cognitive evaluative, which refers to the benefits of community membership: better finances, community, and health. The groups also provide hedonic experiences. The hedonic experience includes (1) autonomy, (2) relatedness, (3) competence, and (4) self-actualization. The feeling of self-actualization and better life experiences due to better living

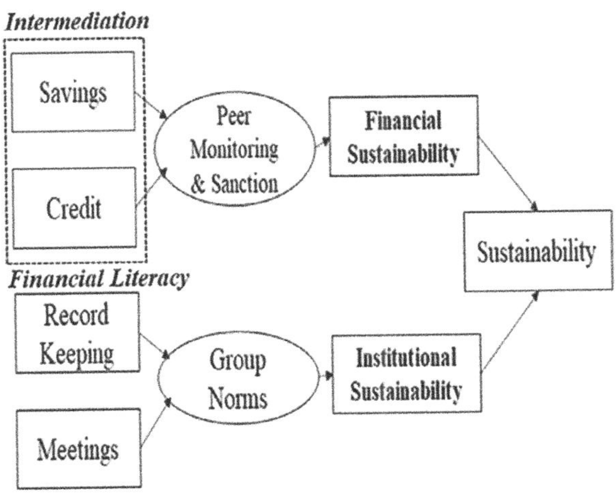

Fig. 23. Category 4 Sustainability. *Source*: By the authors.

standards and achievement in life, family, and community are included in the cognitive evaluation. Debt can cause (1) depression and (2) worry. The procedural utility is defined as (1) autonomy, (2) connectedness, (3) trust, and (4) competitiveness. Thus, joint liability groups through microcredit provide procedural utility, leading to women's empowerment and self-determination. In one interview, the member said: 'The government is helping the women members gain confidence, self-efficacy, and trust'.

In a group, regular savings and credit lead to financial inclusion, and social upliftment leads to women empowerment. Further, joint liability groups generate livelihood and eliminate the money lenders, reducing poverty. In an interview, the respondent highlighted:

> We make small, big diyas, a lamp made of mud, and it becomes terracotta when baked in the fire. The group members get letters from Patan vihbaag, NRLM exhibition, and NRLM vihbaag, and if we do not get funds, we get loans from these agencies. Even the honorable Chief Minister has visited our facility to see our work. Since joining the group, the self-efficacy of the group has improved.

In another interview, the member highlighted that 'Group lending has far reached social impacts including the better standard of living, better income. Common vocation and all women make bedsheets on a common khadi and handloom; the members can better peer monitor each other'. Fig. 24 highlights the category of social welfare.

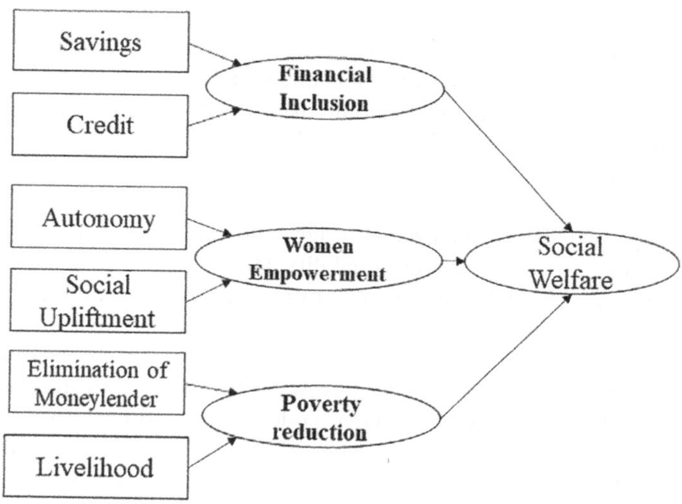

Fig. 24. Category 5 – Social Welfare. *Source*: By the authors.

6.2. Focussed Codes

Through initial coding, it was discovered that the most analytically significant initial codes converge to a common theme. After the first 50 codes, focussed codes were generated. The focussed coding was based on the MACR (meaning, action, challenge, & results) approach (Charmaz, 2006). At this stage of focussed coding, the *constant comparison* method was used to uncover hidden patterns. Through constant questioning, the objective is to shift descriptive data to conceptual abstraction (Kolb, 2012). Glaser and Strauss (1967) suggested four stages of comparison incidents to a category, integrating categories to properties, delimiting, and writing theory were followed. Similarly, this study referred to theoretical literature at the focussed coding stage to build theoretical sensitivity and for conceptual verification (Creamer, 2021). The objective at this point was to delimit the emergent pattern to achieve theoretical saturation. The objective at this stage was to see how the categories relate to the concept. The core category of a unique group dynamic, peer mechanism, started emerging. In this stage, the core category did not emerge directly. At this stage, categories were further refined to extract four concepts: *network relations*, *shared norms*, *trust*, and *motivation*. *Theoretical memoing* was done to identify the *research pattern*.

For example, *the social exchange* category hinges on *network relations* and *trust* types. Within the categories and sub-categories, there are significant differences. The group members in a horizontal structure communicate informally and frequently and socialize. In a linking relationship with the banks, the members share information formally through state-level banking committees, MIS, dashboards, and bank sakhis. In a federation, the groups interact through the leaders and meetings. Similarly, *social control* is informal and personal in the case of group members and highly formal in linking relationships with the bank. Group members exhibit high solidarity in a bonding relationship, which is not demonstrated in the bridging relationship with clusters or federations. And it was found that *influence* and social control depend on *norms and network* relations. It also depends on *motivation*. From the initial code analysis, we find three concepts: social exchange, social control, and social cohesion, which lead to sustainability and social welfare and can be classified as *social capital*. Comparing and memoing data helped bring data together cohesively. What affects the group? Who, what, and how does the peer mechanism work? 'How does the social process work?' From the data analysis shown in Fig. 25, it was discovered that the group works through social capital and norms.

Social capital is operationalized through enforceable trust and motivation, which leads to social welfare and sustainability. These concepts of social exchange, social control, and social cohesion institutionalize relationships and content into norms. Social capital is structural, relational, and cognitive. The structure includes network ties, configurations, and appropriable organization (Burt, 2000). According to network theorists, social network has direct and indirect effects. The cognitive dimension includes shared codes, rules, and narratives (Wellman & Berkowitz, 1988). These two dimensions of social capital interact, that is, the structure and the norms. Social capital varies depending on the external or internal network configuration (Seibert et al., 2001), and relational components refer to trust norms and obligations.

The phenomenon under investigation is peer mechanism and financial access through peer mechanism. The members of the self-help groups are trying to access finance through peer mechanisms. They communicate and influence each other highly or in a limited manner. The members share their experiences and financial decisions and influence others to exercise prudence in managing money and finances. The interviews tell us how the group members communicate, influence, control, and collaborate. The primary structure is of a community group, and the process is the peer mechanism, which comprises peer selection, peer monitoring, and peer sanctions. Fig. 25 highlights the major themes in the development of the focussed codes.

Structural social capital refers to network relations, configurations, and organization forms. These network relations can be (1) closure or bonding, (2) bridging, and (3) linking. Closure or bonding relationships refer to relationships originating from the same social background. The bridging relationship refers to the relationship with other clusters and federations. And the linking relationship refers to the relationship with the banks. These relationships are further classified as internal and external configurations. Internal relations refer to bonding (lateral or horizontal) and bridging relationships in a group context. And the exterior design refers to the linking relationship (vertical relationship). *Cognitive relationship* refers to the enforceable and accepted norms as part of the social contract. *Relational social capital* refers to the expectations and shared perceptions among the group members.

There are enforceable norms that are communicated to the group norms. This is the *cognitive component* of the social capital, that is, codes, rules, and norms. Then there are *relational networks* due to social ties among the members, business correlations among the members, and cultural beliefs embedded or institutionalized in the groups. This is the cultural capital. Social capital, cultural capital, and cognitive norms lead to solidarity, reciprocity, and task contingency. Table 8 provides the focussed codes.

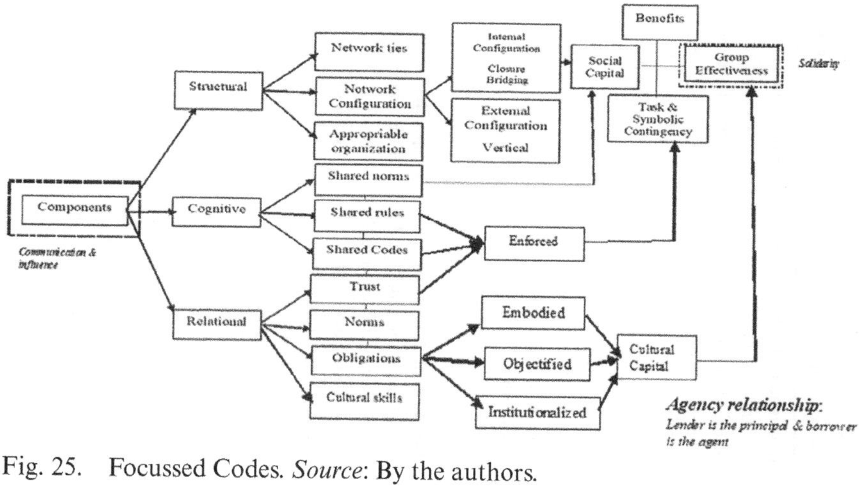

Fig. 25. Focussed Codes. *Source*: By the authors.

Table 8. Focussed Codes.

Shared Norms	Trust	Network Relations	Motivation	Peer Mechanism
Respondent 1: Our members are highly versatile in Madhubani painting, an ancestral art form. And in a group, the repayment rates are high. This is because, on the 10th month, every member contributes the savings. And by the 15th of the month, the bookkeeping is completed for the group	**Respondent 1:** There are ten members in the group. In a successful self-help group, the members are selected based on criteria – members of the same village who know each other	**Respondent 1**: Banyan mat is extremely popular, and we are weaving the mats from the banyan mat. Also, we are making coral mats, and there are groups interested in hand embroidery. This is their family art, and these groups are taking loans from the bank under the self-help group bank linkage programme	**Respondent 1**: Monitoring these groups is done based on the number of meetings in a month, attendance in meetings, books of account, and the low level of literacy, what is the level of savings, debt repayment. This helps enable the achievement of personal finance goals and dreams. In my group, there have not been instances of bad repayment	**Respondent 1:** Members discuss their problems and financial matters with each other. As all the villagers know each other. They discuss their financial matters as and when they meet in the village. The entire society monitors and builds pressure. Family members of SHG ask for and monitor the utilization of the loan amount
Respondent 2: Our SHG is 6 KM from the bank, and the bank is within Mandal. If somebody does not make the payment, there is counselling at the Panchayat level. In the monthly meeting, the Sarpanch bank representative counsels the defaulting member. All groups are linked to the SHG Federations. The interest rate of the group is decided by the group and approved by the leader	**Respondent 2:** In a group, the members are from the same village. Say the candidates from Arifnagar are consolidated in one group, Chole in one group, and we have a team that remains in touch with them and handholds them from the bank linkage till the sustainability phase	**Respondent 2:** SHGs are involved in Bamboo cut work. SHG groups are formed based on certain common ground. In my SHG, members are homogenous. Most groups are of the same gender and are involved in our group [2]. In our group, bank linkage provides them the bank loans. And the groups avail loans from the bank	**Respondent 2:** 640-crafts man pottery artisans are doing this work. For the last 12 years, we have worked with the terracotta artisans' community in Chittoor district, Andhra Pradesh. Six hundred forty craftsman families are doing pottery work in our district. Initially, we promoted SHGs among the artisans' communities, both men and women. It facilitated savings and thrift needs and also provided inter lending to a working capital loan for their handicraft needs	**Respondent 2:** Respondent said they come from a family of bunkers and have been in this profession since the times of his grandfathers. Our group has taken the loan under the self-help group linkage from the bank. Earlier it was Swarn Jayanti Rozgar Yojana, and now it is DAY (Deendayal Antodaya Yojana). As per the respondent, since all the members of the group are from the same profession, this helps in reducing the rate of loan default

Respondent 3: The group members make regular payments and maintain the books of accounts. In the group, we retain registers for savings and loans. Members regularly conduct meetings at least four to five times a month. Financial discipline, cooperation of the members, cohesion in the group and linkages, informal network, and sharing of information among the members lead to better financial performance. Not all people are literate. A group leader is appointed and responsible for maintaining books of account	**Respondent 3**: All 11 members are part of the group. They make bedsheets, and then profits are distributed among the group. Creditworthiness is good because of its sound financial behaviour. Members regularly conduct the meetings. The members work meeting four to five times a month. Member is motivated because of their excellent behaviour. There is no difficulty, and they reap benefits due to their cooperation and good behaviour. Members discuss their financial condition with the members, and the Chairperson coordinates and maintains the books of account. Members of the group stay very close to each other at an approximate distance of 50 meters. The member's peers monitor each other, and there is a positive change in the living standard of the members	**Respondent 3**: 640-crafts man pottery artisans are doing this work. For the last 12 years, we have worked with the terracotta artisans' community in Chittoor district, Andhra Pradesh. Six hundred and forty craftsmen families are doing pottery work in our district. Initially, we promoted SHGs among the artisans' communities, both men and women. It facilitated savings and thrift needs and also provided inter lending to working capital loans for their handicraft needs	**Respondent 3**: SHG groups in the Chhattisgarh district. Some SHGs are involved in bamboo cut work. SHG groups are formed based on specific common ground. In my SHG, members are homogenous. Most of the groups are of the same gender and are involved in our group. In our group, bank linkage provides them the bank loans. And the groups avail loans from the bank	**Respondent 3:** Though members do not generally default, the entire group that stays nearby counsels the member if the member default. Even in monthly meetings, the member is counselled. He drew an analogy that all the fingers in a hand are not the same, and some 10% of people default, and as a result, some members default. The members are all in the same profession, and monitoring ensures they do not misuse the funds. If they do, they are warned and can primarily repay their loan bank

(*Continued*)

Table 8. (*Continued*)

Shared Norms	Trust	Network Relations	Motivation	Peer Mechanism
Respondent 4: The members in the group are from the expected background in the same vocation and village, due to which they have information about each other. The members can peer monitor each other. On a personal level, the relationship is maintained with the members	**Respondent 4:** In one of the interviews, the member of a self-help group mentions that members of the self-help group are from the same vocation, and this benefits them. This helps them get help from the other members. This includes both monetary help and technical help. SHPI does the hand-holding to make them sustainable	**Respondent 4:** We do Sikki handicraft work. We are from Madhubani village and train the members in Sikki art. This house was used as a workshop for making handicrafts. 4 SHGs are joined in the form of the SHG Federation. This includes Jawala, Bhagwati, Bhairav, and Ganesh. Of all the four SHGs combined, 35 members are working together Tula Mohalla comprises Jawala and Bhagwati. Bhairav and Ganesh are far off, and we find it difficult to reach them. There is no loan repayment problem in the group	**Respondent 4:** Our groups are financially sustainable. Banks monitor only members who have taken loans. One of my artisans visited America for an international exhibition with the CM Birsa Munda. We have excellent repayment rates and remind our members to pay back the amount. In our group, we sanction bad credit behaviour with the threat of expulsion. This reinforces excellent credit behaviour as they value the credit extended by the members. The members share a social bond, and they discuss their financial problems	**Respondent 4**: Yes, we have taken a bank loan, and members are generally members of the same village. These women know each other, and they peer monitor each other. Banks generally do not peer sanction our group. Banks are very cooperative, and the group members do meetings and maintenance of books of accounts. This meeting is conducted once a week. Rarely do the members default on the payment of bank loans? If some women members cannot pay the loan, all the members get together and visit the home of the said member. Through cooperation and peer pressure, repayment is retrieved from the defaulting members

Source: Author's own work.

Note: [2] indicates the reply from the respondent.

Table 11 provides the theoretical codes for the study.

Table 8 highlights the interview excerpts for focussed codes. Table 9 represents the focussed codes for the Grounded Theory. Table 10 provides an example of the theoretical codes. At this stage, the coding has started achieving a higher abstraction as the research study progresses. The emerging pattern became more apparent during this stage, and the core 'peer mechanism' phenomenon started emerging. This category is a core category because (1) there are at least two stages in the process, (2) this process evolves or changes over time, (3) preferable for qualitative research, and (4) it represents a gerund.

(1) *Shared norms*: Shared norms refer to the group's cognitive understanding of adhering to regulations and norms. Norms are accepted by specific guidelines relating to group activities, etc. The group members share an understanding of the maintenance of books of accounts, bookkeeping, and record keeping. These norms are the foundation of social capital. These norms are the group's preamble and derive from the group's strategic intent and vision. They ensure financial control and reinforcement, leading to more efficient networks. This social collateral

Table 9. Memo for Focussed Codes.

Memo – Focussed Code 1
The comment by participant 1 is critical as it highlights the importance of peer monitoring and joint liability. It shows how the group of similar people got together. Homogeneity of the members in the group ensures peer monitoring and control and facilitates financial discipline and regulation. It also shows how important social collateral is in the form of group homogeneity and information about its members, which makes it easier for people to get access to financial services. The interview highlights the presence of network relations as bonding, horizontal relationship, and vertical relationship as SHPI. Besides, it highlights the importance of Trust and shared norms to ensure enough social capital facilitates access to Microcredit. Increased outreach helps the group to achieve the long-term goal of financial inclusion

Source: Author's own work.

Table 10. Memo for Focussed Code 2.

Memo – Focussed Code 2
The existing interview highlights the presence of network relations among the group. It highlights the importance of bonding and horizontal relationship among the group members. It also highlights the presence of shared norms, trust, and rules that facilitate achieving the developmental goals of poverty reduction through financial inclusion. Besides network relations and social structures, the interview also highlights the importance of solidarity and cohesiveness among the members to facilitate the achievement of objectives of financial inclusion

Source: Author's own work.

Table 11. Theoretical Codes.

Cognitive Social Capital		Affective Social Capital			
Content	**Structure**				
Shared Norms	**Network Relations**	**Trust**	**Sustainability**	**Social Welfare**	**Motivation**
Record keeping	Group formation	Homogenous groups	Lack of financial literacy	Financial security	Competence
Meetings	Institutional structures	Account keeping by Kosh Adhyaksh	Progressive lending	Better living standards	Competence
Attendance registers	Homogeneity of groups	Collective benefits – increased income, family development, and mobility	Bridging through federation	Sense achievement	Competence
Peer monitoring	Delegated monitoring	Social collateral	Misutilization of loans	Community recognition	Relatedness
Peer sanction	Monitoring by NRLM	Social ties	Social ntermediation	Family welfare	Autonomy
Leadership	Bonding	Generalized reciprocity	Monitoring by SHPI	Worries	Competence (negative reinforcement)
Joint liability	Linking	Beliefs	Social intermediation	Depression	Competence (negative reinforcement
Peer learning	Bridging	Business correlations	Handholding by SHPI	Respect	Relatedness
Savings	Closure	Cohesiveness	Regular saving	Care	Relatedness

Repayment of loan	Establishing information networks	Shared feelings	Thrift	Inclusiveness	Relatedness
Social contract	Information asymmetry	Culture	Profit making on group activities	Acknowledgement of needs	Relatedness
Progressive lending	Heterogenous groups	Business correlation	Training on credit norms	Rewards	Competence
Terms of intralending	Communication channels	Collective efficacy	Moral hazard	Sanctions	Competence (negative reinforcement)
Terms for distribution of profits	Banking channels	Generalized trust	Adverse selection	Joint liability	Relatedness
Noticing, discussing	The agency relationship of borrowers with banks	Social cohesion	Financial inclusion of women	Threat deadlines	Competence (negative reinforcement)
Knowledge sharing	Embedded power relations	Interpersonal relations	Regular savings	Women empowerment	Autonomy
Tacit knowledge	Market relations	Collective action	Working together		
Financial planning	Hierarchal relations	Cooperation	Cooperative working of women		
Reporting	Incubation by SHPI	Working together	Financial training for women		
Size of group	Market relations	Emotionally supporting the women	Bank Saathi channel for the collection of data		

(Continued)

Table 11. (*Continued*)

Cognitive Social Capital		**Affective Social Capital**
Instituting obligations	Nearness to banks	Social exchange
Exerting pressure on women		Drawing on socio-cultural institutions
Collective approval of the loan		Supporting defaulting members
Levelling through norms		Motivating payments
Social contracting		
Financial training		
Saving today for tomorrow		
Discussing financial matters with the family members		
Social sanctions		
Certifying women on digital literacy		
Imposing fines		
Instituting obligations		

Source: Author's own work.

helps the group achieve its goals. These groups are cultural groups not part of the more extensive financial system. They have a skilled workforce but are not part of the market due to a lack of access to finance. Social norms can be defined as a social structure or cultural capital which comprise: (i) behaviour patterns that do not change over time, (ii) legal elements that govern the social behaviour, (iii) social relationships and hierarchy of social relationships, and (iv) group rules that define the behaviour in the group. These could be (1) cognitive, which includes an understanding of bookkeeping, attendance, and minutes of meetings, or there could be (2) affective, which refers to group sanctions and group control. These norms work as motivation and lead to sustainability in the group. Fig. 26 highlights the theoretical construct for the shared norms. Fig. 27 highlights the three-level codes for the shared norms which are part of the economic system.

The initial data analysis found that the homogenous members (based on profession or domicile) integrate into a group. Based on common ground, the members discover the purpose of the group. They share knowledge through interactions, leading to a strong *group identity* and *social exchange*. Moreover, the group members develop a consensus on the performance attribute metrics to monitor the

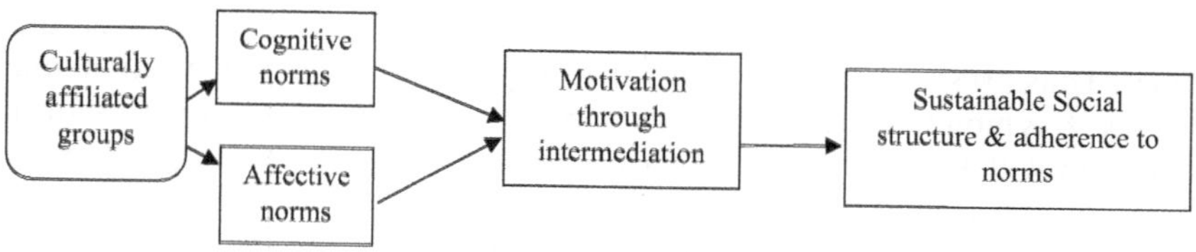

Fig. 26. Operational Model for Shared Norms. *Source*: By the authors.

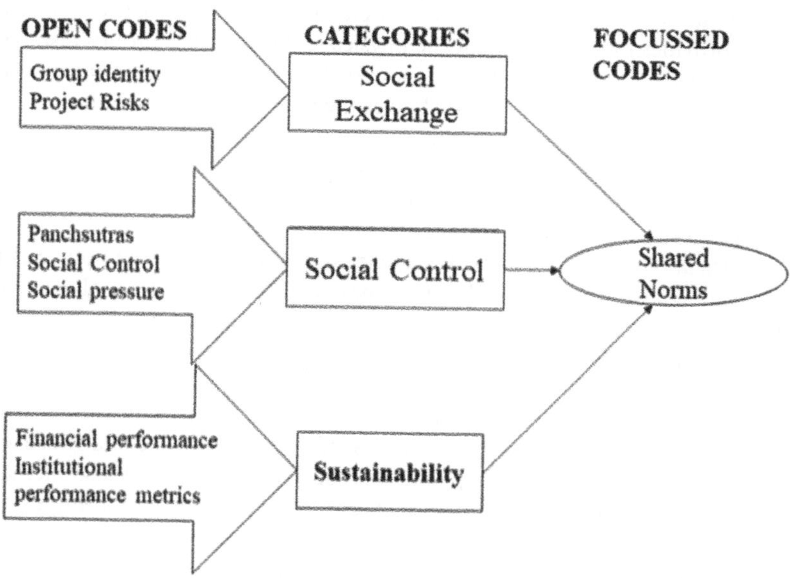

Fig. 27. Three-level Codes for Shared Norms. *Source*: By the authors.

group's performance. The group exerts influence through adherence to a group norm, peer monitoring, and peer pressure. They also use delegated monitoring to exert pressure and influence. This leads to *social control*. And adherence to norms and monitoring leads to institutional and financial *sustainability*. Thus, *shared norms* emerged as an important focussed code. The shared norms are based on social exchange to exercise social control and ensure sustainability.

(2) *Trust*: Trust underpins all social relationships in a community. To show solidarity, the group must exhibit good financial behaviour, even without access to the physical collateral. The members can access financial services through trust. Trust refers to delivering the promised performance by the agent, that is, the borrower, to the lender or the principal. It relates to the perception of members about the performance attributes of other team members. It operates within the agency relationship of the agent, that is, the borrower, and the lender, that is, the principal. It also refers to the perception of performance and is mentioned as a social contract term.

The group's strategic intent is to provide finance to the poor at a low cost. Members possess trust and commit to making regular loan repayments. In the group lending scenario, the members are self-selected in a homogenous group. They formulate policy frameworks, rules, and regulations to maintain trust between the entities. Thus, trust is a hygiene factor that originates from communication and influence. It is monitored to ensure adherence to group norms. The members form groups only with known members. This informal trust from knowledge about each other leads to perceived trust. Social linkage is provided by mutual assurance and insurance in the team. Social capital enables group lending to the poor through mutual trust, shared values, networks, and peer monitoring. The agent in agency theory is the borrower, and the principal is the lender. Financial institutions use social evaluation to lend money to borrowers, and the mutual trust among the members provides the substitute for the physical collateral. The groups also build trust through mediators or SHPI. Agency relationships reduce self-interest and promote repayment integrity. The trust gives the poor access to capital.

As given in Fig. 28, Trust is naturally occurring or in a lateral or *horizontal relationship* and is operational through *social capital*. Being vulnerable to other people's expectations is a psychological state of mind. The trust further helps develop generalized reciprocity among the group members.

In a *vertical relationship* with banks, the trust is enforced through policies, procedures, and enforceable norms. In an agency relationship, control plays a vital role in building trust.

The trust can further be defined as (1) narrow or (2) broad trust.

(a) Narrow trust: In the case of a joint liability contract, the members select members from the family, friends, and co-workers, members with similar backgrounds and traits. This soft creditworthiness information ensures financial access and is the *narrow trust* in the group. Narrow social capital or trust also increases loan repayment. This bonding capital includes social and cultural affinities, values, cohesiveness, and ties. The narrow trust among members in a joint liability group leads to cooperation. This limits opportunistic behaviour. 'Members rush to a non-paying member's door and start a big fight. Defaulters face social

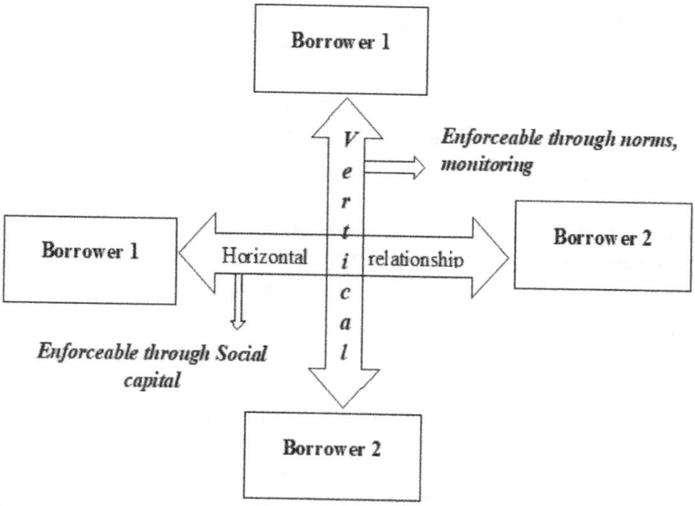

Fig. 28. Operational Model for Trust. *Source*: By the authors.

pressure. Mutual trust in a group comes from joint liability bonds, not altruism. Friendships, social networks, and business ties build trust'. Thus, it was inferred that social networks, ties, joint liability, and information sharing lead to mutual trust. Mutual trust is reinforced through the performance of the social contract:

> We all work together. It makes me feel good; they also feel good and can pass the time. We also make eco-friendly Ganesh Ji. We get the mitti in March, making the eco-friendly Ganesh Ji. We established it in September. There is no repayment problem. We do not take women who are not creditworthy. Our leader is Komalben. Komal ben is known all over the village. There has never been an issue regarding the non-repayment of a loan. Even if there is a default due to medical reasons or any disease in the family, we support them and counsel them regarding the importance of timely repayment. In our group, members attend meetings regularly. Komalben manages the distribution of the money. This is Komalben's ancestral business, and her mother taught them this skill. She handles all the tasks, like the distribution of money. Pach's work has been passed on to Komal ben from generation to generation. Members do cooperate and encourage each other. In the initial days, women were constrained by the needs of their members and children. They owe their success to the money, emotional support, and efforts of Komalben. Komalben has traveled worldwide from Delhi, Bangalore, Chennai, and Hyderabad to make an exhibition. This provides the member with so much happiness, and they feel delighted that their work is so good and recognized worldwide. Slowly and slowly, they explore whether they are willing to learn or not.

Thus, it was inferred that the homogenous groups lead to ex ante perfect information about the group's creditworthiness. The perfect information about the creditworthiness of members leads to higher trust. Leadership leads to better control and motivation and directs the group members. Better control, motivation, and direction lead to the financial sustainability of the group. Thus, leadership also leads to trust in a group:

> There are 12 to 13 ladies and 7 to 8 men. They all work in their home and make items from silver. Since all the members make silver jewelry, they are experts and train new members. Groups are a perfect structure; earlier, we used to take loans from the money lender who charged extremely high-interest rates, but now we are self-reliant. This helps to increase the interactions among the members. In each meeting, the member is apprised of the savings and loans. All the members are not literate but know the importance of loan repayment. If someone needs a loan for an emergency, we help the person defaulting to pay. In the melas, demand for the Adivasi design is very high. These products are available on the web under the Adivasi brand, and the government has launched this. Group has led to a vast improvement in the standard of living. Today men earn to save for tomorrow; earlier, they could not do that. Earlier, if someone could not pay, we paid them money from the group for emergency needs. Earlier, Mahajan used to charge some amount, and money used to return to Mahajan. Now the money is increasing.

Thus, it was inferred that a homogenous group leads to a pooling of financial resources. The pooling of resources is solely achieved from the mutual trust in a group. Mutual trust is achieved through financial autonomy, which leads to financial inclusion and freedom from informal sources like money lenders. Thus, homogenous groups lead to higher trust in the group:

> There are ten people, and they work regularly. They start at 11 a.m. and till 5 p.m. Terracotta pottery is our ancestral job. The members in the same group help each other. If some member makes the Ganesh Ji chair or the statue, then the women making the craft are guided and helped by other members. If the members need a loan, we all pool together and permit loan sanctions to the needy. And our membership is not restricted to the Kumhar community; anybody can join. But they are from this village. Since joining the group, my self-efficacy of the group has improved. Since joining the group, the big officials have started coming, and our group is near Khajuraho, and foreigners have also been coming to Khajuraho. Our group meeting is conducted per week. In each meeting, members maintain accounts and records. Banks visit the site and the Ajeevika officials to inspect the work and find out if

> the work is as per the standard. Members are confident in each other that if the loan is taken, it will be paid off. In our group, the members understand that if a loan is taken, it has to be paid back. We also show our accounts to Ajeevika and books to the other group members. We make small, big diyas, lamp from mud, and it becomes terracotta when baked in the fire. And if we talk about utensils like handi, plates, we do not color it.

Thus, it was inferred that the homogeneity of the members in a group leads to cooperation. Cooperation leads to higher self-efficacy. Higher self-efficacy leads to an increase in the income of the members. Also, group formation leads to market access and better peer control. Better peer control leads to financial sustainability. Thus, trust in a group is a significant force that increases the members' self-efficacy and the group's financial sustainability.

(b) Broad trust: Broad trust refers to the extrinsic trust with the banks. Social capital enables the members to borrow from the bank. Based on cultural capital, members peer monitor and control each other. Thus, the banks trust the group members and provide them the loan due to the narrow trust. Once the loan is availed, the members develop a relationship with bankers, leading to broad trust. Peer monitoring is motivated by dynamic contract enforcement with sanctions and joint liability. This enables the self-help group members to connect to banks and financial institutions. Thus, with norms, network relations, and narrow trust, access to bank loans is ensured. This trust posed by the banks in groups is called broad trust.

An interviewee stated, 'Bank DM gives a loan to a member of the Didi (leader) group'. *This leads to a personalized banker–group leader relationship. Mutual trust is critical to accessing financial capital.* Thus, good leadership leads to trust with the banker. Trust leads to access to financial services. SHPI enables the group to access finance through formal financial institutions and banks. Thus, leadership and intermediation lead to broad trust:

> The bank trusts members of a group, and if an individual member approaches the bank from the group, the bank remains skeptical that they might not pay. Yes, we have taken a bank loan, and members are generally members of the same village. These women know each other, and they peer-monitor each other. Banks generally do not peer-sanction our group. Banks are very cooperative, and the group members do meetings and maintenance of books of accounts. This meeting is conducted once a week. Rarely do the members default on the payment of bank loans. Our group has pursued this vocation of making handicrafts since we came from Pakistan. These women have pursued the vocation of making handicrafts since their independence. In many Karkhanas, Karigars pursue handicrafts as an ancestral art form in markets. We make leather products etc.

Thus, it was inferred that the social contract and knowledge-sharing lead to higher trust between the bank and the microborrowers. Higher trust leads to higher financial services. Leadership leads to higher trust in the bank, and trust leads to access to financial services. Fig. 29 represents the three-level code for the focussed code of trust.

Thus, it was inferred that members in a group exhibit solidarity and *social cohesion* through bonding relationships, social capital, homogeneity of relationships, and information about their peers. Communication about the performance attributes, purpose, and group identity leads to *social exchange* and trust solidarity. Adherence to Panchsutras, leadership, and shared norms leads to *social control and* trust. Thus, trust emerged as a crucial focussed code derived from open social cohesion, social exchange, and social control codes. Or social cohesion, social exchange, and social control in a group lead to trust.

(3) *Network relations:* Our research suggests two types of network relations in the context of self-help groups for the poor. Societal capital is created ex ante through (1) profession-relatedness, domicile, and shared interests and ex post through (2) joint liability and self-help promoting institutions. Borrower–lender network relationships are structured. As shown by the data, there are two types of relationships between members, that is, (1) lender–borrower relationships are vertical. It connects the banker and the borrower; (2) Horizontal bonding involves intralending and borrowing; (3) Bridging relationship – a grouping of the formal groups into a federation or cluster. The relationships between the members of the group and self-help groups can be explained at three levels:

(i) *Relationship within the groups*: Members of the group are homogenous regarding vocation, domicile, and interests. They are connected and have perfect information about the other member of the group. This leads to bonding capital between the members of the group.

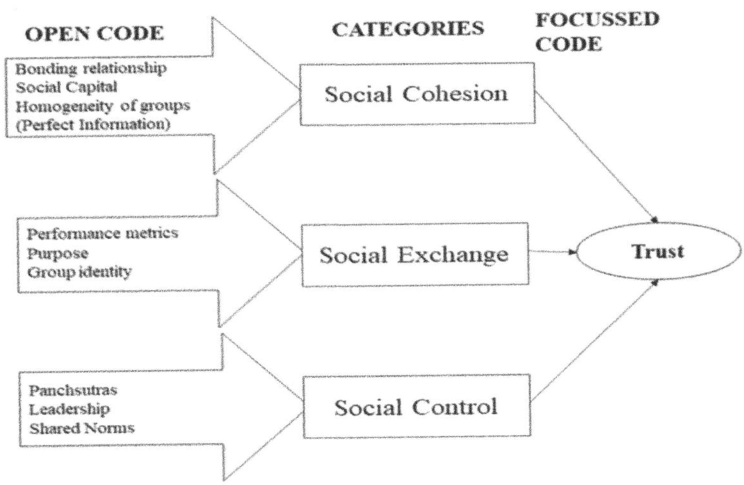

Fig. 29. Three-step Process for Pre-group Formation Trust. *Source*: By the authors.

(ii) *Relationship between the groups:* Members develop a close affinity with each other. The groups develop a separate group identity. This builds a relationship between the groups in the form of bridging capital.

(iii) *Relationship with financial institutions:* Members develop relationships with the financial institutions and banks from which they take loans. This is referred to as linking capital.

Fig. 30 highlights the theoretical relationship for the focussed code of network relation.

The network relations between the lender and the borrower can be called vertical and horizontal relationships. A *vertical relationship* is high on power and also high on control. A *horizontal relationship* is low on power and low on control. An example of a horizontal relationship is the bonding between the group members. A vertical relationship refers to the relationship of authority or agency between the principal, that is, the lender, and the agent, that is, the borrower. But with self-help group bank linkage, the social contract facilitates high social control and power that facilitates financial sustainability. The focussed code of network relation was identified from data analysis of social control and social cohesion categories. Within the categories of social control, homogeneity of members, social ties, vertical relationships, and bridging relationships are the main codes that led to the focussed code of network relations. And within the category of social cohesion, the open codes of joint liability, task dependencies, and bilateral dependencies lead to a focussed code of network relations. The nature of network relations is discussed as horizontal and vertical relationships existing in the group.

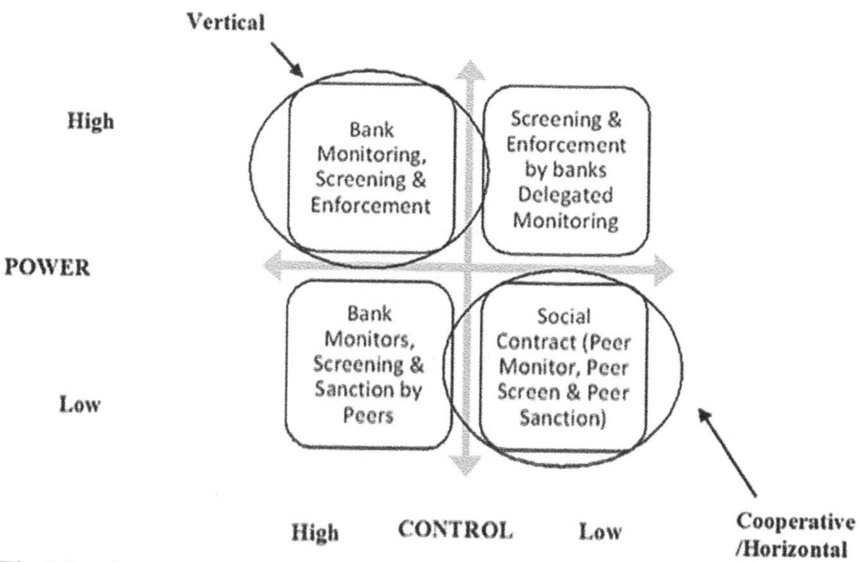

Fig. 30. Operational Model for Network Relations (Interplay of Power and Control). *Source*: By the authors.

6.2.1. Horizontal Relationship

The relationship between the borrowers is called the horizontal relationship. This relationship is low on power and control. This is called a cooperative or bonding relationship.

> Our organization helps in the formation of SHGs. We provide training to like-minded people who have an interest in handicrafts and then help them open a bank account. Most people are from handicrafts, and only they are included. Banks look at the records of SHG and the repayment history, then provide the loans. Our SHGs are not graded, but grading is done for the artisans. These people are like-minded, so they remain in consensus. Whenever they have meetings, they all get together, but once in a while, they cannot pay, but that does not happen that often. This is the reason that groups are financially sustainable.

Thus, it was inferred that the horizontal relationship refers to the bonding relationship among the same group members. Groups are homogenous. They are homogenous either in terms of vocation or in terms of domicile. Homogenous members can cooperate, and cooperation leads to social capital. This social capital leads to access to a higher amount of bank loans. *At the formation stage, the members are grouped based on their like-mindedness. The group members make regular payments and maintain the books of accounts. There is a tally application for updating the loan amount. Members of the group monitor each other. Every month there is a meeting and discussion around financial transactions.* Thus, horizontal relationships based on homogeneity are the driving force behind the formation of groups. These relationships are a significant source of social control and lead to horizontal network relations in the group.

6.2.2. Vertical Relationship

Vertical relationships refer to the relationship between the group members and the bank. In indigenous banking, based on social capital, the members leverage capital from the bank (Matin, 1997). In the case of the self-help group, based on the six-month repayment history, the bank provides a loan to the group. This loan is based on the premise of joint liability of the group members. However, the members distribute the loan among themselves. They share a limited individual liability for the loan. The relationship between the member and the bank is vertical. This relationship is high on power and control. Thus, vertical relationship leads to network relations in the group. An interview with the SHPI director elaborated on how self-help groups create social capital. And SHPI enables the groups to link the groups with the banks. This is an example of vertical linkages and financial intermediation. This refers to the vertical relationship with banks, external institutions, and SHPI. He highlighted that intermediary financial help in group formation, norming, and accessing finance from banks through bank linkage.

> DAY NRLM Circular provides for the credit linkage of the women to the banks. The group is graded after six months based on the repayment of internal loans, savings, and credit-linked. In the first year, they get a loan of eight times of savings or Rs 8 Lakhs. In this loan, the default rate is minimal. If your loan goes bad, then the bank will come for recovery. And the females get scared of this. The groups that have been bank-linked for over three years face no problems or issues accessing bank loans.

Thus, the vertical relationship with the bank is a source of social control. This open code of vertical relationship within social control leads to a focussed code of network relations.

In another interview, the respondent said:

> Our organization, SHPI, helps to form SHGs. We provide training to like-minded people who have an interest in handicrafts and then help them open a bank account. Most people are from handicrafts, and only they are included. The groups are trained on the maintenance of books of accounts and conducting meetings. We help the members by training them in book maintenance and record-keeping. The designs are very time-consuming, which leads to increased costs. Banks look at the records of SHG and the repayment history and then provide them with the loans. Our SHGs are not graded, but grading is done for the artisans. SHPI helps them get linked to the bank.

Thus, SHPI is important in helping the group members access bank loans. They largely control the formation of network relations with banks.

> Banks track a member's progress over five months. Banks fund only successful SHGs. By getting a bank loan, the social status of the member increases. Trust is important for the success of the SHG. The biggest strength of the SHG is that they have trust. After the first loan, the progressive lending by banks depends on the repayment of earlier loans. Monitoring, financial literacy, and training by the group to ensure loan repayment. In Mathura, there's Fareb. In that district, 700 village women are formed as SHGs. The government gives them money when their equity reaches 5 Lac. The government provided eight crore rupees for goat maintenance and sheds. Direct payments to suppliers reduce the misappropriation of funds when monitoring is lacking. One of the major worries of the members is loan repayment. But handholding and intermediation help the members to repay the loan. Loan repayment is key to project success.

Thus, it was inferred that with financial intermediation, the group members get financially disciplined and can access the financial loan. Also, the network relations with banks lead to higher social control in the group. 'Knowing that the members have joint liability, they return their loan in time. They fear bank sanctions and the debarment of the group. Also, the group exerts social pressure on the members to repay'. Thus, the bonding and vertical relationship with banks and horizontal relationship with members give rise to network relations.

In Chaatikraha, Vrindavan, bankers formed a Tulsimala cluster. *And the HOD of Mechanical IIT visited the village. He developed a method to make Tulsimala malas from the seeds in a few hours. This impressed and helped members. Social innovation helps change society. If the government doesn't help, members won't be trained, and the SHG will be unable to innovate. SHG gets the required training and guidance from a government agency*. Thus, vertical relationships with banks and external agencies such as IIT enable SHGs to innovate and select members to form the group and undertake entrepreneurship. This helps the member to access loans from the banks. This is yet another form of network relation.

> Members don't know how to conduct meetings, organize each other, keep a register, or organize business at first. And the banks want to know how to help SHGs generate business. In one area, if the work is done on a large scale, for example, in Saharanpur, the artisans do Pittal work; in Hathras, its metal Zari work, Glass work, and Stonework, then they automatically get buyers. Market planning is crucial after production. Mathura has spillways run by private agencies. The government gave them spillers, but low-quality products could not sell because members were not trained. The group can't succeed if all ten members work on different things. SHPI provides 4-year handholding. The goal is to maximize progressive lending from the banks. When women travel 100 places, they gain confidence, learn how to handle things, and how to talk. One hundred women were sent to meet Anandipatel, and 4 were leaders. Big units worked together.

> Fareb unit towards Agra has many goat-rearing women's units. Incubating credit planning takes five months. SHPI facilitates intermediation, and the members start developing the habits of savings and regular payments in the initial incubation period. SHPI helps the members in financial planning.

Thus, vertical relationships with banks and intermediaries like self-help promotion led to network relations. In another interview, the respondent stated:

> Our SHG is 6 KM from the bank, and the bank is within the Mandal. If somebody does not pay, there is counseling at the Panchayat level. In the monthly meeting, the Sarpanch bank representative counsels the defaulting member. All groups are linked to the SHG Federations.

The groups also have network relations in the form of linkages with federations.

The state government machinery oversees the grant of bank loans. This committee includes the state level banking committee, block level banking committee, and district mission management unit. In the case of the self-help groups, the group members borrow money. So, district mission managers, block level officials, and CRPs monitor and motivate them to repay the loan.

The borrower has horizontal relationships among its members and standing relationships with the lender. Saving and lending occur in a perfect information setting where everyone knows everyone, reducing the adverse selection problem. Aside from that, the group shares a common profession and village. So, they know each other. Members can monitor each other. Members from the same society and village share financial concerns. The needy person gets a loan from the group's savings. Peers watch each other because of their social networks. We convene a meeting and suggest the leader punish the member who accepts and misuses the loan:

> Locals know each other well. Every time the villager gathers, they discuss money. The whole society keeps an eye on things. Family and SHG members monitor the loan amount used. A person who has borrowed Rs 1 lakh will be asked about repayment by the members. Our Group is a family of four houses. There were times of counseling and disagreement, but it helped us improve loan repayment.

Thus, joint liability and task dependencies lead to solidarity.

Fig. 31. highlights the three-level code for the focussed code of network relation.

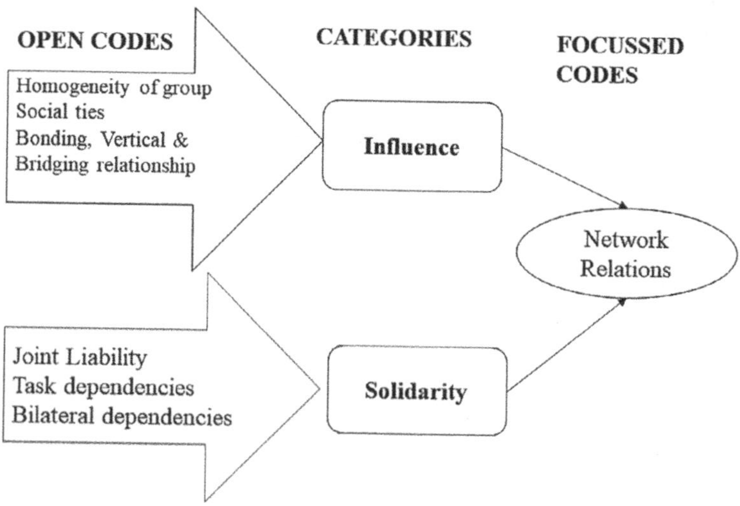

Fig. 31. Three-level Codes for Network Relations. *Source*: By the authors.

The data analysis inferred that the homogenous members have social ties in horizontal relationships. They also have a vertical relationship with the banks. They can *influence* each other. Similarly, members with joint liability, task, and bilateral dependencies exhibit *solidarity*, which leads to network relations. Thus, the focussed code of network relations is derived from open codes of influence and solidarity.

(4) *Motivation:* By institutionalizing existing relationships, trusts, and social ties through network relations, norms, and beliefs, it was found that social capital is operationalized. How the borrowers mobilize social capital during the group lending process is determined by their motivation. The members are motivated by affiliation, power, and achievement needs, as explained by the McClelland Theory. In our theory, motivation can be (1) affective (hedonic experience) or latent (social connectedness or relatedness) or (2) cognitive (competence or autonomy).

Shared norms, trust, and networked relations emerged as critical concepts related to the core phenomenon of motivation and social capital. These ideas synthesize and capture data patterns. These three phenomena highlight social capital, the central force that leads to the peer mechanism phenomenon. More data analysis was done to explain the core phenomenon till the data saturation. Social capital is further defined as cognitive and affective social capital. Shared norms and network relations form *cognitive and social capital. Affective*, hedonic motivation refers to the feeling of *autonomy and competence* in the group. Thus, this study examined two aspects of motivation: procedural (affective factors) and instrumental (cognitive factors). Fig. 32 highlights the model for the focussed code of motivation.

Based on the data, self-help groups help provide financial access without physical collateral. The groups also have an institutional mechanism for peer selection, monitoring, and sanctioning. On a group level, the peer mechanism and joint liability lead to financial sustainability – better repayment and savings. This is the *instrumental utility* or cognitive motivation to join a self-help group.

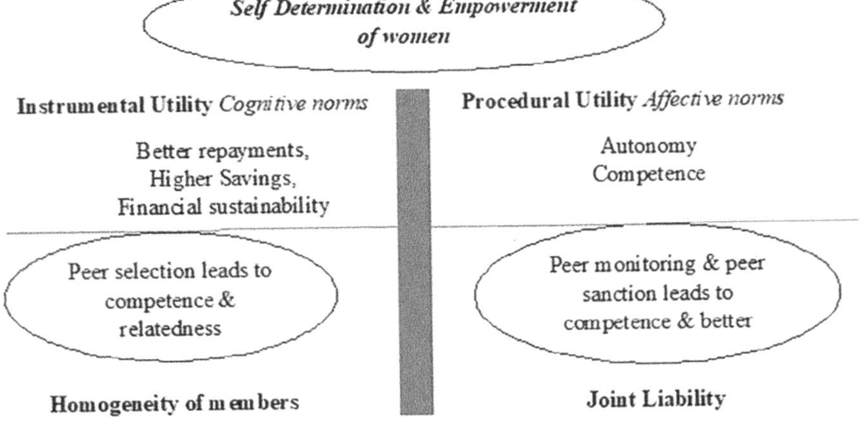

Fig. 32. Operational Model for Motivation. *Source*: By the authors.

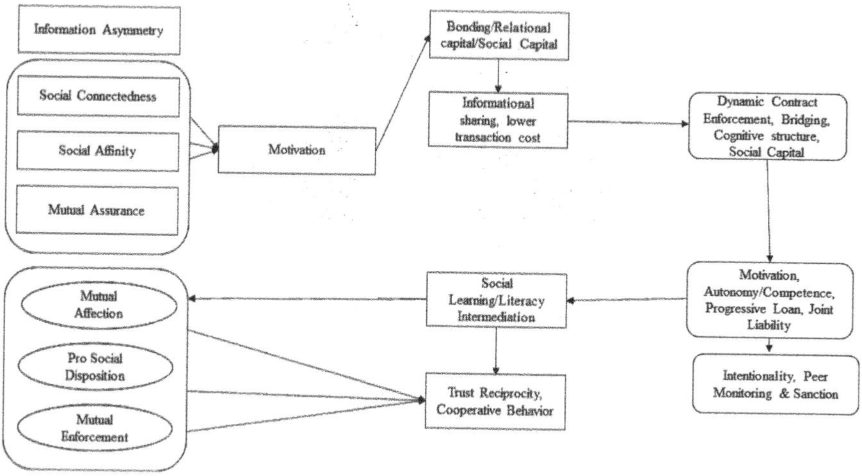

Fig. 33. Role of Motivation in Joint Liability Groups. *Source*: By the authors.

On an individual member level, the group peer mechanism leads to *autonomy and competence*. Financial sustainability and better repayments lead to competence and autonomy, which refers to *procedural utility* or affective motivation in the group. This entire mechanism empowers and self-determines members. Fig. 33 represents the role of motivation in a joint liability group.

From the data analysis, social affinity and mutual assurance lead to relatedness, and this motivation leads to the relationship in the form of bonding, which refers to the horizontal relationship among the group members. Thus, it further leads to affective social capital. This reduces information asymmetry and transaction costs. This relationship is further enforced as a dynamic contractual relationship in bridging and linking relationships. This dynamic contract further leads to motivation in the form of autonomy and relatedness. The cultural capital in a group operationalizes the social capital through peer monitoring and sanction. It further leads to financial unsustainability. Fig. 34 represents the three-level code for motivation.

Thus, the relatedness and homogeneity of members lead to *solidarity*, which motivates them to be part of a group. Further, the financial and institutional sustainability of the group leads to faith in the power of the group to reduce poverty and mitigate the woes of poverty. This *sustainability* functions as motivation. Besides, the *social welfare* promoted by the group in the form of women empowerment, rural development, and financial inclusion leads to motivation. Thus, the open codes of solidarity, sustainability, and social welfare lead to the focussed code of motivation in the group.

6.3. Hypothesis Testing

6.3.1. Hypothesis 1: Role of Peer Selection in Mitigating Adverse Selection

In a group of homogenous members, 'information sharing' is easy. Through the initial interviews, the codes of 'homogeneity of members', 'business correlation',

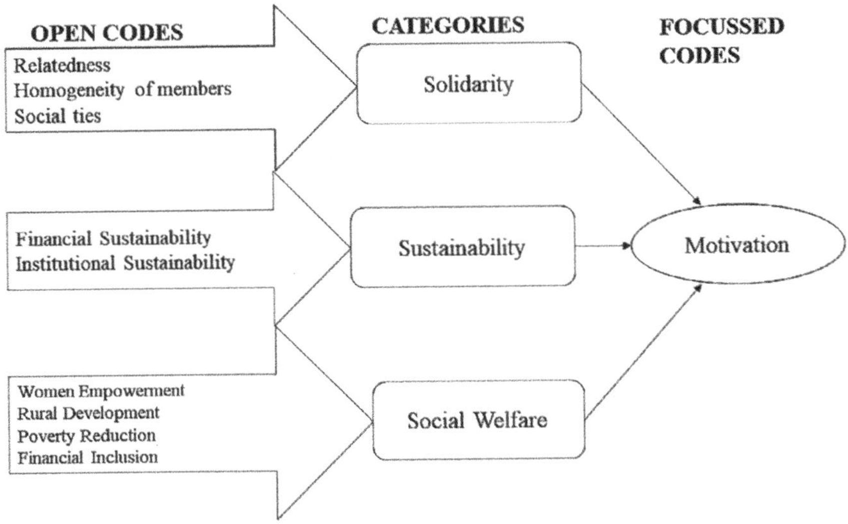

Fig. 34. Three-level Codes for Motivation. *Source*: By the authors.

'social ties', and 'cultural affinities' are generated. The group's underlying rationale for information sharing is the homogeneity of profession, domicile, or risk. The nearness and typical village facilitate ease of communication and exercising influence. This lattice of relations leads to a social structure called a social group or group identity. The properties of the code 'homogeneity' combine, and a new concept appears: 'network relations' that facilitate communication and influence among group members. This also promotes 'solidarity' and 'social cohesion'. A group's 'information flow capability' leads to 'generalized reciprocity' among its members. The members agree to 'provide credentials' based on 'trustworthiness'. The 'social collateral' created by 'generalized reciprocity' and 'group identity' is the basis for credit and loan access. A group peer mechanism reduces information asymmetry and provides access to bank credit. Based on the interviews conducted, the study concludes that group members self-select each. Self-selection implies prior knowledge of members. Social ties form when people share a common ground like a home, profession, or vocation. This is known as assortative matching, allowing members to see the group's business risk. This member information leads to the group's success. The first stage in the self-help group is group formation through 'peer selection'. Thus, the group formation theory conceptual framework was used for the analysis. It comprises group forming, norming, storming, and performing stages. This part of the study deals with group formation.

Fig. 35 enumerates peer selection criteria such as risk matching, business correlation, social ties, signalling, reporting, joint liability, and incentives that mitigate the adverse selection and lemon problem. The first stage in the group lending process is peer selection or group formation. Adverse selection is when the lender has no information about the borrowers and cannot screen them based on their creditworthiness. In other words, certain unobservable traits of borrowers are

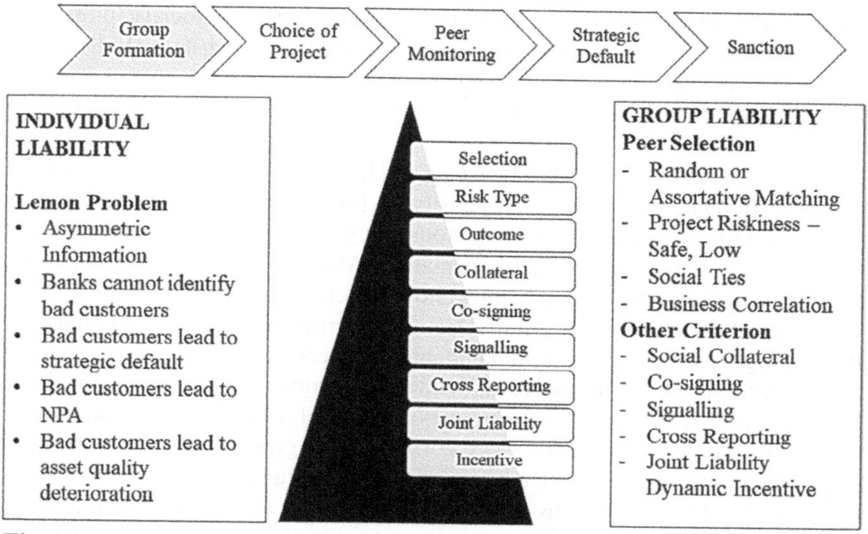

Fig. 35. Akerlof Lemon Problem and Agency Theory Problem (Criterion for Self-selection) to Mitigate Adverse Selection. *Source*: By the authors.

known to the borrowers, not the lender. These traits might affect the probability of default. If the bank knows the risk type of a member, the risky borrower can choose to pay a higher interest rate and less collateral.

In contrast, the safe borrower can deposit higher collateral and pay less interest. But this increases the cost of selection by the banks, and due to the lack of returns on loans to microborrowers, banks might not be willing to spend on selecting members in joint liability groups. Thus, it can lead to the lemon problem, where risky and safe borrowers pay the exact cost, leading to inefficiency. Agency problem crops up due to information asymmetry, which is the root cause of adverse selection. Social capital is a panacea to the problem of information asymmetry and high selection costs in JLGs. According to social capital, local information networks help in risk hedging. Social capital is described as social networks, and the relationships among group members that establish norms for collective conduct are based on the principles of trust and reciprocity. Existing literature offers three distinct theories on social capital: relational and informational capital and groups with inherent properties of joint liability.

Social capital is defined as social ties among group members influencing compensation. As social ties, the same gender, ethnicity, and activity or occupation have been used to self-select the group members. Religion is a proxy for social links; work, domicile, or neighbourhood is also cited as a proxy for social relations. Formal lenders do not have perfect information about the borrowers in the capital markets. Researchers emphasize that if borrowers can classify each other based on risk type, the lender can use Joint liability and various social contract types to select members in a group for lending. In rural markets, borrowers lack collateral. Still, group lending by peer monitoring allows them to keep track of each other, and it is used as the self-selection criteria for the group. Higher linkages and networks can ensure better group repayment. The social capital helps lower transaction costs, which are dispersed across the pre-disbursal, disbursal, and post-disbursal stages of credit delivery. The wealth distribution and financial incentives affect monitoring intensity among credit-constrained individuals.

6.3.1.1. Assortative or Random Matching. Thus, the selection issue in a group is primarily related to the risk propensity of borrowers. Hence, the problem is whether all members can risk homogenous in a group, that is, all safe or all risky. This occurs in the case of perfect information. Alternatively, in case of imperfect information, the group can be heterogenous, where some members are safe, and some are risky. Homogenous group selection is termed Assortative matching, and the heterogeneous group is random matching. Adverse selection is the problem of a bank selecting a high-risk borrower with a high probability of default. In a joint liability group scenario, when borrowers know each other, safe borrowers will group with safe borrowers, and risky borrowers will group with risky borrowers only. This reduces the issue of adverse selection and raises debt repayment rates in the groups. In a collaborative group, members know about each other, and the safe borrowers will not be willing to cross-subsidize the risky borrowers and use the peer mechanism. Safe members will screen out risky borrowers and not borrow until a cut-off point. Joint liability is an incentive to monitor other members of the group. So, in a homogenous group, given joint liability, the safe member will group with the safe borrower and use the peer mechanism to ensure loan repayment. In this scenario, the banks can use different contracts as safe members will be more inclined to take higher joint liability and pay the lower interest rate. Risky members will be willing to accept lesser joint liability and higher interest payments. Also, safe borrowers will be less inclined to borrow than risky borrowers. This is called the underinvestment problem in the case of a joint liability group. Thus, the authors argue that banks can screen members by the company they keep in joint liability as risky borrowers will not be willing to assume joint liability, which is greater than individual liability contracts. In this scenario, non-defaulting members pay default members' loans and penalties; if the output is more significant than a penalty, all the borrowers default. Assortative matching is the most popular group formation method compared to random matching. A detailed process flow of peer selection in homogenous groups through assortative matching is given below in Fig. 36.

This is a simple lending model for borrowers with limited liability who have private information on the quality of their investment projects. When the risk type of borrowers is related, group lending contracts are a powerful tool for rent extraction and subtle discrimination. However, in assortative matching, since all the members are of the same risk type if even one member defaults due to similar riskiness, there is a probability of collision or strategic default. But at the same time, groups with safe borrowers will be less willing to collude or take on risky projects. Strategic default will be an issue for members with complex tasks. In the context of assortative matching, the importance of non-monetary signalling mechanisms to address the issue of adverse selection and underinvestment is very high. In a homogenous group with joint liability, the borrowers will

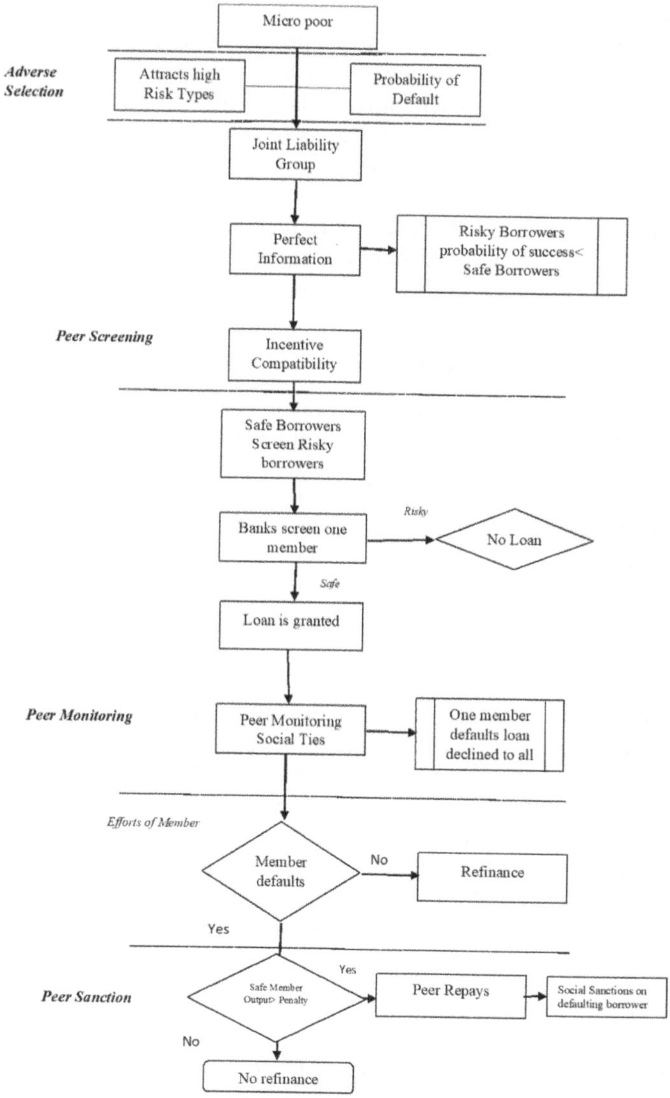

Fig. 36. Peer Mechanism to Address Adverse Selection and Moral Hazard (Assortative Matching). *Source*: By the authors.

gladly accept the added burden of verification and screening the risky borrowers by using non-monetary side payments as a signalling mechanism due to their existing social ties. Since the contracts are joint liability, borrowers must repay their loans and are responsible for the loans of their group members if any of them default. The welfare properties of homogenous group formation outperform random matching or individual lending with information asymmetry. This implies that signalling-based homogeneous group formation may help reduce under-investment. Therefore, since joint liability groups are formed from the same group of people, the group can exert social pressure to ensure regular repayment.

Contrary to assortative matching, groups are formed through random matching or pooling mechanisms when individuals do not know each other in a group lending situation. Random matching refers to a heterogeneous group in which the borrower's riskiness is not a criterion for selection. This group comprises all borrowers with different risk types. In a pooling risk mechanism, if the cost of ex post bank verification is high, the safe members will be prepared to cross-subsidize the risky borrowers. Group lending will be feasible through the social collateral effect. Table 12 provides supporting codes.

6.3.2. Hypothesis 2: Peer Monitoring Leads to the Reduction of Moral Hazard

According to existing literature, peer monitoring and sanctioning reduce the misuse of funds. Social collateral reduces moral hazard (Simtowe & Zeller, 2006). A moral hazard is the risk of behaviour change after the group takes the loan. This risk arises after taking out a bank loan through the self-help group bank linkage programme. This refers to the stage of norming and performing. The problem has a behavioural dimension that can be solved by social intermediation and training.

6.3.2.1. Social Contract and Moral Hazard. A social contract with joint liability emerges from the data. The main reason for moral hazard is the members' limited liability and the group's joint liability. Knowing that other members will pay on behalf of defaulting member, the member can wilfully default. In this context, what becomes essential is whether a member is not paying due to the negative income shock (externality) or wilfully commit fraud (intrinsic behaviour change). There are cognitive and affective terms in the social contract. Contracting's cognitive component implies joint ability and progressive lending. And the 'affective bonds' refer to the relationship and social ties among the members.

As mentioned in Fig. 37, through the conceptual framework of Gadamer hermeneutics and agency theory, peer mechanism has emerged as a significant theme

Table 12. Codes for Hypothesis 1.

Open Code	Focussed Code	Theoretical Code
• Forming a group of homogenous members	• Network relations	Peer selection
• Forming a group based on like-mindedness or common ground	• Shared norms	

Excerpts from the interview: These groups are formed by people with similar characteristics, that is, they go to the wells to fetch water or spend time together. This affinity helps the members come together

Source: Author's own work.

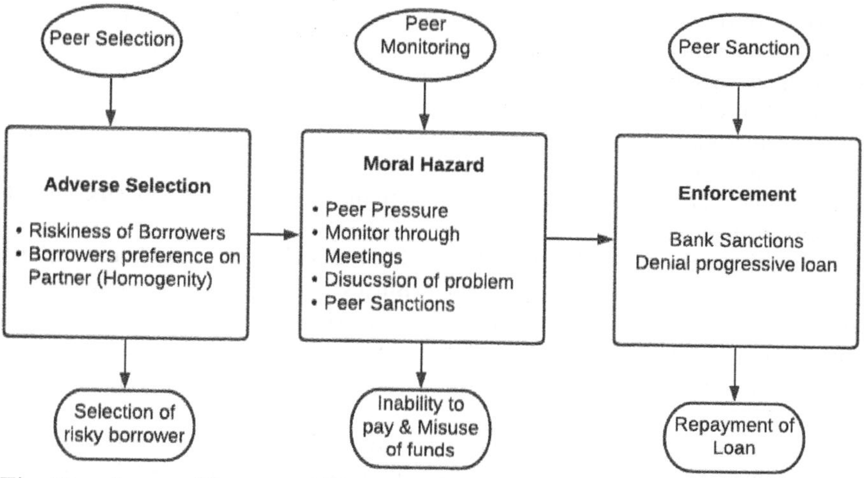

Fig. 37. Agency Theory and Framework for Moral Hazard. *Source*: By the authors.

to mitigate moral hazard. Peer selection reduces the selection of risky borrowers, peer monitoring reduces the inability to misuse funds, and peer sanction leads to loan repayment. Formal financial institutions are cautious of lending to the micro-poor due to a lack of collateral and costly monitoring. Alternatively, due to limited liability, there is a moral hazard effect, in which borrowers are enticed to take the kinds of risks that lead to bankruptcy. Ex post moral hazard is a big challenge in the credit markets. Once a financial institution has granted a loan to the borrower, a moral hazard arises, and social collateral mitigates the moral hazard. After peer selection, things depend on group productivity, peer monitoring, the strength of social ties, peer pressure, dynamic incentives, and social cohesion as the factors impacting moral hazard. Since members in a group know each other, they can better monitor, exert pressure, and sanction the members, reducing the probability of misuse of funds borrowed from the bank and reducing moral hazard. Peer monitoring and social ties play an essential role in mitigating moral hazards. The borrowers' risk propensity and group information influence the moral hazard problem in a group lending situation. Suppose there is a correlation between the returns of different borrowers; the benefits of peer-based monitoring in terms of enhanced payback are not the same. Selection criteria, that is, random or assortative, the riskiness of the project, and the correlation of returns do impact the outcomes of peer monitoring. Very few existing studies clarify the impact of borrowers' output distributions on the success of peer monitoring in mitigating strategic default. The project's riskiness affects the tendency for strategic default. Risky borrowers prefer to default because their output probability distributions have fatter tails.

A dynamic refinancing incentive helps in mitigating the ex ante moral hazard problem. Due to joint liability, the entire group will be debarred from further loans even if one borrower defaults. Due to this, the safe borrower will monitor the risky borrowers and use social ties and pressure to inculcate financial discipline. Despite this, data analysis reveals the free-rider problem in the context of self-help groups. Because of limited liability, members lack the incentive to repay on behalf of other group members, which leads to strategic default. Other studies mention factors responsible for moral hazard problems, such as project output and penalty costs. In the case of the unobservable action of an agent, the borrower's financial contract cannot be operationalized, and only the social contract can ensure economic sustainability.

Thus, the main reason for moral hazard in the social contract, that is, unlimited joint and limited individual liability. But dynamic incentives in progressive lending and peer sanction mitigate moral risk. Also, the cause of moral hazard should be wilful default, not externality or negative income shock. Peer selection also determines the level of moral hazard.

6.3.2.2. Mitigation of Moral Hazard. The joint liability group aids in transferring liability and the cost of monitoring from financial institutions to borrowers. Peer monitoring can successfully improve group performance. Peer monitoring can reduce moral hazards in joint liability lending. It is assumed that by using joint liability, group members jointly liable for the loan will monitor each other's investment decisions and efforts, lowering the monitoring costs for the lending institution and reducing moral hazard. So, safe borrowers will be reluctant to cross-subsidize the risky borrowers and monitor their peers to avoid repayment issues. Peer monitoring shifts risk from the bank to the group members, who are better equipped to bear it by social ties. This chapter shows that the transfer of risk leads to an improvement in borrowers' welfare. Peer monitoring with peer sanction helps in mitigating strategic default.

This study also refers to the problem of moral hazard as the problem of strategic default. Thus, research highlights the importance of *social sanctions* in reducing moral hazards. If a borrower defaults on a personal loan, all the bank can do is issue sanctions. But in group lending, he may face the anger of his fellow group members. In instances where the market and non-market institutions interact, calling on specific agents' punishment power to achieve better outcomes has broader importance in contract design.

Further, the borrowers' strategic default is determined by penalties and output. Borrowers will strategically default if the production of successful members is less than the penalty of defaulting members. If a borrower refuses to repay his portion of the loan, the entire credit group is regarded as in default, preventing access to future loans. This causes the group to either compensate or socially pressurize the delinquent member.

It is difficult to encourage members of disorganized groups, such as self-help groups, to attain the group's goals without motivation. The data analysis highlights the importance of *specialization and authority in leadership & centralized structure* in promoting cooperative behaviour. Risk aversion also has an impact on various types of monitoring techniques. Further, the members' action determines the probability of success. In a joint liability group, the marginal cost of the project is not equal to the marginal return, as, in the absence of collateral and

Table 13. Codes for Hypothesis 2.

Open Coding	Focussed Coding	Theoretical Coding
• Pressurizing members to repay loans • Knowing that the bank will not give a loan if one defaults, members monitor other members • Going to the door of the defaulter and counselling him to pay the loan	• Shared norms • Motivation	• Peer monitoring • Peer sanction
Excerpts from the interview: In many of the Karkhanas in markets, Karigars pursue handicrafts as an ancestral art form. We make leather products. If some women members cannot pay the loan, all the members get together and visit the home of the said member		

Source: Author's own work.

information asymmetry, the cost of failure is not internalized by the member. The study propagates that members of joint liability act either cooperatively or non-cooperatively. If all members work cooperatively, they choose a safe project. Even if one member chooses a risky project, the other will select a risky one due to joint liability. Also, the group size affects the outcome of monitoring the groups. Large group sizes are difficult to monitor, and large groups with uncorrelated project returns have more states of the world. Small group sizes are easy to monitor. Dynamic incentives are also significant in determining the impact of joint liability groups. In a joint liability group, a peer mechanism through peer monitoring ensures that members utilize credit for only income-generating activities. Table 13 provides codes for hypothesis 2.

6.3.3. Hypothesis 3: Enforceable Trust Mitigates Moral Hazard

In agency theory, sanctions punish or reward agents and align their interests with those of principals. In microfinance, the lender punishes defaulting group members by using social sanctions to control opportunistic behaviour. It is further contended that social sanctions encourage clients to pay on time. This relationship is mentioned below in Fig. 38. It exhibits the progressive lending model in a joint liability group. Borrowers, who are agents of formal financial institutions, get higher refinancing if they pay on time, which acts as an incentive to promote good financial behaviour or *stewardship behaviour* through peer pressure.

The primary issues with lending money to the group are moral hazards and bad payback behaviour. If all borrowers in the group return their loans, they can access more outstanding loans (dynamic incentives). Afraid of being barred from future loans if one (or more) of its members cannot repay, each member will keep an eye on others and pressure them if they misuse their loans. As a result, repayment is improved because joint liability contracts transfer risk from lenders to borrowers. Groups allow a member with a high-return project to pay off a partner with a poor-return project. However, if social ties among members

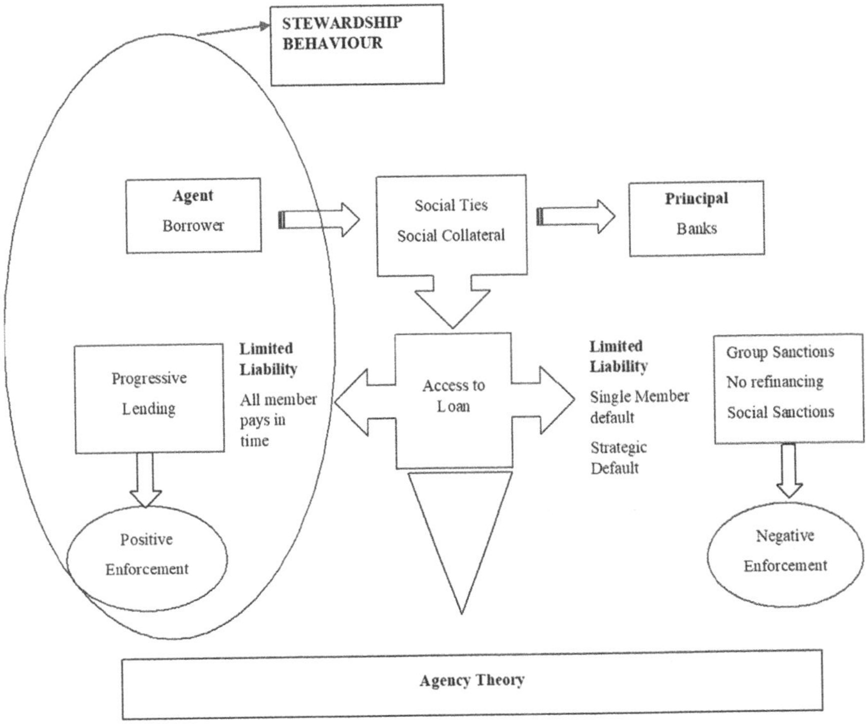

Fig. 38. Agency and Stewardship Theory. *Source*: By the authors.

are strong enough, the net effect is beneficial because borrowers who default willingly face punishment from the bank and the community. A borrowing group with enough social capital enforces payback better than an individual. In these groups, if the business connection of the borrowers is not too great, more than one borrower will be unable to repay their loan. Clients with group liability are incentivized to pressure other clients to improve enforcement. As a result, group liability effectively shifts responsibility from the lender to the clients, overcoming knowledge asymmetries common in credit markets, particularly for households without collateral.

6.3.3.1. Mitigation of Risk Through Sanctions. The conventional reason for high group loan payback rates is peer group pressure in the form of potential sanctions and denial of future loans. If other group members don't follow the rules, they risk being sanctioned. Others pay if a member fails to make a weekly payment or repay the loan. To ensure prompt repayment, the threat of potential punishment is a strong motivator for the researchers. Group sanctions might include indirect or outright criticism of an individual, social exclusion, and financial sanctions on prospective loans. In agency theory, sanctions punish or reward agents and align their interests with those of principals. It is contended that social sanctions generally encourage clients to pay on time. Clients can benefit from and enjoy different aspects of group participation, including meeting content, information, idea-sharing, and social interaction with other group members. According to empirical microfinance research, peer mentorship, intragroup learning, shared decision-making, attendance, and timeliness are all characteristics of influential groups. For exerting social pressure, word of mouth can also be significant.

Moreover, group meetings can enable the members to improve their productivity. Therefore, members can monitor each other in a group and sanction the defaulting members to ensure financial discipline. Table 14 provides code for this hypothesis.

6.4. Theoretical Coding

From the data analysis, through open coding and focussed coding, the theoretical code of peer mechanism was derived as the significant factor that leads to the success of the self-help groups in the form of higher repayments and savings. A core category of 'peer mechanism', a core phenomenon of stage-wise functioning of the groups, and peripheral concepts of network relations, shared norms, trust, and motivation, are discovered in the data and used as elements on which theory is constructed. As per the data analysis, the theoretical code of *peer mechanism comprises peer selection, monitoring, and sanction.*

Peer mechanism: In a self-help group, members have limited individual liability and unlimited joint liability. Due to the lack of physical collateral, banks, and formal financial institutions are unwilling to give loans to the marginalized poor. The members of a group peer select each other. The safe borrowers are reluctant to support the risky borrowers in a group. Due to this, the safe borrower group with the safe borrowers only. Moreover, the banks do not find it profitable to

Table 14. Codes for Hypothesis 3.

Open Codes	Focussed Codes	Theoretical Codes
• Seeking like-mindedness in other members	• Social exchange	• Network relations
• Noticing, discussing, reporting, and applying social pressures	• Social control	• Shared norms
• Regular savings and repayments	• Sustainability	• Trust
		• Motivation

Excerpt from the interview: These groups comprise around 10 to 20 members. They make leather Jutties. This is their ancestral art, and all the members are from the same profession. These members save regularly, and they do not take external loans, but they do internal lending. The educated women counsel the other members and maintain the books of accounts. This leads to the success of the group

Source: Author's own work.

monitor the borrowers. However, the members have joint liability and are willing to watch each other. They peer monitor, each other, and in case of default, they also peer sanction each other. The banks are wary of lending to the micro-poor due to the lack of physical collateral. The formal financial institutions do not have any information about these poor borrowers. SHPI agency enables the members to the group. This financial intermediary helps the group to enter into a social contract. The members with shared backgrounds or homogenous members group together. After six months, based on the group's performance, the members enable the group to get a bank loan under the self-help group bank linkage programme. They formulate shared norms such as maintaining books of account, attending meetings, saving regularly, and contributing a sum to the repayment of loans. Due to the joint liability of the group and the limited individual liability, members peer, monitor, and each other. The members are not willing to insure the risky borrowers. If a member defaults, all members must bear the loan burden. The peer mechanism of peer selection, peer monitoring, and peer sanction enable the group to achieve self-sustainability, that is, financial and institutional sustainability.

6.4.1. Cs Approach to Theoretical Coding

In brief, *trust, norms, motivation, and network relations* in the form of social capital led to social capital. This leads to social contract enforcement. The focussed code of network relations and trust lead to the code of peer selection. In one of the interviews, the member stated, '*The members stay together* because they belong to the same group'.

The focussed codes of shared norms, network relations, motivation, and trust lead to peer monitoring. In another interview, the member stated:

> The members of the group Peer monitor each other by conducting regular meetings and through regular record keeping through the maintenance of the books of accounts. This leads to better financial control and reporting.

In another interview, the respondent states, '*A late payer should return the loan in time. Otherwise, he is socially sanctioned*'. Using axial coding through the six Cs approach, the *network relations* are the *cause* of the phenomenon of peer selection, peer monitoring, and sanction. The homogenous members have joint liability and are bound by the social contract, leading to peer monitoring and sanction. The *homogeneity of members or network relations* is the *condition* for operationalizing the peer mechanism. All the members in the group know each other ex ante. *Motivation* is the *contingency*, and *trust* is the *consequence* of this peer mechanism. Table 15 represents the six Cs approach to theoretical coding.

Table 6 represents the functioning of the joint liability group through the peer mechanism.

Table 15. 6C's Approach to Theoretical Coding.

Categories	Theoretical Coding	Coding Families	Codes Derived from the Literature
	Phenomenon: Peer Mechanism in Group Lending		
Social exchange	*Network relations* *Trust*	The six Cs (consequences, contexts, conditions); unit (homogeneity of members in the group, homogenous profession, geographic proximity, social ties) (bank linkages = consequence of network relations)	Horizontal and vertical social relations (Sanae, 2003) *Theory*: Peer selection; peer monitoring
Social control	*Shared norms* *Network relations* *Trust*	The six Cs (conditions, context, cause); unit (existing social beliefs, culture, accepted norms) in the group	Group dynamics (Shaw, 1961) Peer monitoring in credit markets (Stiglitz, 1990) *Theory*: Peer monitoring and peer sanction
Social cohesion	*Trust* *Motivation* *Network Relations*	the six Cs (condition, cause) unit: (existing social relations, social contract, profit sharing	Social contracting (Hobbes, 1588–1679; Locke & Whiting, 1974; Rousseau, 1978) *Theory:* Peer control, sanction
Social welfare	*Motivation*	the six Cs (cause, condition, consequence) unit: (affiliation, autonomy, competence)	McClelland's acquired need motivation theory, 1961 *Theory*: Peer monitoring and sanction
Sustainability	*Motivation* *Shared norms*	The Six Cs Unit: Consequence, Cause, Condition	Sustainability Colonius et al. (1993) *Theory*: Peer monitoring and sanction

Source: Author's own work.

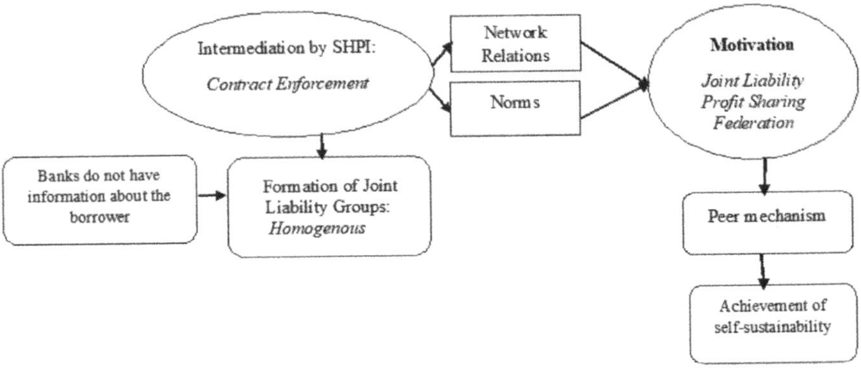

Fig. 39. Functioning of the Joint Liability Groups Through the Peer Mechanism. *Source*: By the authors.

In a group, members are self-selected. The banks are wary of investing in the selection of members. The group has joint liability; if one member does not pay, all are denied the bank loan or must pay for the defaulter. Due to the joint liability and risk of adverse selection, members peer select other group members. The members select only homogenous members for the group and form network relations. This leads to risk homogeneity as the safe members screen out the risky members. Then after selection, due to the individual limited liability, the members are incentivized to commit moral hazards. Thus, members peer monitor each other through adherence to group norms. They leverage social capital and ties to gather information and follow up with the members. In case of wilful default by a member, the members of the group apply social sanctions on the members. The group members get together based on some network relations and common ground. These members conceptualize network relations through shared norms and trust. Trust in the form of the group emerges from the bilateral and task dependencies, which act as motivation to peer monitor other members. Thus, group identity enables these members to assume joint liability and peer monitor each other. This leads to the financial sustainability of the group.

(1) *Peer selection*: The data revealed peer selection as risk matching based on business correlation, social ties, signalling, reporting, joint liability, and incentives. It is a problem of ex ante selection. The lenders have no information about the borrowers and cannot screen out the bad borrowers. Only homogenous members with a common background in profession or geography come together to form the group. The analysis sought to understand the emerging data to develop a theory relevant to the self-help group bank linkage programme's microfinancing objectives. The data analysis shows that peer selection reduces adverse selection through the assortative matching problem. Due to the perfect information about the members' creditworthiness, the safe member's group and the safe members screen out the risky members. This reduces the risk of adverse selection among the members of the group.

(2) *Peer monitoring*: Peer selection reduces risky borrower selection. No member can misuse the fund because peer monitoring prevents moral hazard. Formal financial institutions are wary of lending to borrowers due to a lack of collateral and costly monitoring (Conning & Morduch, 2011). The limited liability creates a moral hazard. But in a group, the members have joint liability, leading to peer monitoring. This peer monitoring helps to instil financial discipline among group members. In a group, if one member does not pay, the rest must pay on behalf of the defaulter. This leads to peer monitoring, where members monitor each other's activities. This peer monitoring can be either through informal modes like interactions and meetings in the village or through a formal mechanism such as meetings. This peer monitoring improves the financial sustainability of the group. Peer monitoring transfers risk from the bank to the group members, who are better equipped to bear it.

(3) *Peer sanction*: In a self-help group, the members have joint liability, which implies that if one member does not pay, the others must spend on his behalf. Therefore, to obtain more loans from banks, group members must apply peer pressure on one another to ensure prompt loan payback. This pressure is applied to ensure loan repayment and is operationalized by affinity, trust, and solidarity. This peer sanction reduces the risk of moral hazard in a group. This reduces the likelihood of misappropriation of funds because group members know each other. The safe borrower will monitor a risky borrower and use social relations and pressure to ensure the repayment of loans. The study found that peer sanction improves group performance.

Through peer selection, less risky borrowers are selected, peer monitoring reduces the ability to misappropriate funds, and peer sanction results in loan repayment. Traditional financial institutions avoid lending to micro-poor people without collateral and high monitoring costs (Conning, 2005). Due to a lack of accountability, borrowers are attracted to take risks that lead to bankruptcy (Busetta & Zazzaro, 2006). Ex ante moral hazard is a significant issue in the credit markets. Banks lack information about borrowers' creditworthiness. Project risk is shared among members of a homogeneous group. They are jointly liable, and if even one member defaults, the whole group is barred. Thus, the members develop group norms. The group members hold meetings, keep records of the sessions, apply peer pressure, and apply sanctions in monetary penalties.

6.5. Hypothesis Testing

6.5.1. Hypothesis 4: Social Capital Operationalizes the Peer Mechanism in the Group

Social capital is another major factor that leads to peer mechanisms in a group. Social capital refers to the relationship and social ties among the members. This social capital reduces monitoring costs and transaction costs. The members of the group have *information* about each other. They can influence each other, leading to *solidarity* among the group. With information about the members, the group can exercise *influence* among the members. The relationship among the members

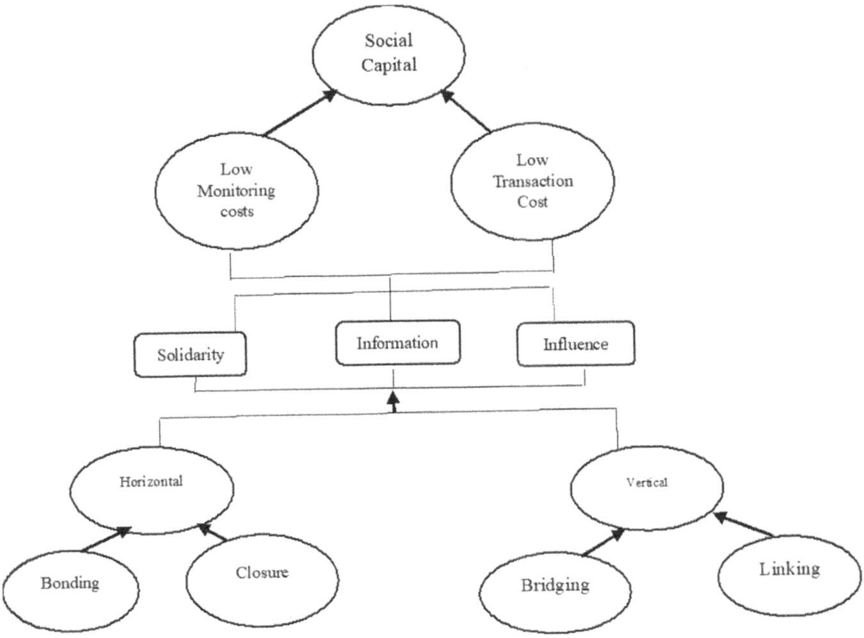

Fig. 40. Social Capital through Horizontal and Vertical Linkages (Sandefur & Laumann, 1998) – Benefits and Risk. *Source*: By the authors.

in the form of bonding and closure is called a horizontal relationship. And the relationship of power and control between the banks, clusters, and members is vertical and called bridging and linking. Thus, the existing relationships among the homogenous members based on solidarity, information, and influence lead to social capital. This social capital becomes the substitute for physical collateral and reduces the cost of transactions and monitoring for the banks. This leads to group formation and the group's sustainability through peer mechanisms.

Fig. 40 represents the social capital generated in the form of horizontal and vertical linkages.

In a group, the agents or borrowers are sanctioned to align their interests with the principals or the lenders. The lender uses social contracts to punish the defaulter. The members achieve a consensus to pay back on time. And the borrowers who pay on time get a higher loan amount. Due to the existing social capital in the form of networks, joint liability, trust, and norms, the group members peer select each other, monitor each other, and sanction each other.

Fig. 41 highlights the peer mechanism in the joint liability group (see Fig. 39). This leads to the success of self-help groups.

The norms represent cognitive components and networks in a group to describe structural components in the emerging model. The groups achieve better solidarity, information, and influence with adherence to norms and network relations. Social capital leads to peer mechanisms in the group. The peer mechanism

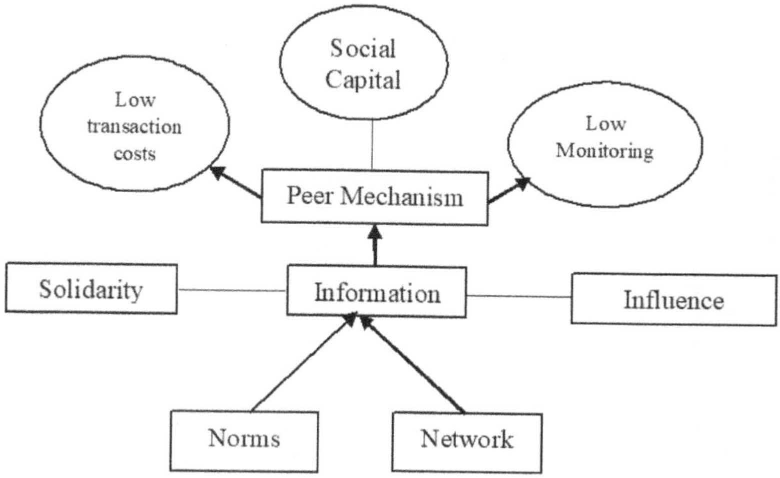

Fig. 41. Peer Mechanism. *Source*: By the authors.

reduces the transaction and monitoring costs and increases the impact of solidarity and cohesion among the group. The members monitor each other due to the nature of the social contra joint liability. This monitoring through cognitive elements such as attendance bookkeeping leads to better repayments. Thus, the emerging theory proposes that social capital leads to better peer mechanisms. This peer mechanism in the group reduces adverse selection through peer selection and moral hazard through peer monitoring. Further peer sanction also leads to reduce moral hazard in the group. Table 16 provides coding for hypothesis 4.

Table 17 provides descriptive codes for the study.

7. Process View of Peer Mechanism

Fig. 42 provides a detailed process view of the peer mechanism as a three-step process. Adverse selection is mitigated through peer selection or self-selection and social contracts with individual or limited liability based on criteria such as the riskiness of projects or personal characteristics. The selection can be made by the lender or the borrower himself. Banks do not find it worthwhile to screen the

Table 16. Code for Hypothesis 4.

Open Coding	Focussed Coding	Theoretical Coding
Forming groups with people with a common background	Trust	Peer mechanism
Excerpts from the interview: All the members make bedsheets on the handloom. Due to this, the members can monitor each other, and we members stay together. There is transparency in our operations, leading to social capital		

Source: By author.

Table 17. Descriptive Coding for Interviews.

Line-by-Line Analysis	In Vivo Coding	Descriptive coding	Analytical Coding
SHG is linked to Ajeevika NRLM and is involved in manufacturing the Madhubani paintings. There are 15 members in my group, and all do Madhubani painting. There are more than 40 members who are part of the Kala Kriti SHG. And all of us are involved in Madhubani painting, and we do an exhibition in various states such as Kerala, Mumbai, Karnataka, and Patna	Forming a homogenous group based on profession Clustering members through SHG Federation	The criterion for selection in the group is a homogenous profession	Peer selection based on homogeneity
		Groups are bridged through the formation of SHG Federations	Bridging of members through clustering in SHG Federation
And all of us are involved in Madhubani painting, and we do an exhibition in various states such as Kerala, Mumbai, Karnataka, and Patna. Not all but a few women members are selected who can talk to the people outside the SHG. We make paintings, and this style commands an excellent price and involves a lot of hard work and labour	Exploring international markets and getting recognition	Collective benefits through representation on international forum	Collective benefits
	Creating products of high quality that have market	Economic benefits through income increase and selection of good members	Economic benefits
			Market expansion
	Selecting members based on extrovert personality		Group selection and group benefits

The Government of India has started the Ajeevika programme, under which the members initially join the group to earn a livelihood. Then the members from the Ajeevika group, who are self-selected, join the self-help group. We have not taken the bank loan, but we have taken the loan under the CLF Ajeevika programme. We do not face any difficulties in making payments or savings amounts	Linking through Government scheme Ajeevika	Government schemes provide easy access to a loan	Network relations – bridging
	Financial inclusion through Government scheme	The hassle-free loan disbursement process	Financial inclusion
	Getting access to financial services		
Our members are aligned to households and are not part of any organization. Our members are versatile in Madhubani painting, a traditional art form. It is a heritage art and is passed on from generation to generation. My mother, grandmother, and great-grandmother used to pursue this art form, and we have become proficient in this. Ajeevika has given a push to this, and our group deposits Rs 10 per member per month, and then we became eligible for the loan	Homogenous groups of Karigars from the community pursuing Madhubani Art	Local artisan community organized in the form of groups	Homogenous groups of the Madhubani community
	Regular savings and bonding	Members of the group save regularly under Ajeevika	Bonding through regular savings
	Linking with Ajeevika	Ajeevika loans are based on social capital and savings	Linking with Ajeevika
			Social collateral

(Continued)

Table 17. (*Continued*)

Line-by-Line Analysis	In Vivo Coding	Descriptive coding	Analytical Coding
And our women members are very proactive. In our group, the CM or the Chief (Kosh Adhyaksh) maintains the books of accounts. Members of the group are not literate and are made aware by the Kosh Adhyaksh. All the members are not literate, and illiterate members are apprised of their savings and outstanding loan amount by the chief accountant	Appreciating group control through books preparation, leadership, and peer monitoring	Members prepare regular books of accounts	Shared norms – Book keeping and meetings
	Leadership and collaborative effort	Supervision and control of the Kosha Adhyaksh	Leadership
		Regular savings by members	Bonding – regular savings
		Information sharing by the accountant	Linking on the basis of social capital
Our group members are hard-working and collectively work extremely hard from 11 p.m. to 4 a.m. None of the members have received any help from any of the members. Ajeevika NRLM block officers come and assist the members in making the loan repayment	Access to loan based on social capital	Members receive loans and assistance in repayment based on social capital	Collective benefits of solidarity in the form of access to a loan
	Delegated monitoring by members	Delegated monitoring through NRLM	Delegated monitoring

Source: By the authors.

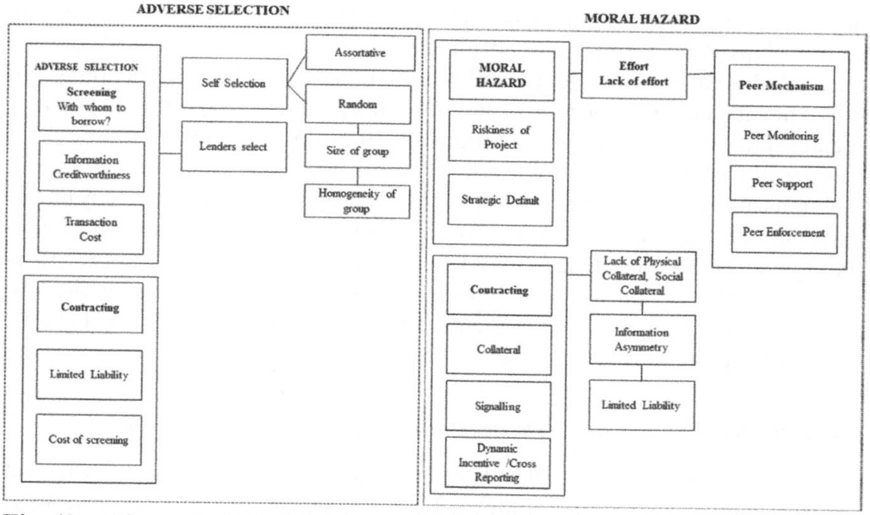

Fig. 42. Theoretical Model – Process View of Peer Mechanism. *Source*: By the authors.

members. The screening of the members can be assortative or random. Assortative matching refers to the selection of members with the same risk type. During the peer selection stage in a self-help group, the members screen out the risky borrowers and group only with the safe borrowers. This screening is done based on perfect information about creditworthiness. This assortative matching of the members with the same riskiness reduces the transaction costs and mitigates adverse selection. The members are selected into a social contract with joint liability.

After selection, the main challenge is moral hazard, where members choose risky projects. The issue concerns the project's riskiness and the probability of strategic default. Peer monitoring, sanctions, and enforcement through social contracts based on social collateral mitigate moral hazard. Contracting in group lending can use signalling, cross-reporting, and refinancing incentives to mitigate moral hazard. Joint liability in a group works as a dynamic incentive and prevents the members from defaulting on their loans. The members know that if even one member defaults, all the members will have to repay the loan; they monitor each other and sanction the defaulting members.

8. Emergent Theory

An emergent theory based on empirical data is presented here using the peer mechanism framework. On a higher level of abstraction, the concept and categories were integrated to derive the emergent theory of peer mechanism. In the earlier part, it was inferred that the group has four stages: forming, storming, norming, and performing. Using this conceptual framework, it was concluded that group formation is based on peer selection, mainly on the homogeneity of members – homogenous business relations, geographic proximity, and working relationships. And storming and norming refer to the terms of the social contract that include debt covenant, joint liability, sanctions, terms of internal lending, and group norms regarding meetings and books of account. The self-help group uses social capital to create network relations which can be horizontal with the peers or vertical with the banks. These relations and joint liability with norms about sanctions motivate members to perform. Motivation is cognitive, driven by norms and common weaknesses, affective through social relationships, and behavioural through intermediation. Due to joint liability, the safe members monitor the risky members and sanction the defaulting members. This is the reason for the sustainability of groups. Fig. 43 represents the peer mechanism's theoretical coding through the group formation process lens.

8.1. External Validity and Trustworthiness of the Qualitative Study

This external validity refers to whether the causal relationships or the internal fact can be generalized to multiple contexts. These contexts include different measures, persons, settings, and times. The interviews were taken with the respondents in different scenarios and contexts to generalize the research findings across different contexts. We have validated various empirical measures, such as the selection of peers and the loan repayment amount. They have to be tested across multiple contexts. Thus, through deduction, we articulate various generalizations. Also, we tried these generalizations or relationships between the concepts in multiple contexts. However, the internal validity was not compromised to achieve the external validity. To ensure credibility and trustworthiness in the qualitative study, we used triangulation as we collected data from multiple sources. Besides the participant observation, we used historical document analysis. We used prolonged engagement and negative case analysis, and after open coding, we went back to the members during focussed coding to reconfirm our findings. Thus, the findings

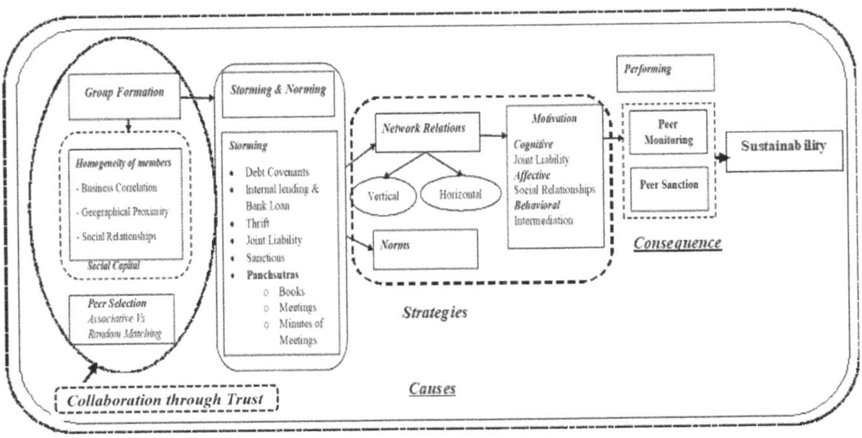

Fig. 43. Theoretical Coding in Team Formation Conceptual Framework.
Source: By the authors.

of our study are generalizable, replicable, creditworthy, dependable, and authentic (Lincoln & Guba, 1985). Though, the study does not propagate that it can be generalized in all contexts and situations. Further research can be conducted by considering other contexts to extend the scope of the theory (Calder et al., 1982).

9. Conclusion

The study provides a theoretical framework for evaluating peer mechanisms' impact on the financial outcome of the joint liability group. It also provides a process view of the peer mechanism that helps to resolve the information asymmetry problem. In a joint liability group, peer selection reduces adverse selection issues in a community group, and peer monitoring minimizes the issue of moral hazard in a community group. In the case of a lack of physical collateral, the community group provides a substitute to ensure financial access. This study will add to the current research on joint liability groups and peer monitoring in the context of self-help groups in India. It will theoretically corroborate the current financial intermediation and microfinance literature in group lending. Further, more research can be conducted on the impact of digitization on peer mechanisms in the group.

References and Further Reading

Abdallah, W., Goergen, M., & O'Sullian, N. (2015). Endogeneity: How failure to correct for it can cause wrong inferences and some remedies. *British Journal of Management*, *26*(4), 791–804.

Adhikary, S., & Papachristou, G. (2014). Is there a trade-off between financial performance and outreach in South Asian microfinance institutions? *Journal of Developing Areas, Tennessee State University, College of Business*, *48*(4), 381–402.

Aguirre-Urreta, M. I., Rönkkö, M., & McIntosh. (2019). A cautionary note on the finite sample behavior of maximal reliability. *Psychological Methods*, *24*(2), 236–252. https://doi.org/10.1037/met0000176

Ahlin, C., & Jiang, N. (2008). Can micro-credit bring development? *Journal of Development Economics*, *86*(1), 1–21.

Ahlin, C., & Townsend, R. M. (2007). Using repayment data to test across models of joint liability lending. *The Economic Journal*, *117*(517), F11–F51.

Aiyar, T. T. (1984). Informal credit markets in India. *Economic Development and Cultural Change*, 43–59.

Ajzen, I. (1991). The theory of planned behavior. *Organizational Behavior and Human Decision Processes*, *50*, 179–211.

Akerlof, G. A. (1970). The market for "lemons": Quality uncertainty and the market mechanism. *The Quarterly Journal of Economics*, *84*(3), 488–500.

Anderson, F. (2020). Women's entrepreneurship in the global south: Empowering and emancipating? *Administrative Sciences*, *10*(4), 87.

ANZ. (2008). *ANZ survey of adult financial literacy in Australia*. http://www.anz.com/Documents/AU/Aboutanz/AN_5654_Adult_Fin_Lit_Report_08_Web_Report_ful

Angelucci, M., & Karlan, D. (2015). Microcredit impacts: Evidence from a randomized microcredit program placement experiment by Compartamos Banco. *American Economic Journal: Applied Economics*, *7*(1), 151–182.

APMAS. (2006). *Self help groups in India: A study of the lights and shades*. CARE, Catholic Relief Services, GIZ Deutsche Gesellschaft für Internationale Zusammenarbeit GmbH, USAID.

APMAS. (2017). *Impact and sustainability of self help group bank linkage programme in India*. APMAS.

Arellano, M., & Bond, S. (1991). Some tests of specification for panel data: Monte Carlo evidence and an application to employment equations. *Review of Economic Studies*, *58*(2), 277–297.

Armendáriz, B. (1999). Development banking. *Journal of Development Economics*, *58*(1), 83–100.

Armendáriz, B., & Morduch, J. (2010). *The economics of microfinance*. MIT Press.

Asli, D.-K., Klapper, L., & Singer, D. (2017). *Financial inclusion and inclusive growth: A review of recent empirical evidence* [Policy series 8040, Research working paper]. The World Bank. https://openknowledge.worldbank.org/handle/10986/26479

Atkinson, A., & Messy, F. (2012). *Measuring financial literacy: Results of the OECD/international network on financial education (INFE) pilot study* [OECD Working papers on finance, insurance and private pensions no. 15]. OECD Publishing. http://www.oecd-ilibrary.org/finance-and-investment/measuring-financial-literacy_5k9csfs90fr4-en

Ayayi, G. A., & Maty, S. (2010). What drives microfinance institution's financial sustainability. *Journal of Developing Areas, Tennessee State University, College of Business*, *44*(1), 303–424.

Baag, P., & Malhotra, N. (2021). Finance literacy as a tool for microfinancing: A literature review. *International Journal and Business Economics*, *6*(2), 189–215. https://doi.org/10.5281/zenodo.5711125

Baker, T., & Nelson, R. E. (2005). Creating something from nothing: Resource construction through entrepreneurial bricolage. *Administrative Science Quarterly*, *50*(3), 329–366. https://doi.org/10.2189/asqu.2005.50.3.329

Bagozzi, R. P., & Yi, Y. (1998). On the evaluation of structure equation models. *Journal of the Academy of Marketing Science*, *16*, 76–94.

Baland, J. M., Somanathan, R., & Vandewalle, L. (2008). Microfinance lifespans: A study of attrition and exclusion in self-help groups in India. *The IDEAS*, *4*(1), 159–210.

Bandura, A. (1977). *Social learning theory*. Prentice Hall.

Banerjee, A., Besley, T., & Guinnane, T. (1994). Thy neighbor's keeper: The design of a credit cooperative with theory and a test. *The Quarterly Journal of Economics*, *109*(2), 491–515.

Banerjee, A. V. (2013). Microcredit under the microscope: What have we learned in past and what we need to know? *Annual Review Economics*, *5*, 487–519.

Banker, R. D., Lee, S.-Y., & Potter, G. (1996). A field study of the impact of a performance-based incentive plan. *Journal of Accounting and Economics*, *21*(2), 195–226.

Baruah, P. B. (2012). Impact of microfinance on poverty: A study on twenty SHGs in Nalbari District, Assam. *Journal of Rural Development*, *31*(2), 223–234.

Bastelaer, T. (1999). *Does social capital facilitates the poor's access to credit: A review of microfinance literature* [Social Capital Initiative working paper no. 8; IRIS World Bank working paper no. 234]. http://dx.doi.org/10.2139/ssrn.260058

Basu, P., & Srivastava, P. (2005). *Scaling-up microfinance for India's rural poor* [World Bank policy research working paper no. 3646]. https://openknowledge.worldbank.org/handle/10986/8311

Bateman, M. (2014). *The rise and fall of Muhammad Yunus and the microcredit model*. http://www.microfinancegateway.org/sites/ default/files/mfg-en-paper-the-rise-and-fall-of-muhammad-yunus-and-the-microcredit-model-jan-2014.pdf https://doi.org/10.2139/ssrn.2385190

Battilana, J., & Dorado, S. (2017). Building sustainable hybrid organizations: The case of commercial microfinance organizations. *Academy of Management Journal*, *53*(6), 1419–1440. https://doi.org/10.5465/amj.2010.57318391

Beal, D. J., & Delpachitra, S. B. (2003). Financial literacy among Australian university students. *Economic Papers*, *22*(1), 65–78.

Beck, T. A.-K. (2004). Bank competition. *Journal of Money, Credit and Banking*, *36*(3), 627–648.

Bec, A., Moyle, B., & Moyle, C. (2018). Resilient and sustainable communities. *Sustainability*, *10*(12), 4810. https://doi.org/10.3390/su10124810

Bell, S., & Morse, S. (2000). *Sustainability indicators: Measuring the immeasureable?* Earthscan.

Benjamin, D. J., Choi, J. J., & Strickland, A. J. (2010). Social identity and preferences. *American Economic Review*, *100*(4), 1913–1928. https://doi.org/10.1257/aer.100.4.1913

Bernheim, B. D. (1996). *Financial illiteracy, education, and retirement saving* [Working paper (pp. 38–67)]. Wharton Pension Research Council.

Bernheim, B. D., Garrett, D. M., & Maki, D. M. (1997). *Education and saving: The long-term effects of high school financial curriculum mandates*. [NBER Working papers 6085]. National Bureau of Economic Research, Inc.

Besanko, D., & Thakor, A. (1987). Collateral and rationing: Sorting equilibria in monopolistic and competitive credit markets. *International Economic Review*, *28*(3), 671–689.

Besley, T. (1995). Property rights and investment incentives: Theory and evidence from Ghana. *Journal of Political Economy*, *103*(5), 903–937. http://www.jstor.org/stable/2138750

Besley, T., & Coate, S. (1995). Group lending, repayment incentives, and social collateral. *Journal of Development Economics*, *46*(1), 1–18.

Besley, T., & Coate, S. (1995). Group lending, repayment incentives and social collateral. *Journal of Development Economics*, *46*, 1–18.

Bhaduri, A. (2006). Endogenous economic growth: A new approach, *Cambridge Journal of Economics*, *30*(1), 69–83.

Bhanot, D., & Bapat, V. (2019). Contributory factors towards sustainability of bank-linked self-help groups in India. *Asia-Pacific Sustainable Development Journal*, *26*(2), 25–55. https://doi.org/10.18356/be394dc2-en

Bhanot, D., Bapat, V., & Bera, S. (2012). Studying financial inclusion in North East India. *International Journal of Bank Marketing*, *30*(6), 465–484. https://doi.org/10.1108/02652321211262221

Bhanot, D. & Bapat, V. (2019). Contributory factors towards sustainability of bank-linked self-help groups in India. *Asia-Pacific Sustainable Development Journal*, *26*(2), 25–55.

Bhatt, N., & Tang, S. Y. (1998). The problem of transaction costs in group-based micro-lending: An institutional perspective. *World Development*, *26*(4), 623–637.

Bijli, H. K. (2012). Financial literacy: An essential tool for empowerment of women through micro-finance. *Studies on Home and Community Science*, *6*(2), 77–85.

BIRD. (2019). *Trend report on Financial Inclusion in India*. Centre for Research on Financial Inclusion and Microfinance.

Birks, M., Chapman, Y., & Francis, K. (2008). Memoing in qualitative research: Probing data and processes. *Journal of Research in Nursing*, *13*(1), 68–75.

Blumer, H. (1969). *Symbolic interactionism perspectives and methods*. University of California Press.

Bogdan, R. C., & Biklen, S. K. (2006). *Qualitative research for education: An introduction to theory and methods* (5th ed.). Allyn & Bacon.

Borden, L., Lee, S. A., Serido, J., & Collins, D. (2008). Changing college students' financial knowledge, attitudes, and behavior through seminar participation. *Journal of Family and Economic Issues*, *29*(1), 23–40.

Bos, J. W. B., & Millone, M. (2015). Practice what you preach: Microfinance business model and operational efficiency. *World Development*, *70*, 28–42.

Bourdieu, P. (1986). The forms of capital. In J. Richardson (Ed.), *Handbook of theory and research for the sociology of education* (pp. 241–258). Greenwood.

Braunstein, S. F., & Welch, C. (2002). Financial literacy: An overview of the practice, research, and policy. *Federal Reserve Bulletin*, *88*, 445–447.

Bruhn, M., Luciana, D. S. L., Legovini, A., Marchetti, R., & Zia, B. (2013). *The impact of high school financial education: Experimental evidence from Brazil* [Policy research working paper no. 6723]. World Bank. https://openknowledge.worldbank.org/handle/10986/16940

Brundtland, G. H. (1987). Our common future: Report of the world commission on environment and development. *Geneva, UN-Dokument* A/42/427. http://www.un-documents.net/ocf-ov.htm

Burgess, R. G. (1982). *Field research: A sourcebook and field manual*. Routledge.

Burke, J., Angela, A., & Hung, A. (2015). *Trust and financial advice* [Working papers WR-1075]. RAND Corporation.

Burt, R. S. (2000). The network structure of social capital. In R. S. Burt (Ed.), *Research in organizational behavior* (pp. 345–423). Elsevier.

Busetta, Z. (2006). *Mutual loan-guarantee societies in credit markets with adverse selection: Do they act as a sorting device?* RePEc.

Calder, B. J., Phillips, L. W., & Tybout, A. M. (1982). The concept of external validity. *Journal of Consumer Research*, *9*, 240–244.

Campbell, D. T., & Fiske, D. W. (1959). Convergent and discriminant validation by the multitrait-multimethod matrix. *Psychological Bulletin*, *56*(2), 81–105. https://psycnet.apa.org/doi/10.1037/h0046016

Carpenter, J., & Williams, T. (2014). Peer monitoring and microcredit: Field experimental evidence from Paraguay. *Oxford Development Studies, Taylor & Francis Journal*, *42*(1), 111–135.

Carpenter, W. J. (2014). *Peer monitoring & credit field experimental survey from Paraguay*. Oxford Developmental Studies.

Chakravarty, S. R. (2003). A generalized human development index. *Review of. Development Economics*, *7*(1), 99–114.

Charmaz, K. (2000). *Objectivist and constructivist methods*. In *The handbook of qualitative research*. Sage Publications.

Charmaz, K. (2006). *Constructing grounded theory: A practical guide through qualitative analysis*. Sage Publication.

Charmaz, K. (2014). Grounded theory in global perspective: Reviews by international researchers. *Qualitative Inquiry*, *20*(9), 1074–1084. https://doi.org/10.1177/1077800414545235

Che, Y. K. (2002). *Joint liability and peer monitoring under group lending*. Columbia University Publications.

Cheah, J.-H., Sarstedt, M., Ringle, C. M., Ramayah, T., & Ting, H. (2018). Convergent validity assessment of formatively measured constructs in PLS-SEM: On using single-item versus multi-item measures in redundancy analyses. *International Journal of Contemporary Hospitality Management*, *30*(11), 3192–3210.

Chen, H., & Volpe, R. P. (1998). An analysis of personal financial literacy among college students. *Financial Services Review*, *7*(2), 107–128.

Chen, Q., Clifford, S. J., & Wells, W. D. (2002) Attitude toward the Site II: New information. *Journal of Advertising Research*, *42*, 33–45. https://doi.org/10.2501/JAR-42-2-33-45

Cherryholmes, C. H. (1992). Notes on pragmatism and scientific realism. *Educational Researcher*, *21*(6), 13–17. https://doi.org/10.3102/0013189X021006013

Cheryl, J., MacKenzie, S., & Podsakoff, P. (2003). A critical review of construct indicators and measurement model specification in marketing and consumer research. *Journal of Consumer Research*, *30*, 199–218.

Chicagobooth. (2020, May 11). *Chicago Rustandy Center for Social Center Innovation*. Chicago Booth. https://www.chicagobooth.edu/research/rustandy/stories/indian-households-coping-with-covid19-lockdown-8-findings

Chidambaranathan, M., Smith, P., & Raj, M. (2013). Community-based microfinance: The potential and challenges of self-reliant, self-help group cooperatives. *Enterprise Development and Finance*, *24*(2), 1755–1986.

Chin, W. W. (2010). How to write up and report PLS analyses. In V. E. Vinzi, W. W. Chin, J. Henseler, & H. Wang (Eds.), *Handbook of partial least squares: Concepts, methods and applications in marketing and related fields* (Springer Handbooks of Computational Statistics Series, pp. 171–193). Springer.

Christen, R., & Ivatury, G. (2007). *Sustainability of self-help groups in India: Two analyses* [Occasional paper 12]. CGAP.

Colonius, T., Lele, S. K., & Moin, P. (1993). Boundary conditions for direct computation of aerodynamic sound generation. *AIAA Journal*, 31, 1574–1582. http://dx.doi.org/10.2514/3.11817

Cole, S., & Shastry, G. K. (2009). *If you are so smart, why aren't you rich? The effects of education, financial literacy, and cognitive ability on financial market participation* [Working paper, 09-071]. Harvard Business School.

Coleman, J. S. (1988). Social capital in the creation of human capital. *American Journal of Sociology*, *94*, S95–S120. http://www.jstor.org/stable/2780243

Connelly, L. (2008). Pilot studies. *Medsurg Nursing*, *17*, 411–412.

Connelly, L. M. (2016). A review of educational attainment measures for social research survey. *Methodological Innovations*, *25*(6), 435–436.

Conning, J. (1999). Outreach, sustainability and leverage and monitoring and peer monitored lending. *Journal of Development Economics*, *60*(1), 229–248.

Conning, J. (2005). *Monitoring by peers or by delegates? Joint liability loans and moral hazard* [Economics working paper archive 407]. Hunter College, Department of Economics.

Conning, J., & Morduch, J. (2011). *Microfinance and social investment*. FAI, Hunter and IVY League reports.

Consumer Pyramids Household Survey. (2020). *Household groups*. Centre for Monitoring Indian Economy Pvt Ltd.

Corbin, J., & Strauss, A. (2015). *Basics of qualitative research*. Sage Publications.

Creamer, E. G. (2021). *Advancing grounded theory with mixed methods*. Routledge.

Creswell, J. W. (1994). *Research design: Qualitative & quantitative approaches*. Sage Publications.

Creswell, J. W. (2012a). *Research design: Qualitative, quantitative, and mixed methods approach*. Sage Publication.

Creswell, J. W. (2012b). *Educational research: Planning, conducting, and evaluating quantitative and qualitative research* (4th ed.). Pearson.

Crotty, M. (1998). *The foundations of social research: Meaning and perspective in the research*. Sage Publications.

Cull, R., Demirguç-Kunt, A., & Morduch, J. (2007). Financial performance and outreach: A global analysis of leading microbanks. *The Economic Journal*, *117*(517), F107–F133.

Das, T., & Guha, P. (2019). Measuring women's self-help group sustainability: A study of rural Assam. *International Journal of Rural Management*, *15*(1), 116–136. https://doi.org/10.1177/0973005219836040

David, B., & Thakor, A. (1987). Collateral and rationing: Sorting equilibria in monopolistic and competitive credit markets. *International Economic Review*, *28*(3), 671–689.

De Aghion, B. A., & Gollier, C. (2010). Peer group formation in an adverse selection. *The Economic Journal*, *110*(465), 632–643.

Deininger, K. & Liu, Y. (2009). *Longer-term economic impacts of self-help groups in India* [Policy research working paper series 4886]. The World Bank.

Dembel, B., & Abdulselam, M. (2019). The effect of corporate governance mechanism on the financial performance of microfinance institutions evidence from Ethiopian microfinance institutions. *Research Journal of Finance and Accounting, 10*(21), 19–31. https://doi.org/10.7176/RJFA/10-21-03

Demirgüç-Kunt, A., Klapper, L., & Singer, D. (2017). *Financial inclusion and inclusive growth* [Policy research working paper]. World Bank. https://openknowledge.worldbank.org/bitstream/handle/10986/26479/WPS8040.pdf?sequence=1

Demrigüç-Kunt, A., & Singer, D. (2017). *Financial inclusion and inclusive growth: A review of recent empirical evidence* [Policy research working paper no. 8040]. World Bank. https://openknowledge.worldbank.org/handle/10986/26479

Demirgüç-Kunt, A., Klapper, L., Singer, D., Ansar, S., & Hess, J. (2017). *Global finance – The global Findex report*. World Bank.

Demirgüç-Kunt, A., Klapper, L., Singer, D., Ansar, S., & Hess, J. (2018). *The global Findex database 2017: Measuring financial inclusion and the fintech revolution*. The World Bank.

D'Espallier, B., Hudon, M., & Szafarz, A. (2013). Unsubsidized microfinance institutions. *Economics Letters, 120*(2), 174–176.

de Quidt, J., Fetzer, T., & Ghatak, M. (2016). Group lending without joint liability. *Journal of Development Economics, 121*(C), 217–236.

Diagne, A. (1999). *Determinants of household access to and participation in formal and informal credit markets in Malawi* [FCND discussion papers 67*]*. International Food Policy Research Institute (IFPRI).

Diamantopoulos, A., Sarstedt, M., Fuchs, C., Wilczynsk, P., & Kaiser, S. (2012). Guidelines for choosing between multi-item and single-item scales for construct measurement: A predictive validity perspective. *Journal of the Academy of Marketing Science, 40*, 434–449.

Dichter, T. (1999). *Non-governmental organizations in microfinance: Past, present and future*. World bank.

Dijkstra, T. K., & Henseler, J. (2015). Consistent partial least squares path modeling. *MIS Quarterly, 39*, 297–316.

Dissanayake, D. (2012). *The determinants of return on assets: Evidences from micro finance institutions in Sri Lanka*. SSRN. https://ssrn.com/abstract=1990281 or http://dx.doi.org/10.2139/ssrn.1990281

Dorjana, N. (2015). The interrelationship between financial attitude, financial behavior and financial knowledge. *International Journal of Business and Technology, 4*(1), 1–7.

Douglas, D. (2003). Grounded theories of management: A methodological review. *Management Research News, 26*(5), 44–52.

Dryden, I., & Mardia, K. V. (1998). *Statistical analysis of shape*. John Wiley and Sons.

Easterby-Smith, M., Thorpe, R., & Lowe, A. (2002). *Management research: An introduction*. Sage Publication.

Edmondson, A. C., & McManus, S. E. (2007). Methodological fit in management field research. *The Academy of Management Review, 32*(4), 1155–1179.

Eisenhardt, K. M. (1989). Building theories from case study research. *The Academy of Management Review, 14*(4), 532–550.

Eisenhardt, K. M. (2021). What is Eisenhardt method, really? *Strategic Organization, 19*(1), 147–160.

Eisenhardt, K. M., & Graebner, M. E. (2007). Theory building from cases: Opportunities and challenges. *Academy of Management Journal, 50*, 25–32. http://dx.doi.org/10.5465/AMJ.2007.24160888

Eisenhardt, P. O. (2009). Origin of alliance portfolios: Entrepreneurs, network strategies, and firm performance. *The Academy of Management Journal*, 246–279.

Ellison, G., & Fudenberg, D. (1995). Word of mouth communication and social learning. *The Quarterly Journal of Economics, 110*(1), 93–125.

Emmons, W. R. (2005). *Consumer-finance myths and other obstacles to financial literacy* [Policy analysis working papers 2005-03].

Ferrero-Ferrero, I., Fernández-Izquierdo, M. Á., & Muñoz-Torres, M. J. (2015). Integrating sustainability into corporate governance: An empirical study on board diversity. *Corporate Social Responsibility and Environment Management, 22*(4), 193–207.

Floro, S. L., & Yotopoulos, P. A. (1991). *Informal credit markets and the new institutional economics: The case of Philippine agriculture*. Westview Press.

Fornell, C. G., & Larcker, D. F. (1981). Evaluating structural equation models with unobservable variables and measurement error. *Journal of Marketing Research, 18*(1), 39–50.

Geertz, C. (1962). The rotating credit association: 'A middle rung in the development'. *Economic Development and Cultural Change, 10*(3), 241–289.

Greenwald, B. C., Stiglitz, J. E., & Weiss, A. (1984). *Informational imperfections in the capital market and macro-economic fluctuations* [Working papers 1335]. NBER.

Gangopadhyay, S., & Lensink, R. (2001). *Joint liability lending: A note*. RePEc.

Gangopadhyay, S., Ghatak, M., & Lensink, R. (2005). Joint liability lending and the peer selection effect. *The Economic Journal, 115*(506), 1005–1015.

Geertz, C. (1962). The rotating credit association: A middle rung in the development. *Economic Development and Cultural Change, 10*(3), 241–289.

George, D., & Mallery, P. (2016). *IBM SPSS statistics 23 step by step: A simple guide and reference* (14th ed.). Routledge. https://doi.org/10.4324/9781315545899

Gehman, J., Glaser, V. L., Eisenhardt, K. M., Gioia, D., Langley, A., & Corley, K. G. (2017). Finding theory – Method fit: A comparison of three qualitative approaches to theory building. *Journal of Management Inquiry, 27*(3), 284–300. https://doi.org/10.1177/1056492617706029 (Original work published 2018)

Ghatak, M. (1999). Group lending, local information and peer selection. *Journal of Development Economics, 60*(1), 27–50.

Ghatak, M. (2000). Screening by the company you keep: Joint liability lending and the peer selection effect. *Economic Journal, 110*(465), 601–631.

Ghatak, M., & Guinnane, T. (1999). The economics of lending with joint liability: Theory and practice. *Journal of Development Economics, 60*(1), 195–228.

Glaser, B. (1978). *Theoretical sensitivity: Advances in the methodology of grounded theory*. Sociology Press.

Glaser, B. (1998). *Doing grounded theory: Issues and discussions*. Sociology Press.

Glaser, B., & Strauss, A. (1967). *The discovery of grounded theory: Strategies for qualitative research*. Sociology Press.

Greaney, B., Kaboski, J. P., & Leemput, E. V. (2016). Can self-help groups really be 'self-help'? *The Review of Economic Studies, 83*(4), 1614–1644. http://www.jstor.org/stable/26160250

Guba, E. G. (1990). The alternative paradigm dialog. In E. G. Guba (Ed.), *The paradigm dialog* (p. 170). Sage Publication.

Gugerty, M. K. (2007). You can't save alone: Commitment in rotating savings and credit associations in Kenya. *Economic Development and Cultural Change, 55*(2), 251–282.

Guinnane, T. (1994). A failed institutional transplant: Raiffeisen's credit cooperatives in Ireland, 1819-1914. *Explorations in Economic History, 31*(1), 38–61.

Gutiérrez-Nietoa, B., Serrano-Cincaa, C., & Molinero, C. M. (2007). Microfinance institutions and efficiency. *International Journal of Management Sciences, 35*(2), 131–142.

Guttman, J. M. (2008). Assortative matching, adverse selection, and group lending. *Journal of Development Economics, 87*(1), 51–56.

Hammersley, M., & Traianou, A. (2012). *Ethics in qualitative research: Controversies and contexts*. SAGE Publications. https://doi.org/10.4135/9781473957619

Harris, M., & Raviv, A. (1979). Optimal incentive contracts with imperfect information. *Journal of Economic Theory, 20*(2), 231–259.

Harriss, J, & Renzio, P. (1997). Policy arena: Missing link or 'analytically missing'? The concept of social capital. An introductory bibliographic essay. *Journal of International Development*, *98*(7), 919–937.

Henseler, J. (2018). Partial least squares path modeling: Quo vadis? *Quality & Quantity*, *52*, 1–8. https://doi.org/10.1007/s11135-018-0689-6

Henseler, J., Ringle, C. M., & Sarstedt, M. (2015). A new criterion for assessing discriminant validity in variance-based structural. *Journal of the Academy of Marketing Science*, *43*(1), 115–135.

Hermes, N., Lensink, R., & Meesters, A. (2011). Outreach and efficiency of microfinance institutions. *World Development*, *39*(6), 938–948. https://doi.org/10.1016/j.worlddev.2009.10.018

Hertzog, M. A. (2008). Considerations in determining sample size for pilot studies. *Research in Nursing & Health*, *31*(2), 180–191.

Hira, T. K., & Loibl, C. (2005). Understanding the impact of employer-provided financial education on workplace satisfaction. *Journal of Consumer Affairs*, *39*(1), 173–194. https://doi.org/10.1111/j.1745-6606.2005.00008.x

Hobbes, T. (1588–1679). In D. S. Clark (Ed.), *Encyclopaedia of law & society: American and global perspectives* (Vol. *3*, pp. 705–705). Sage Publications, Inc. https://doi.org/10.4135/9781412952637

Hoff, K., & Stiglitz, J. E. (1998). Introduction: Imperfect information and rural credit markets- puzzles and policy perspectives. *The World Bank Economic Review*, *40*(3), 235–250. https://doi.org/10.1093/wber/4.3.235

Hulme, D., & Mosley, P. (1996). *Finance against poverty, 1 and 2*. Routledge.

Hung, A., & Parker, A. M., & Yoong, J. (2009). *Defining and measuring financial literacy*. [Working papers]. RAND Corporation Publications Department. https://papers.ssrn.com/sol3/papers.cfm?abstract_id=1498674

Hunter, S. T., Tate, B. W., Dzieweczynski, J. L., & Bedell-Avers, K. E. (2011). Leaders make mistakes: A multilevel consideration of why. *The Leadership Quarterly*, *22*(2), 239–258. https://doi.org/10.1016/j.leaqua.2011.02.001

Huston, S. J. (2010). Measuring financial literacy. *The Journal of Consumer Affairs*, *44*(2), 296–316. https://doi.org/10.1111/j.1745-6606.2010.01170.x

Imai, K., King, G., & Stuart, E. A. (2008). Misunderstandings among experimentalists and observationalists in causal inference. *Journal of the Royal Statistical Society Series A*, *171*(2), 481–502.

Isern, J. A. (2007). *Sustainability of self-help groups in India: Two analyses*. [Occasional paper no. 12]. Consultative Group to Assist the Poor (CGAP).

Ito, S. (2003). Microfinance and social capital: Does social capital help create good practice. *Development in practice*, *13*(4), 322–332. http://www.jstor.org/stable/4029657

Jacob, Y. (1992). Assessing development finance institutions: A public interest analysis [Discussion paper no. 174]. World Bank.

Jensen, M. C., & Meckling, W. H. (1976). Theory of the firm: Managerial behavior, agency costs and ownership structure. *Journal of Financial Economics*, *3*(4), 305–360.

Johnson, S., & Rogaly, B. (1997). *Microfinance and poverty reduction*. Oxfam.

Kahn, C. M., & Mookherjee, D. (1998). Competition and Incentives with nonexclusive contracts. *The RAND Journal of Economics*, *29*(3), 443–465.

Kaiser, T., & Menkhoff, L. (2017). Does financial education impact financial literacy and financial behavior, and if so, when? *Finance and Financial Sector Development*, *31*(3), 611–630. https://doi.org/10.1093/wber/lhx018

Karlan, D. S. (2005). *Social connections and group banking*. [Working papers 913]. Economic Growth Center, Yale University.

Kavita, S. (2011). Determinants of financial inclusion in India: A literature review. *Indian Journal of Finance*, *13*(11), 53–61. https://doi.org/10.17010/ijf/2019/v13i11/148417

Katzur, T., & Lensink, R. (2012). Group lending with correlated project outcomes. *Economics Letters, 117*(2), 445–447.

Kelle, U. (2007). "Emergence" vs. "forcing" of empirical data? A crucial problem of "Grounded Theory" reconsidered. *Historical Social Research, 19*, 133–156.

Kempson, E. (2006). *Policy level response to financial exclusion in developed economies: lessons for developing countries*. World Bank.

Kempson, H. E, Whyley, C. M, Caskey, J., & Collard, S. B. (2000). *In or out? Financial exclusion: A literature and research review*. Financial Services Authority.

Kinde, B. A. (2012). Financial sustainability of microfinance institutions (MFIs) in Ethiopia. *European Journal of Business and Management, 26*(4), 2628–2639.

Kock, N. (2015). Common method bias in PLS-SEM: A full collinearity assessment approach. *International Journal of e-Collaboration, 11*(4), 1–10. https://doi.org/10.4018/ijec.2015100101

Kolb, S. M. (2012). Grounded theory and the constant comparative method: Valid research strategies for educators. *Journal of Emerging Trends in Educational Research and Policy Studies, 3*, 83–86.

Kotz, J. C., Treichel, P., & Weaver, G. C. (2006). *Chemistry and chemical reactivity*. Thomson Brooks Cole.

Kumari, A., & Malathi, N. (2009). Micro credit and rural development. In A. K. Thakur & P. Sharma (Eds.), *Micro-credit and rural development* (pp. 1–10). Deep & Deep Publications.

Kunt, A. D. (2017). *Global finance: The global Findex report*. World Bank.

Kunt, D. A., Klapper, L., & Singer, D. (2017). *Financial inclusion and inclusive growth: A review of recent empirical evidence* [Policy research working paper no. 8040]. World Bank. https://openknowledge.worldbank.org/handle/10986/26479

Laffont, J. J., & Rey, P. (2003). *Moral hazard, collusion and group lending* [Working paper 122]. Institut D'Économie Industrielle (IDEI), Toulouse.

Leavy, P. (2014). *The Oxford handbook of qualitative research*. Oxford University Press.

Ledgerwood. (1997). *Microfinance handbook: An institutional and financial perspective*. World Bank. https://openknowledge.worldbank.org/handle/10986/12383

Lewin, K. (1938). *The conceptual representation and the measurement of psychological forces*. Duke University Press.

Liébana-Cabanillas, F., de Luna, I. R., & Ríos, F. J. M. (2017). Intention to use new mobile payment systems: A comparative analysis of SMS and NFC payments. *Economic Research, 30*(1), 892–910.

Lincoln, Y. S., & Guba, E. G. (1985). *Naturalistic inquiry*. Sage Publications.

Lincoln, Y. S., & Guba, E. G. (2000). Paradigmatic controversies, contradictions, and emerging confluences. In Y. S. Guba (Ed.), *Handbook of qualitative research* (pp. 163–188). Sage.

Lincoln, Y. S., & Guba, E. G. (Eds.). (2008). What comes naturally? In *Naturalistic enquiry* (pp. 187–208). Sage Publication.

Locke, E. A., & Latham, G. P. (1990). *A theory of goal setting & task performance*. Prentice Hall.

Locke, E. A., & Whiting, R. J. (1974). Sources of satisfaction and dissatisfaction among solid waste management employees. *Journal of Applied Psychology, 59*(2), 145–156. https://psycnet.apa.org/doi/10.1037/h0036531

Lusardi, A., & Mitchell, O. (2011). *Financial literacy around the world: An overview* [Working paper no. 17107]. National Bureau of Economic Research.

Lusardi, A., & Mitchell, O. (2006). *Financial literacy and retirement preparedness: Evidence and implications for financial education programs* [CFS working papers 42]. University of Michigan, Michigan Retirement Research Center.

Mahapatra, M. S., & Dutta, S. (2016). Determinants of sustainability of microfinance sector in India. *Journal of Rural Development, 35*(3), 507–522.

Majumdar, K. K. (2011). N. Srinivasan, microfinance India: State of the sector report. *South Asia Economic Journal*, *12*(2), 342–343. https://doi.org/10.1177/139156141101200209
Man ski, C. (1993). Identification of endogenous social effects: The reflection problem. *Review of Economic Studies*, *60*(3), 531–542.
Maria, K. V. (1970). Measures of multivariate skewness and kurtosis with applications. *Biometrika*, *57*(3), 519–530. https://doi.org/10.2307/2334770
Matin, I. (1997). Repayment performance of Grameen Bank borrowers: The "unzipped" state. *Savings and Development*, *4*.
McDonald, R. M., & Eisenhardt, K. M. (2020). Parallel play: Startups, nascent markets, and effective business-model design. *Administrative Science Quarterly*, *65*(2), 483–523. https://doi.org/10.1177/0001839219852349
McIntosh, C., & Wydick, B. (2005). Competition and microfinance. *Journal of Development Economics*, *78*(2), 271–298.
Meckling, J. A. (1976). Theory of the firm: Managerial behavior, agency costs and ownership structure. *Journal of Financial Economics*, *3*(4), 305–360.
Memona, M. A., Cheah, J., Ramayah, T., Ting, H., & Chuah, F. (2018). Mediation analysis issues and recommendations. *Journal of Applied Structural Equation Modelling*, *2*(1), 1–9.
Memona, M. A., Ramayahb, T., Cheahc, J.-H., Tingd, H., Chuahe, F., & Chamf, T. H. (2021). PLS SEM statistical programs: Review. *Journal of Applied Structural Equation Modelling*, *5*(1), 1–14.
Mersland, R., & Strøm, R. Ø. (2010). Microfinance mission drift? *World Development*, *38*(1), 28–36.
Mieno, F., & Kai, H. (2012). Do Subsidies Enhance or Erode the Cost Efficiency of Microfinance? Evidence from MFI Worldwide Micro Data. *PRIMCED Discussion Paper Series 26*, *Institute of Economic Research, Hitotsubashi University*.
Miles, M. B., Huberman, A. M., & Saldana, J. (2014). *Qualitative data analysis: A methods sourcebook*. Sage Publications.
Minnesota University. (2017). Organization behaviour. In *Open textbook library (Chapter 1)*. https://open.umn.edu/opentextbooks/textbooks/30
Montogomerry, H., & Weiss, J. (2011). Can commercially oriented microfinance help meet the millennium development goals evidence from Pakistan. *World Development*, *39*(1), 87–109.
Moore, D. (2003). *Survey of financial literacy in Washington State: Knowledge, behavior, attitudes and experiences* [Technical Report 03-39]. Social & Economic Sciences Research Center, Washington State University.
Morduch, J. (1999). The microfinance promise. *Journal of Economic Literature*, *37*(4), 1569–1614.
Morgan, D. L. (2007). Paradigms lost and pragmatism regained: Methodological implications of combining qualitative and quantitative methods. *Journal of Mixed Methods Research*, *1*(1), 48–76. https://doi.org/10.1177/2345678906292462
Morgan, G., & Smircich, L. (1980). The case for qualitative research. *The Academy of Management Review*, *5*(4), 491–500. https://doi.org/10.2307/257453
Morse, J. M. (2001). Toward a praxis theory of suffering. *Advances in Nursing Science*, *24*, 47–59.
Morse, S. B. (2008). *Sustainability indicators measuring the immeasurables*. Routledge.
Mosley, P., & Hulme, D. (1998). Microenterprise finance: Is there a conflict between growth and poverty alleviation? *World Development*, *26*(5), 783–790.
NABARD. (2003). *Progress of self help group bank linkage programme 2003-04*. NABARD.
NABARD Department of Economic Analysis. (2020). *Impact Assessment of COVID 19 on Indian agriculture and rural economy*. NABARD.
Nair, T. S., & Tankha, A. (2013). *Microfinance India – State of the sector report*. Access Development Services in association with Sage Publications India Pvt.

Nair, T. S., & Tankha, A. (2015). *Inclusive finance India report*. Oxford University Press.

Navajas, S., Schreiner, M., Meyer, R. L., Gonzalez-vega, C., & Rodriguez-Meza, J. (2000). Microcredit and the poorest of the poor: Theory and evidence from Bolivia. *World Development*, *28*(2), 333–346.

Nunnally, J. C., & Bernstein, I. H. (1994). The assessment of reliability. *Psychometric Theory*, *3*, 248–292.

Nurmakhanova, M., Kretzschmar, G., & Fedhila, H. (2015). Trade-off between financial sustainability and outreach of microfinance institutions. *Eurasian Economic Review, Springer Eurasia Business and Economics Society*, *5*(2), 231–250.

OECD. (2013). *How's life? 2013: Measuring well-being*. OECD Publishing. https://doi.org/10.1787/9789264201392-en

Oxford, R. (2021). Gregory Hadley: Grounded theory in applied linguistics research. *Applied Linguistics*. *42*, 363–366. 10.1093/applin/amy038

Ozcan, P., & Eisenhardt, K. M. (2009). Origin of alliance portfolios: Entrepreneurs, network strategies, and firm performance. *The Academy of Management Journal*, *52*(2), 246–279. http://www.jstor.org/stable/40390287

Parida, P. C., & Sinha, A. (2010). Performance and sustainability of self-help groups in India: A gender perspective. *Asian Development Review*, *27*(1), 80–103.

Pati, A P. (2008). Subsidized micro financing and financial sustainability of SHGs. *The Indian Journal of Commerce*, *61*(4), 137–150.

Patton, M. (2005). *Qualitative research & evaluation methods* (4th ed.). Sage Publication.

Peirce, C. S. (1958). *Collected papers of Charles Sanders Peirce*. In C. Hartshorne & P. Weiss (Eds.), (Vols. 1–8). Harvard University Press.

Phillippi, J., & Lauderdale, J. (2018). A guide to field notes for qualitative research: Context and Conversation. *Qualitative Health Research*, *28*, 381–388.

Pischke, J. D. (1996). Measuring the trade-off between outreach and sustainability of microenterprise lenders. *Journal of International Development*, *8*(2), 225–239.

Pischke, V. (1991). *Finance at the frontier: Debt capacity and the role of credit in the private economy*. The World Bank.

Pitt, M., & Khandekar, S. (1998). The impact of group-based credit programs on poor households in Bangladesh: Does the gender of participants matter? *Journal of Political Economy*, *106*(October), 958–996.

Potrich, A. C. G., Vieira, K. M., & Mendes-Da-Silva, W. (2016). Development of a financial literacy model for university students. *Management Research Review*, *39*(3), 356–376.

Puhazhendi, V. (2006). *SHG-bank linkage programme for rural poor – An impact assessment*. esocialsciences.com, Working Papers.

Puhazhendi, V., & Badatya, K. C. (2002). SHG-bank linkage programme for rural poor an impact assessment (pp. 25–26). SHG-Bank Linkage Programme Seminar.

Puhazhendhi, V., & Satyasai, K. (2000). *Micro finance for rural people: An impact evaluation, microcredit innovations department*. National Bank for Agriculture and Rural Development.

Putri, A. (1998). IPCT-J Robin hill SampleSize. *Interpersonal Computing and Technology: An Electronic Journal for the 21st Century*, *6*(3–4), 1–10.

Quayes S. (2012). Depth of outreach and financial sustainability of microfinance institutions. *Applied Economics*, *44*(25–27), 3421–3433.

Rahman, M. W., Luo, J., Hafeez, A. S. M., & Sun, T. (2015). A comprehensive review of microfinance impacts sustainability and outreach. *Asian Journal of Agricultural Extension, Economics and Sociology*, *6*(2), 64–76.

Rai, A. K., & Rai, S. (2012). Factors affecting financial sustainability of microfinance institutions. *Journal of Economics and Sustainable Development*, *3*(6), 1–9.

Ranjani, K. S., & Kumar, S. (2018). An investigation of mission drift in Indian MFIs. *International Journal of Social Economics*, *45*(9), 1305–1317.

Ravishankar, M. N. (2011). Examining the strategic alignment and implementation success of a KMS: A subculture-based multilevel analysis. *Information Systems Research, INFORMS*, *29*(3), 39–59. https://doi.org/10.1287/isre.1080.0214

Ray, D. (1997). *Development economics*. Princeton University.

Ray, D. (1998). *Development economics*. Oxford Press.

Rankin, K. N. (2002). Social capital, microfinance, and the politics of development. *Feminist Economics*, *8*(1), 1–24. https://doi.org/10.1080/13545700210125167

Rasoolimanesh, S. Mostafa & Seyfi, Siamak & Hall, Colin & Hatamifar, Pezhman. (2021). Understanding memorable tourism experiences and behavioural intentions of heritage tourists. *Journal of Destination Marketing and Management*. *21*. 10.1016/j.jdmm.2021.100621.

Remund, D. L. (2010). Financial literacy explicated: The case for a clearer definition in an increasingly complex economy. *The Journal of Consumer Affairs*, *44*(2), 276–295. https://doi.org/10.1111/j.1745-6606.2010.01169.x

Rennie, D. L. (2000). Grounded theory methodology as methodical hermeneutics: Reconciling realism and relativism. *Theory & Psychology*, *10*(4), 481–502.

Rhyne, E. (1988). The Yin and Yang of microfinance: Reaching the poor and sustainability. *MicroBanking Bulletin*, *2*, 6–9.

Rhyne, E., & Otero, M. (2006). The changing face of microfinance: Closing the quality gap. *Micro Banking Bulletin*, *13*, 1–7.

Robinson, M. S. (2001). *The microfinance revolution: Sustainable finance for the poor*. World Bank.

Roldán, J., & Sánchez-Franco, M. J. (2012). Variance-based structural equation modeling: Guidelines for using partial least squares in information systems research. In M. Mora, O. Gelman, A. Steenkamp, & M. Raisinghani (Eds.), *Research methodologies, innovations and philosophies in software systems engineering and information systems* (pp. 193–221). IGI Global. https://doi.org/10.4018/978-1-4666-0179-6.ch010

Rousseau, D. M. (1978). Relationship of work to nonwork. *Journal of Applied Psychology*, *63*(4), 513–517. https://doi.org/10.1037/0021-9010.63.4.513

Rehman, H., Moazzam, D. A., & Ansari, N. (2020). Role of microfinance institutions in women empowerment: A case study of Akhuwat, Pakistan. *South Asian Studies*, *30*(1), 107–125.

Remund, D. L. (2010). Financial literacy explicated: The case for a clearer definition in an increasingly complex economy. *The Journal of Consumer Affairs*, *44*(2), 276–295. https://doi.org/10.1111/j.1745-6606.2010.01169.x

Rennie, D. L. (2000). Grounded theory methodology as methodical hermeneutics: Reconciling realism and relativism. *Theory & Psychology*, *10*, 481–502.

Rey, J. J. (2003). *Moral hazard, collusion and group lending*. RePEc.

Rosenberg, R. (2009). *Measuring results of microfinance institutions: Minimum indicators that donors and investors should track*. CGAP.

Rosenbaum, P. R., & Rubin, D. (1985). Constructing a control group using multivariate matched sampling methods that incorporate the propensity score. *The American Statistician*, *39*, 33–38.

Rosenberg, R., Gonzalez, A. & Narain, S. (2009). *The new moneylenders are poor being exploited by high microcredit interest rates* [Occasional paper number 10 (pp. 145–181)]. CGAP.

Roy, M. (2010). Microfinance mission drift? *World Development*, *38*(1), 28–36.

Rutherford, S. (2000). Raising the curtain on the 'microfinancial services era. *Small Enterprise Development*, *11*(1), 13–25. https://doi.org/10.3362/0957-1329.2000.005

Sacerdote, B. (2001). Peer effects with random assignment: Results for Dartmouth roommates. *The Quarterly Journal of Economics*, *116*(2), 681–704.

Sajjad, Z., & Matin, I. (2004). Wider impacts of microfinance institutions: Issues and concepts. *Journal of International Development*. https://doi.org/10.1002/jid.1080

Saldaña, J. (2009). *The coding manual for qualitative researchers*. Sage Publications Ltd.
Samuelson, P. A. (1949). *Economics*. McGraw Hill.
Sanae, I. (2003). Microfinance and social capital: Does social capital help create good practice? *Development in Practice*, *13*(4), 322–332.
Santos, F. M., & Eisenhardt, K. M. (2009). Constructing markets and shaping boundaries: Entrepreneurial power in nascent fields. *Academy of Management Journal*, *52*, 643–671. https://doi.org/10.5465/amj.2009.43669892
Sandefur, R. L., & Laumann, E. O. (1998). A paradigm for social capital. *Rationality and Society*, *10*, 481–501. http://dx.doi.org/10.1177/104346398010004005
Sarstedt, M., Hair, J. F., Nitzl, C., Ringle, C. M., & Howard, M. C. (2020). Beyond a tandem analysis of SEM and process: Use of PLS SEM for mediation analysis. *International Journal of Market Research*, *62*(3), 288–299.
Sarstedt, M., Hair, J. F., Pick, M., Liengaard, B. D., Radomir, L., & Ringle, C. M. (2022). Progress in partial least squares structural equation modeling use in marketing research in the last decade. *Psychology & Marketing*, 1035–1064.
Sarstedt, M., Ringle, C. M., & Hair, J. F. (2021). Partial least squares structural equation modeling. *Handbook of Market Research*, *15*(2), 1–47.
Saunders, M. N. K., Lewis, P., & Thornhill, A. (2009). *Research methods for business students* (5th ed.). Pearson Education.
Seibert, S. E., Kraimer, M. L., & Liden, R. C. (2001). A social capital theory of career success. *Academy of Management Journal*, *44*, 219–237. http://dx.doi.org/10.2307/3069452
Shadish, W. R., Cook, T. D., & Campbell, D. T. (2001). *Experimental and quasi-experimental designs for generalized causal inference*. Houghton Mifflin.
Sharma, M., & Zeller, M. (1997). Repayment performance in group-based credit programs in Bangladesh: An empirical analysis. *World Development*, *25*(10), 1731–1742.
Shaw, F. (1961). Houses in multi-occupation. *Royal Society of Health Journal*, *81*(4), 214–220. https://doi.org/10.1177/146642406108100472
Shazia, J. (2014). Qualitative research method-interviewing and observation. *Journal of Basic and Clinical Pharmacy*, *5*, 87–88.
Sharma, R. (2021). Empowering women self help groups through microfinance during the COVID 19. *Indian Journal of Finance and Banking*.
Silverman, D. (2010). Doing qualitative research: *A practical handbook* (3rd ed.). Sage Publications.
Simtowe, F., & Zeller, M. (2006). *The impact of access to credit on the adoption of hybrid maize in Malawi: An empirical test of an agricultural household model under credit market failure*. MPRA Paper, *45*.
Spence, M., & Zeckhauser, R. (1971). Insurance, information and individual action. *American Economic Review*, *61*, 380–387.
Spradley, J. P. (1979). The ethnographic interview. Holt Rinehart & Winston.
Starks, H., & Trinidad, S. B. (2007). Choose your method: A comparison of phenomenology, discourse analysis, and grounded theory. *Qualitative Health Research*, *17*, 1372–1380. https://doi.org/10.1177/1049732307307031
Stiglitz, J. (1990). Peer monitoring and credit markets. *The World Bank Economic Review*, *4*, 351–366. http://dx.doi.org/10.1093/wber/4.3.351
Srivastava, P. B. (2005). *Scaling-up microfinance for India's rural poor* [Policy Research Working Paper 3646]. World Bank.
Stiglitz, J., & Weiss, A. (1981). Credit rationing in markets with imperfect information. *The American Economic Review*, *71*, 393–410.
Strauss, A., & Corbin, J. (1998). *Basics of qualitative research: Techniques and procedures for developing grounded theory* (2nd ed.). Sage Publications.
Streubert, H. J., & Carpenter, D. R. (2011). *Qualitative research in nursing: Advancing the humanistic imperative*. Wolters Kluwer.

Sutton, R. I., & Staw, B. M. (1995). What theory is not. *Administrative Science Quarterly*, *40*(3), 371–384.
Tankha, A. (2002). *Self-help groups as financial intermediaries in India: Cost of promotion, sustainability and impact*. Sa-Dhan A Study Prepared for ICCO and Cordaid, The Netherlands. https://www.academia.edu/1915039/Self-help_Groups_as_Financial_Intermediaries_in_India_Cost_of_Promotion_Sustainability_and_Impact
Tankha, T. S. (2013). *Microfinance India – State of the sector report*. Sage Publications.
Tashakkori, A., & Teddlie, C. (2003). *Handbook of mixed methods in social and behavioral research*. Sage Publications.
Tassel, E. V. (1999). Group lending under asymmetric information. *Journal of Development Economics*, *60*(1), 3–25.
Thomson, S. B. (2011). Qualitative research: Validity. *Journal of Administration and Governance*, *6*(1), 77–82.
Thorsten, B., Asli, D. K., & Vojislav, M. (2004). Bank competition and access to finance: International evidence. *Journal of Money, Credit and Banking*, *36*(3), 627–648.
Timberg, T. A., & Aiyar, C. V. (1984). Informal credit markets in India. *Economic Development and Cultural Change*, *33*, 43–59.
Timothy, B., & Coate, S. (1995). Group lending, repayment incentives and social collateral. *Journal of Development Economics*, *46*(1), 1–18.
Tripathi, G. (2000). Review of econometric methods. In J. Johnston & J. DiNardo (Eds.), *Econometric theory* (pp. 139–142). Cambridge University Press.
Tushman, M. L., & Romanelli, E. (1994). Organizational transformation as punctuated equilibrium: An empirical test. *Academy of Management Journal*, *37*(6), 1141–1166.
Verhelle, C., & Berlage, L. (2003). *Determinants of microfinance group performance: An empirical analysis of self help groups in India*. http://citeseerx.ist.psu.edu/viewdoc/download?doi=10.1.1.201.4032&rep=rep1&type=pdf
Vigenia, A. K. (2005). *Key factors of joint-liability loan contracts: An empirical analysis*. RePEc.
Vigenina, D., & Kritikos, A. S. (2004). The individual micro-lending contract: Is it a better design than joint-liability? Evidence from Georgia. *Economic Systems*, *28*(2), 155–176.
Von Pischke, J. D. (1991). *Finance at the frontier: Debt capacity and the role of credit in the private economy*. World Bank Institute.
Von Pischke, J. D. (1996). Measuring the trade-off between outreach and sustainability of microenterprise lenders. *Journal of International Development*, *8*(2), 225–239.
Vroom, V. H. (1964). *Work and motivation*. John Wiley & Sons.
Walker, D., & Myrick, F. (2006). Grounded theory, an exploration of process and procedure. *Qualitative Health Research*, *16*, 547–559. https://doi.org/10.1177/1049732305285972
Walshe, C., Ewing, G., & Griffiths, J. (2012). Using observation as a data collection method to help understand patient and professional roles and actions in palliative care settings. *Palliative Medicine*, *26*(8), 1048–1054.
Weber, O., & Ahmad, A. (2014). Empowerment through microfinance: The relation between loan cycle and level of empowerment. *World Development*, *62*, 75–87. 10.1016/j.worlddev.2014.05.01
Wellman, B., & Berkowitz, S. D. (1988). *Social structures: A network approach*. Cambridge University Press.
Woolrdige J. (2002). *Econometric analysis of cross section and panel data*. MIT Press.
Wry, T., & Zhao, E. Y. (2018). Taking trade off seriously: Examining the contextually contingent relationship between social outreach intensity and financial sustainability in global microfinance. *Organization Science*, *29*(3), 507–528.
Xiao, J. J., Serido, J., & Shim, S. (2010). *Financial education, financial knowledge and risky credit behavior of college students* [NFI working papers 2010-WP-05]. Indiana State University, Scott College of Business, Networks Financial Institute.

Yanyan, D. K. (2009). *Economic and social impacts of self-help groups in India* [Working policy paper 4884]. World Bank

Yaron, J., Benjamin, M. P., Jr., & Piprek, G. L. (1997). *Rural finance: Issues, design, and best practices, environmentally and socially sustainable development*. World Bank.

Yin, R. K. (2003). *Case study research: Design and methods*. Sage Publication.

Yunus, M. (2008). Turning beggars into entrepreneurs. *New Perspectives Quarterly*, *25*(2), 88–89.

Yunus, M., & Jolis, A. (2003). *Banker to the poor: Micro-lending and the battle against world poverty*. New York Public Affairs.

Zeckhauser, M. S. (1971). Insurance, information and individual action. *American Economic Review*, *61*(2), 380–387.

Zhao, X., Lynch, J. G., & Chen, Q. (2010). Reconsidering Baron and Kenny: Myths and truths about mediation analysis. *Journal of Consumer Research*, *37*(2), 197–206.

Zimmerman, D. J. (2003). Peer effects in academic outcomes: Evidence from a natural experiment. *The Review of Economics and Statistics*, *85*(1), 9–23.

Zott, C., & Huy, Q. N. (2007). How entrepreneurs use symbolic management to acquire resources. *Administrative Science Quarterly*, *52*(1), 70–105.

Chapter 7

Savings Groups in Kenya – Chamas: A Case Study

Abstract

Savings groups in Kenya work on the principle of collectives and joint liability. These groups have played an important role in the financial inclusion of the poor. In case of the savings groups in Kenya, the financial intermediation by the local non-government organizations (NGO) has played an important role in fostering community development and poverty reduction. These groups also play an extremely important role in the women empowerment and knowledge sharing. This study will mainly aim to develop a compelling case on unique phenomenon of financial savings through the savings groups.

Keywords: Community lending groups; chamas; harambee; financial inclusion; self-help groups

1. Introduction

According to various studies, self-help groups play an extremely important role in promoting group savings, leadership, and income-generating activities. The government should lay more emphasis on the financial literacy and awareness of women to reduce financial disparities and woes. Further, training given to women regarding financial management plays an important role in promoting self-reliance and independence. The literature highlights the brief history of the self-help groups as structures and institutional designs that help marginalized women cope with labour shortages and often help the women meet social obligations such as funerals and childbirths. The existence of the self-help group projects in Kenya started with the initiation of the Harambee self-help development

Global Perspectives on Financial Inclusion: Case Studies in Microfinance and Women's Empowerment, 195–206

Published under exclusive licence by Emerald Publishing Limited
doi:10.1108/978-1-83708-080-920251007

projects, which include community self-help projects (Muasya, 2013). During the colonial period, non-government organizations emerged as intermediaries such as Maendeleo Ya Wanawake Organisation (Organisation for Development of Women), which strengthened women's participation in rural communities. Various international conferences, such as the United Nations World Conference for Women in Mexico City, Copenhagen, and Nairobi, emphasized the cause of women's empowerment and female emancipation. The Kenyan Government has highlighted the importance of sensitizing society to the cause of women through a change in attitude and helping women overcome the evil of traditional and archaic cultural practices. The forum such as the Forum of African Women Educationists believes that education is a socialization process by which women get an opportunity to participate in the financial system. According to several studies, groups and collective institutional structures have come to play an important role in the financial sector. Through merry-go-round, saving institutions offer opportunities for financial inclusion of the women at the bottom of the pyramid. Social intermediation and training as per the member have come to play an important role in the empowerment of women in rural India. Johnson (2004) highlights that self-help groups play an important role in impacting loan delinquency among the members of the group. Further, the existing data highlight the importance of the organizational culture in promoting a sustainable competitive advantage among the members of the group. Moreover, as per the previous studies and literature organizational culture plays an important role in ensuring the strategic fit between the organization and the external environment of a financial services firm. The cerebral culture is referred to as a set of knowledge, beliefs, ethics, habits, and customs that are gathered through socialization and education (Geertz, 1973). This work aims to use the *Competing Value Framework* (CVF) to study how the culture enables the group of marginalized women to consolidate their resources and work towards the achievement of the group goals and missions. It also highlights how the culture helps in the alignment of the external environment and the internal dynamics of working of a group through state intervention, marketing, communication, and leadership development. This work specifically aims to use the case study method to explore the institutional design of Harambee projects in Kenya, and their role in achieving this sustainable development goal of poverty reduction and development (Chitere, 2018).

2. Literature Review

CVF is the conceptual framework to identify the effectiveness of the organization (Quinn & Rohrbaugh, 1981). Organizational behaviour is subject of various competing organizational thoughts and theoretical views. Goulder (1950) in his study highlights that the organizations are not closed systems, which are immune from external impacts and factors. Rather, the organizations continuously interact with the external environment and the external environment has a vast impact on the functioning of these organizations. Self-help groups are semi-formal organizations that provide loan to the people at the bottom of the pyramid, using the social capital generated by the members of the group. These semi-formal organizations interact with the social, economic, political, and business environment. Thus, the interactions between the external environment and the structures of an organization impact the effectiveness of the organizations. The community lending programmes and self-help groups are basically open systems that interact continuously with the other forces in the external environment. The socio-cultural dynamics and the political factors including state policies have a vast impact upon the working of the semi-formal organizations like community lending programmes.

2.1. Conceptual Framework for Clan Management – Competing Value Framework

Clan culture in the participatory groups in Kenya emphasizes the importance of creating a strategic alignment between the external environment and the internal organizational culture. The internal culture highlights the importance of the various attributes. The leadership, communication, leadership processes, structures, and systems depict the culture of an organization. According to various studies, organizational culture has a deep impact on the performance of the clans or the groups. The literature corroborates that the success of an organization is impacted by the alignment of the strategy, structure, and culture. The competing framework is based on two sets of values flexibility and discretion versus stability and control. An internal focus versus external focus and differentiation. Four different types of culture include clan culture, adhocracy culture that promotes innovation, market culture, and hierarchy culture. Within a participatory group, members work closely with each other and are selected by each other. Global financial crisis and the liberalization and privatization have highlighted the importance of regulation and state intervention for balanced economic development and growth. Various studies highlight that the institutional design has a major role to play in increasing the innovativeness of an organizational structure. Within the institutional design are embedded the important components such as organizational culture. The culture within an institution or organization has a vast impact upon the attitude and behaviour of the individuals. Rowe et al. (1994) have introduced various dimensions of culture such as creativity, quality, and supportive and productive culture that have an impact upon the success and financial sustainability of the organization. Quinn and Rohrbaugh (1983) in their research study highlighted importance of CVF, which emphasize the importance of cultural typology of adhocracy, hierarchy, market, and clan culture. The existing studies highlight the important role of the CVF in promoting the performance through the mediating role of various variables such as innovation and social capital to name a few. Most of the theoretical studies in this domain highlight the positive impact of the CVF on outcomes and performance of the institutions. The CVF highlights that the two major sources of tension within an organization are internal versus external tensions and flexible versus stable tensions.

Fig. 44 highlights that how difference in leadership effectiveness and behaviours creates different kinds of competencies and cultures. And how different cultures give rise to different kinds of value systems. The values in an organization

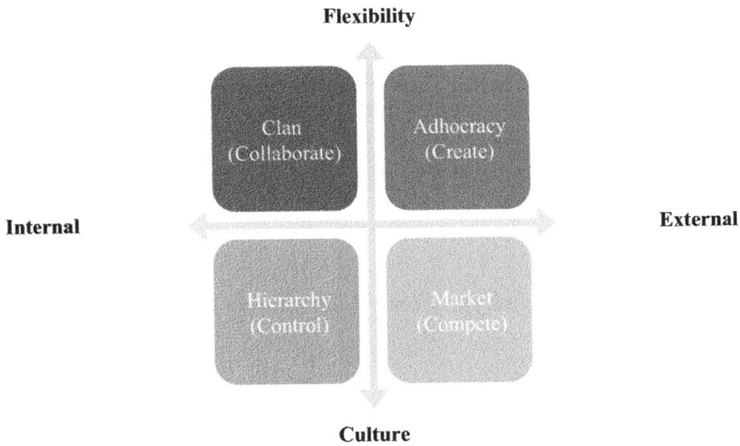

Fig. 44. Competing Value Framework. *Source*: Quinn.

span across two dimensions: (1) flexibility versus focus and (2) internal versus external orientation. The chamas community lending programmes in Kenya fall within the first quadrant – clan culture to collaborate. This culture is marked by the importance of people-to-people connect. All the members in the *chamas* community lending programme are known to each other, and this gives rise to culture of team building, participation, and consensus. These groups come together and work collaboratively to extend common good and social capital. A Clan shows and exhibits a large amount of overlap with group culture. In these organizations, the members of the organizations are mentors and creators, who work towards to attainment of the group goals. The leaders provide direction and motivation to the group and ensure that the group members adhere to group norms. They set the vision and mission for the attainment of group goals and ensure that the organizational commitment is kept intact.

Internal versus external tensions: The cultures that are internally dominant focus on collaborating and coordinating to facilitate the development and deployment of resources. The internal locus refers to the core competencies and sustained capabilities that enable the organizations to attain their end objectives. External tensions or externally dominant culture refers to the focus on the broader market level changes such as technological changes, customer tastes, and preferences. Generally, stable organizations promote internal oriented culture, whereas the volatile and new start-ups have more externally oriented culture. Within the CVF, the Harambee self-help development project is more internally oriented with a clan culture that highlights importance of cohesiveness, collaboration, and solidarity. The groups are formed on the principle of *espirit de corps*. The members are united through the social capital that exists among the homogenous members. In a group, the members are selected from the same geography/neighbourhood or the same profession. The members of the group select one person as the leader of their group, and he acts as the facilitator, mentor, or collaborator. These groups are driven by the values of commitment and communication. Through a social contract, the group as an institutional design assumes joint liability for the members, which implies that if one of the members does not pay, then all other members will have to pay. Whereas the members individually bear the limited liability. This unique social innovation called self-help group promotes solidarity among the members to save together and rotate the savings from one member to another. Theory of effectiveness highlights that the clan culture group leads to better human development and higher level of commitment leading to organizational effectiveness. Thus, in CVF, the groups under Harambee self-help development project lie on left hand quadrant, with low level of individual flexibility and high level of internal maintenance. However, through the leadership and development of organizational practices such as shared norms regarding meeting and maintenance of books, the leaders exercise control and monitor the performance of the individual groups to ensure achievement of the group goals. Moreover, the groups through the entrepreneurial vision and use of technology in the form of network culture and digital transformation provide impetus to the growth and development within an organizational structure. Though the groups reflect the clan culture, with inward looking and flexible approach that is based on team work and collaboration, supportive of each other and responding to the challenges of the world, with an internal focus, with the use of digital technology, these institutions also reflect agility to adapt to the challenges, take risks, and grow. With a democratic leader who is chosen from the members of the group and a secretary and accountant that put in place shared norms for meeting and book keeping that need to be adhered to the groups also reflect the hierarchy. Despite an inward focus, with the support and intermediation by the government, the group reflects market orientation where the government agencies provide training to the members of the group to become competitive and agile. The members of the group are provided the marketing support and are given the training in the use of technology and financial literacy. These improve the quality and reach of the products manufactured by these small entrepreneurs and give the small entrepreneurs to compete with the international players and products. Thus, the modern-day group based or clan-based Harambee self-help development project reflects diversity and span across the four quadrants of the CVF. Besides, the product and process innovation, the organizational innovation or the unique attributes of the institutional designs have an important role to play in the success and achievement of outcomes. Every organization suffers from the constraint of optimal amount of resources and institutional designs that enable the organizational structures to leverage its resources and capabilities to generate core competencies and emerge as competitive advantage. The environment in which the start-ups and the new entrepreneurs operate is highly dynamic and complex. The target segment for the start-ups and micro-entrepreneurs are the marginalized women entrepreneurs, who need core capabilities to enable them to adapt quickly and adopt transformations to facilitate organizational agility. These micro and small business units suffer from the lack of collateral, and none of the banks is willing to provide them loans. Joint liability groups and self-help groups enable the members to leverage the joint liability and the social capital to develop capabilities such as financial prowess to ensure sustainability of the groups.

2.2. Case Study – Harambee and Chamas Self-help Groups in Kenya

Harambee refers to the social phenomenon and a Kenyan tradition that implies *all pull together*. The phrase 'all pull together' is a Swahili phrase and is the official motto of Kenya. In 1963, when Kenya got independence, the nation under the able leadership of the Kenyan president Jomo Kenyatta adopted the concept of 'Harambee' that implies to pull all together. As per the folk narratives, origin of the word Harambee is said to be the Indian labourers, who worked to build the Uganda railway station. Another narrative is about the Swahili porters; when they left the heavy loads, they use the expression Harambee, which implies to pull together. The use of the word Harambee is linked to the blessings of the lord Ambe, the Hindu goddess, who is invoked by the labourers during their weight lift to bestow the energy upon the labourers to lift the weight.

And hence the word *Harambee* is thought to be *Hare Ambeh*, which is accepted to be the coat of arms for the great country Kenya. In any nation, the economic and social development depends upon the literacy levels and access to the social amenities. The constraint of resources is the biggest stumbling block for the people at the bottom of the pyramid. In 1963, when Kenya got the independence, the existing social services and the resources were constrained and not sufficient to meet the needs of the people at the bottom of the pyramid. The resource mobilization and the situational leadership emerged as the panacea for building the nation, which gave rise to the Harambee movement. The word Harambee originated from the word Halambee, which was used by the fishing community in the Kenyan coast and implies 'let's all pull together'. It further refers to the clarion call to the citizens of the country to contribute towards the nation building through cooperation and co-optation. The philosophy of Harambee is based on cooperative work culture that motivates the people to work together towards the achievement of group goals, it refers to the mutual assistance, cooperative behaviour, joint effort, mutual social responsibility, community self-reliance, and the spirit of association. Kenya has adopted the Harambee as the coat of arms, which is testimony to the mutual or cooperative spirit of the indigenous people and their aspirations, where the honourable President Kenya urged the people to make merry and prepare for the tall that is yet to come, which had reference to obstacles such as poverty, disease, and ignorance. At the heart of this project is the scarcity of the resources, which require the members of the society to make a collective effort for the achievement of the group goals. It refers to the bottom-up approach to development, where the projects are motivated by the collective good and emancipation of the millions of people below the poverty line. It also includes various initiatives that include raising money for the important causes like wedding, education, and social welfare projects to name a few.

In the case of Harambee self-help development project, Kenya, it becomes apparent that the social capital, digital innovation, and social contract enabled through joint liability have the ability to cope with the new challenges. Moreover, the culture of an organization has a deep impact upon the success of the organizations. The organizations face the dilemma of allocating the resources among the several competing opportunities to ensure the optimal utilization of resources. However, the resource-based view suffers from various limitations such as Kuhanian incommensurability or different states of nature problem. An optimal allocation in one state might not be the best alternative in another state of nature. In this light, the conceptual framework of *critical realism* is based on metaphysical qualities.

In this regard there is need for redesigning the conceptual framework for allocation of resources using the states of nature. The CVF describes the organizational effectiveness as a goal, achievement of which is dependent on various objective statements such as optimum organizing and deployment of resources, innovation to name a few. However, the deployment or organizational resources and innovation are not performance yardsticks, because the achievement of these objectives is further relative to the purpose, practice, and people in an organization. The purpose refers to the alignment of objectives and goals, practice refers to the dominant organizational routines, and people refer to the leadership and the members of the organization and their organizational commitment. The practice in an organization refers to the incubating the workplace practices, values, and learnings. In the context of a group lending institutional format, practice refers to the adherence to the group norms, shared values, inventing new financial products, and services. To sum it up, the organizational culture forms a very important component of the practices that exist within an organization and impact the achievement of the group goals and objectives. Thus, the acknowledgement that the semi-formal financial institutions like Chamas in Kenya are not standing in isolation, but supported by the organizational routines, processes, leadership pursuits, which lead to achievement of goals. Various studies have highlighted that the cultural practices in an organization might reflect adhocracy, market, clan, or hierarchy culture. The self-help groups or joint liability groups reflect the values of teamwork, collaboration, and participation. These values seem to have a positive impact on the working of the group. Through strong commitment and a psychological contract with the members of the group in a joint liability scenario, the group promotes a significant relationship between the clan culture and the performance. This group culture and organizational format has legitimacy of state endorsement in the form of coat of arms and official national motto. Further, it is argued that the innovative practices such as peer mechanism and the social capital further argument the financial performance of the groups. The purpose refers to the clarity of vision and mission regarding the existence of the organizations. It refers to the underlying motivation that drives the members in the group to collaborate and work together for the achievement of the group objectives. The people refer to most importantly, the leader of the group that provides direction to the other members of the group to work together to ensure financial sustainability of the groups.

2.3. Role of Communication Strategies, Leadership Strategies, and Leadership Behaviour

From the analysis of the extensive literature, communication strategies, leadership strategies, and leadership behaviour have a vast impact upon the success of the community lending groups. The communication strategies have come to play an important role in the success of the harambee community groups. The stakeholders in the implementation group include the government official, locals, and the clan leaders also called *Ithe Ma Mbai*. The basic premise that the cooperation among the various stakeholders leads to focussed and collaborative action is flawed. According to the analysis of the literature, besides the cooperation, there are conflict of interests, competitions, and jealousies among the various members of the groups and the stakeholders. The overlap of the action of the government and the stakeholders led to the massive conflict of interest and spates among the members of the group. Increased coordination among the members of the group is extremely important, an example is where the local people irrigating the farms were requested by the government of the state to breed fishes in the same farm. Without knowing that the fishes were being irrigated along with the crops, the local authorities sprayed DDT in the irrigated farms. This further led to the killing of the fishes. This instance highlights the importance of the communication strategies. Due to the bad communication strategies, the community project failed, leading to major diseconomies for the people at large. Thus, the analysis of the data highlights that the participative groups, where the community officers work in coordination with the clan leaders, the achievement of the group goals is far more easier and convenient for the community. The extensive literature highlights that the construction of the Harambee High School, with participants from the clan, family heads, individuals, and women of all groups has been highly successful, building of the maternity clinics by the group of women leaders, clan leaders has been highly successful, compost making by the communities and farmers has been highly unsuccessful, destocking by the government officials has been a failure, adoption of the cotton communal plantations has been a failure, the maintenance of the irrigation channels has failed, adoption of early maize maturing crop has been a failure, and land allocation to the immigrants has been successful, to name a few. Most of these projects are based upon the age-old indigenous practices and beliefs. The cultural factors provide the coherence and continuity to these kinds of initiatives. The narratives and culture have an important role to play in setting the trajectory of development, and this helps to bridge the gap between past, present, and future. The shared experience of the community development programmes, like Harambee, helps to create shared experience that paves the way for the future development. The major factor impacting the success or failure of the social projects is the communication strategy and the type of leadership. Fig. 45 highlights the various factors impacting the success of Harambee community groups.

Fig. 45. Factors Impacting Success of Harambee Community Groups.
Source: Author's own work.

3. Case Study – Chamas Community Lending Programmes

Chama means the group or body in Kiswahili, which means an informal savings group, or in simple words, a group. In the 1980s, the economic struggles started in East Africa and the origins of Chamas are said to be the Harambee community lending groups, which mean all together. Within these community lending groups, the members contribute the money each period in order to help each other to grow and become financially sustainable. These chamas operate on the principle of all work together, like a merry-go-round. Every period, the members contribute a fixed sum, which is amassed to create a pool of savings. These community groups are marked by a strong sense of friendship and comradery. These groups are formed by the people, who already know each other, due to same domicile, class mates, or profession. Indeed, the chamas self-help groups were prevalent in 1960 as well, where member used to accumulate the savings from each other and these groups became investment groups for economic empowerment and attainment of sustainable development. Earlier studies highlight that the Kenyan society is a traditional society, which is overburdened with old traditions and customs that could lead to the marginalization of the poor women in the society. However, the social innovations, such as *Chamas*, enable the women to get access to credit and financial resources through the pooling of the resources. These social formats enable the women to expand their social networks and acquire necessary life skills and livelihood traits. Thus, the chamas help to financially empower the people at the bottom of the pyramid. These community lending groups provide a social space for the members to meet together, beyond the work place and networks and through the informal banking system, the members not only become shareholder in each other's future but also improvise the financial habits of the other members in the group. Various studies reveal that the Chamas are the community institutional designs that enable the marginalized women without access to collateral to access credit and loans from the banks and financial institutions. Due to stereotyping, social norms, and roles, the women are often excluded from the mainstream finance and credit provided by the banks and financial institutions. Chamas are formed by the marginalized women, who are in poverty, to get access to the financial resource. During the social interactions among each other required for the performance of the duties of the members of the self-help groups, the members generate social capital, which works as a cushion for seeking access to finance. The analysis of the data from the existing studies highlights that when the individual women in these groups come out to participate in Chamas, this gives rise to the interaction between the social realities of the members of the group and the complexities of social world like stereotypes and perceived notions. These interactions lead to reinforcing thoughts and perceptions, and in case of negative interactions, these thoughts and experience take the form of negative values that lead to distractions and decline of savings within the community lending groups. Thus, the shared experiences that members of the group develop with each other have a far-reaching impact upon the sustainability and profitability of the community lending groups. Thus, the social innovations are leading to marginal and incremental improvement in the livelihood of the poor women and such changes are not revolutionaries, rather are incremental. The intersectionality of social realities of marginalized, that include racial oppression, denial of employment opportunities are born out of the structural imbalances of power, which is embedded within the institutional design of the financial services providers. Thus, the external factors such as structural inequalities in the form of caste discrimination and gender discrimination have a negative impact on the living standard of these women. Dismantling of the existing power hegemonies possessed by the structural hegemonies such as the heads of formal financial institutions and inclusion through network structure such as community lending organizations enables the marginalized to get financially included through the access to social capital. These structural inequalities embedded within the community structures are the form of marginalizations. The hierarchy of relationship among the member in rigid financial institutional relationships such as credit providers like bank and members is replaced by the co-optation and cooperation among the members of the group. The study of literature highlights that the trainings, leadership, communication, financial planning, and book keeping have a far-reaching impact on the financial performance of the community lending programmes. Generally, the community lending groups with good leaders are found to be more financially sustainable and institutionally sustainable. The leadership, social intermediation, and communication help to improve the credit terms, credit control, client policy, and credit appraisal for the marginalized and the people at the bottom of the pyramids.

The literature highlights that generally the banks are unwilling to provide loans to the people at the bottom of the pyramid due to the risk of default and lack of information about the credit worthiness of the poor. In the case of the Chamas, the credit policy in the form of providing loan only to the people from the same social background, profession, or some type of homogeneity has helped the community lending groups to achieve financial sustainability. In order to provide for the lack of collateral, the social capital generated in the groups plays an extremely important role to facilitate sustainability of the groups. Through 5 Cs model, *C Collateral* in community lending groups is replaced by the social capital, *character* is supported by the a priori knowledge about the credit riskiness of the members, in the form of homogenity of profession, geographic presence to name a few. *Capacity* refers to the ability of the members to repay back the loan and the mutual guarantee and the ability adds to the capability of the members to repay back their loans in time. *Condition* refers to the external environment such as the macro-economic parameters and state policy. The intervention by the banks enables the members of the groups in Chamas to access loans and credit. Within a semi-formal financial organization like chamas, the diversity of financial goals often leads to various conflicts and adverse use of the peer pressure. Because of joint liability, if one of the members defaults, then all the members apply the social pressure to ensure the recovery of loans, which leads to conflicts in situation where the member is genuinely unable to collect enough money to repay their loans. In this kind of situation, there is a need for a good credit policy and state intervention to protect the interest of the group as well as the members of the group. This kind of experience, where values of the group are at odds with the values or condition of the members of the group is an example of tensions in organization that impede its effectiveness. If a group is flexible and adaptive, the group can train easily and social intermediation can play an important role to enable the members to adhere to group norms and achieve financial sustainability. Chamas, which are more internally focussed with leaders, who pay thrust on financial prudence, financial discipline, and appreciate state role in development are generally performing better, as compared the groups which are competitive, externally focussed and are not cooptative of cooperative. Thus, through the theoretical lens of CVF, a clan behaviour, where the members of the groups and their leaders act as facilitator or mentor, has come to play an important role in the financial growth and sustainability of the groups. Whereas the failure of the community groups can be attributed to the hierarchal structural institutional designs where the leader is focussed on controlling and monitoring the behaviour of the members, adhocracy, or market, which is marked by the competing values and spirit. Thus, on a competing framework, with state intervention and training, internally focussed groups that exhibit clan behaviour are more sustainable and successful as compared to the externally focussed groups.

4. Conclusion

Community lending programmes are the vehicles for facilitating the access to finance for the people at the bottom of the pyramid, particularly women. Tradition of Harambee community groups in Kenya has been existing since 1970 and has been instrumental in empowering the people at the bottom of the pyramid. This type of community lending tradition also gave rise to the Chamas group lending, which has enabled many people at the bottom of the pyramid to get access to finance and credit to earn livelihood and sustainable growth and employment. Through the theoretical lens of CVF, various external factors such as state policy and interventions have a vast impact upon the functioning of these groups. Moreover, the internal dynamics such as good leadership and communication strategies has a vast impact on the success of the group lending programmes.

References

Chitere, P. (2018). Self-help groups as a means for development and welfare: Their characteristics, membership and performance in Kenya. *International Journal of Social Work and Human Services Practice*, *6*, 30–45. http://doi.org/10.13189/ijrh.2018.060202

Geertz (1973). *The interpretation of cultures*. Basic Books.

Johnson, S. (2004). The impact of microfinance institutions in local financial markets: A case study from Kenya. *Journal of International Development*, *16*(3), 501–517.

Muasya, C. K. (2013). *Factors influencing the success of women self-help groups in Pumwani informal settlements* [Master's thesis]. University of Nairobi, Nairobi. UoN Digital Repository. http://erepository.uonbi.ac.ke/bitstream/handle/11295/63484.

Quinn, R. E., & Rohrbaugh, J. (1981). A competing values approach to organizational effectiveness. *Public Productivity Review*, *5*(2), 122–140.

Quinn, R. E., & Rohrbaugh, J. (1983). A spatial model of effectiveness criteria: Towards a competing values approach to organizational analysis. *Management Sciences*, *29*(3), 363–377.

Rowe, A. J., Mason, R. O., Dickel, K. E., Mann, R. B., & Mockler, R. J. (1994). *Strategic management: A methodological approach* (4th ed.). Addison-Wesley.

Chapter 8

Empirical Analysis of Collectives and Microfinance Initiatives in Financial Inclusion

Abstract

Most microfinance and group lending projects in India suffer financial sustainability challenges. The formal financial institutions are hesitant to lend money to microborrowers due to a lack of collateral and a lack of knowledge about the creditworthiness of the poor. The virtues of social capital and social collateral have enabled financial sustainability. No research has been done to assess the impact of other parameters such as portfolio risk on delinquency of loans supplied by microfinance institutions (MFIs). Similarly, there is a dearth of research that examines the many elements that influence microborrowers' operational and financial self-sufficiency in the Indian economy. There is a dearth of research to assess the impact of geographical disparities, profit, bank size, MFI age, and capital asset ratio on the organisations' financial sustainability. The study's data were obtained from the Mix Market database. For the goal of analysis, a dynamic, punctuated equilibrium theory and a resource-based view were used. Operational self-sufficiency was calculated using the average loan gross domestic product (GDP) per capita, the number of active borrowers, and the percentage of female borrowers for this study. The number of female borrowers and the portfolio at risk (PAR) have a negative impact on the microfinance organizations' operational self-sufficiency. MFIs' operational self-sufficiency improves as a result of financial revenue. The type of MFI and its location have an impact on the MFI's operational self-sufficiency.

Keywords: Microfinance; operational self-sufficiency; outreach; group lending; formal finance

Global Perspectives on Financial Inclusion: Case Studies in Microfinance and Women's Empowerment, 207–236

doi:10.1108/978-1-83708-080-920251008

1. Introduction

Globally there are 1.7 billion people who do not have any access to financial services. These people are financially excluded and do not have access to physical collateral. Formal financial institutions do not have any information about the creditworthiness of the rural poor. Till the 1990s, most of the microfinance services were donor-based. This programme was aimed at providing the access to financial services at the doorstep of the people. Due to the economic depression, the reforms were introduced in the 1990s and National Bank for Agriculture and Rural Development (NABARD) introduced the self-help group (SHG) bank linkage programme. This programme aimed to leverage the social capital and social collateral to provide access to the rural poor at their doorsteps. Despite all efforts, this programme suffered from the lack of financial sustainability, and banks providing finance suffered from asset quality deterioration and nonperforming assets. Increasingly, this semi-formal organization structure suffered from the lack of institutional sustainability in terms of lack of adherence to group norms such as maintenance of books of accounts, attendance at the group meetings, and record keeping. The problem of sustainability is often referred to as the issue of outreach and financial sustainability. UN Sustainable Development Goals have adopted Women Empowerment and Poverty reduction as one of the Millennium Development Goals. In this regard, India has adopted financial inclusion as one of the indicators for the achievement of Sustainable Development Goals.

2. Literature Review

(a) *Definition of sustainability*: According to the literature, defining and measuring sustainability is a challenge since sustainability is not quantitative. In the evolving global world order, sustainable development is a major theme. Sustainability does not have the required ideological conditions in the current scenario. Sustainability has become a development theme for international aid organizations. Sustainability is an important term, but it is paradoxically a hollow idea with no real meaning, and it is associated with paternalistic ideological attitudes and content. The lack of metrics for sustainable development makes it difficult to track progress. The conflict is between politics and science; structural flaws must be identified, and organic versus dehumanization must be examined. Serving human needs while keeping natural capital within biological constraints is a dynamic concept. According to the author, hierarchical and rigid organizational structures are commonly rejected, and behavioural solutions that encourage cooperative decision-making to minimize conflict and promote equity and diversity reduce conflict and promote equity and diversity. The authors argue that sustainable development is not the same as growth, notwithstanding the perils of unrelenting growth without development. Unrelenting expansion, according to the author, diverts human resources away from achieving goals and towards chasing selfish human interests, making sustainable development a key goal. Sustainable development, for example, is built on paradigms and frameworks, which provide a theoretical framework within which we can construct laws. The concept of sustainability is context-dependent, according to Lélé (1991). According to the authors, the definition of sustainable development varies depending on the situation. The term 'sustainable' refers to the ability to maintain growth and development in its most literal sense. It also refers to the growth and transformation process. As a result, according to the text, long-term growth is required for sustainable development. Sustainability is defined as the preservation of objects on an ecological basis, whereas social sustainability is defined as the preservation of human existence on a social basis. According to the author, sustainable development refers to a change process that can last indefinitely. Lélé (1991) defined sustainable development as a type of development that is both economically viable and socially relevant. What defines sustainable development is a point of contention. According to the author, development is uneven, and the goal of development and environmental concerns are mutually exclusive. The authors define sustainable growth as 'sustainable growth', 'sustainable development', or 'sustainable change'. It is sustainable if it can continue indefinitely. The term 'sustainable development' refers to changes that can be maintained indefinitely. Long-term economic growth and sustainable development, according to the author, do not contribute to social welfare. Geographical concentration of activity largely demonstrates weaknesses in the idea of 'sustainable development'. To ensure that the benefits of development reach the intended beneficiaries, greater participatory development and grassroots participation are essential (Barbier, 1987). The term 'sustainability' has evolved to mean ecological sustainability or the maintenance of natural conditions and renewable resources to protect human life for future generations. Environmental insufficiency or the inadequacy of social systems may be caused or rooted in social issues. When institutions are unable to preserve the social structures, institutions, cultures, or traits that are essential to maintain the present social structures, institutional sustainability becomes immensely vital and significant. The literature has emphasized the necessity of technological and resource roots to ensure long-term growth. Schaller and Maass (1989) define sustainability as the ability to develop indefinitely and profitably without causing harm to the environment. In 1972, the term 'sustainability' was coined to refer to the future and the utilization of resources in such a way that future generations will have access to them (Kidd, 1992). The five different dimensions of development are ecological capacity root, resource/environment root, biosphere root, technology root, and ecodevelopment root. The United Nations recently approved the Sustainable Development Goal of poverty reduction and women's empowerment through financial inclusion.

2.1. Institutional Sustainability

Institutional sustainability refers to the existence of the institutional structures and designs or processes as defined by the Resource theory and relates to the availability of resources and means for achieving the organization's goals. It refers to the observable processes and structures that enable the organizations to achieve sustained capabilities in the form of optimum utilization of resources (Maher & Gustafson, 2010). It's also on the UN's list of sustainable development indicators (Spangenberg, 2002).

(b) *Theoretical lens of dynamic punctuated equilibrium*: Sustainability is described as a dynamic balance between natural inputs and outputs that has been influenced by external events such as climatic events and natural disasters. There are few markers to measure the sustainability of complex social systems. Punctuated equilibrium in policymaking refers to a time of status growth and equilibrium followed by revolutionary bursts of incrementalism. The author claims that incremental alterations disrupt the equilibrium and stability that has been developed through time. Dynamic punctuated equilibrium is an extremely significant viewpoint and perspective in any form of social welfare scenario. In their research study, Baumgartner et al. (2006) emphasized the importance of this paradigm in public policy. SHG bank connection is a NABARD activity in the context of microfinance. Only the savings group is financially viable during the early stages of group development. Credit-linked groups sometimes struggle to stay afloat either because of a lack of institutional mechanisms and adherence to group norms or because of the groups' inability to repay the loans. In this case, proper legislative measures such as intermediation and financial literacy and digital literacy training pave the path for the initiative's financial viability.

2.1.1. The Resource-based View of Sustainability

Robinson (2001) has referred to sustainability from two perspectives, that is, donor-based and sustainable finance. The author argues that the continuous supply of funds by the donor could lead to instability in the system. From the resource-based perspective (Barney, 1991), the OECD manual for 1969 elucidates that the institutional unsustainability and financial unsustainability are mainly due to the lack of resources and processes. This article particularly deals with the Sustainable Development Goal to achieve financial inclusion through the SHG bank linkage programme.

As a result, unsustainability is defined as the difficulty of putting in place proper processes, such as bookkeeping, record keeping, and meetings, to assure financial and institutional sustainability. The absence of resources and processes is the primary cause of failure in most financially unsustainable SHGs. This is a problem of strategic management and planning, with insufficient financial and organizational resources. During the period of stability, the resources required for the SHG bank linkage in terms of organizational capabilities such as trained staff, credit, seed capital, and literate, and digitally capable personnel is not a problem. Furthermore, the researchers suggest that resource availability is context-dependent (Barney, 1991). During a crisis, the availability of resources such as skilled employees and capital changes. The valuable, rare, imitable, and organization structure and processes in the form of social capital can be a source of competitive advantage when viewed

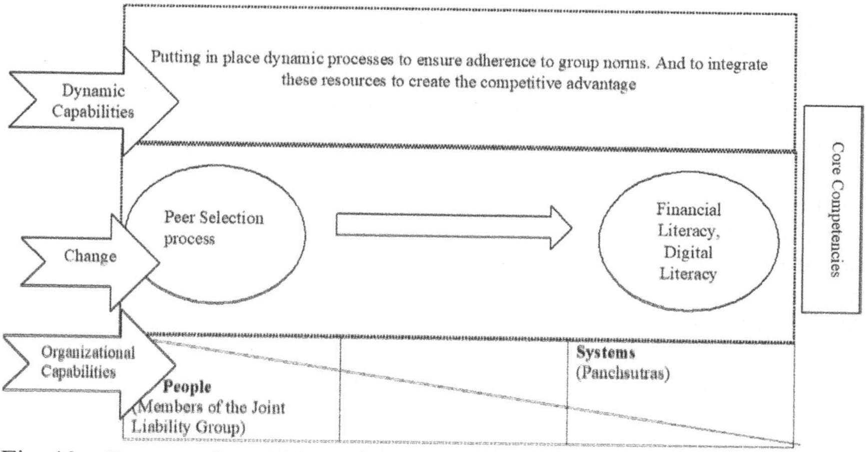

Fig. 46. Resource-based View of SHG Bank Linkage.

through the theoretical lens of resource-based view. The social capital in a SHG refers to the relationship among the members of the group. In this aspect, the microborrowers benefit from the SHG linkage programme. This semi-formal organization can provide finance to the individuals at the bottom of the pyramid by utilizing rare, non-imitable, and valuable social capital. Despite all of the claims, the members of the group still face a problem in terms of long-term viability. There are no institutional structures in place to ensure that books of account are kept up to date, records are kept, and members of the group conform to group standards. This might be contrasted to revolutionary bursts, with progressive improvements such as training and social intermediation being implemented.

Fig. 46 provides the resource-based view of the SHG bank linkage. In a joint liability group scenario, the major resources of the group are composed of the people, who are members of the joint liability group, the institutional mechanisms which comprise the adherence to the group norms. These group norms are the organizational capabilities and the peer mechanism refers to change management. Dynamic capabilities refer to the abilities of the system to integrate the resources to create a competitive advantage.

(c) *Sustainability and microfinance*: Bell and Morse (2008) mention that a large number of women in rural India live below the poverty line. As per the author, the problem of institutional unsustainability is linked to the lack of money. The authors argue that as the loans are to be provided to the poor at a higher frequency and in a much smaller size, this leads to an increase in the processing costs. Thomas (1992) and Soyibo (1996) argue that the banks are not interested in providing finance to the poor people who do not have an access to the resources in terms of physical collateral and banks also lack information about the credit worthiness of the poor. Most of the poor borrowers are dependent on subsidies. This refers to the principle of self-sufficiency. Many of the authors mention that the subsidy dependence index can be used to measure sustainability. Very many banks globally such as Bank Rakyat Indonesia Unit Desa (BUD) have adopted the subsidy independence index as an indicator of financial sustainability. Many other indicators have been adopted by the financial institutions include several savings accounts held, the amount saved, and loan repayment. Berenbach and Guzman (1994) has mentioned the minimalist approach of microcredit as an approach, whereby the revenue earned is sufficient to cover the costs of production. The objective of this approach is to minimize the cost of operation and the cost of loan defaulting. Hulme and Mosley (1996) have defined sustainability as financial sustainability, which is to cover the cost of finance, and social intermediation which is to be donor or subsidy based. From the systems perspective, sustainability refers to the transformation when the systems work collaboratively towards the achievement of the goals. Senge (1994) further promotes the importance of learning organizations. Overall, for a semi-formal organization structure like a SHG, the principles of sustainability can be enumerated as social equity, financial sustainability, and environmental sustainability.

Fig. 47 discusses the three basic tenets of the principle of sustainability, which comprise social equity, environment sustainability, and economic sustainability. In this regard, the study seeks to explore the issue of economic sustainability as financial sustainability and institutional sustainability. Economic sustainability as per the literature refers to the impact of the SHG linkage programme on economic welfare. This includes financial sustainability, which is whether the cost is covered by the revenues of the business. Besides that, it also covers the issue of institutional sustainability, which refers to the internal processes and procedures in a semi-formal organization like SHG linkage. Institutional sustainability, which refers to the adherence to the group norms such as maintenance of attendance registers, bookkeeping, attendance at the meetings helps in increasing the financial sustainability of the SHG.

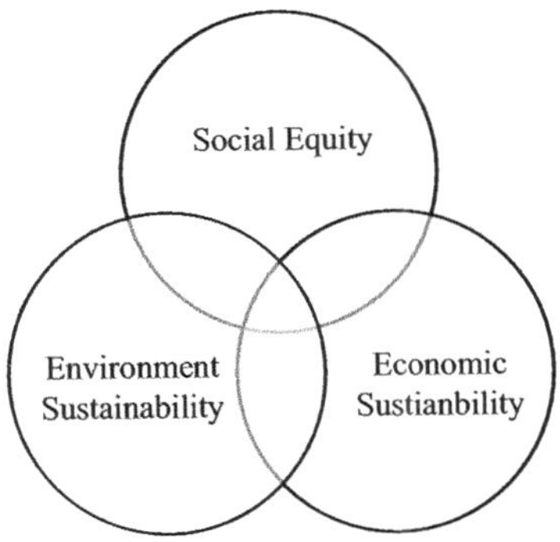

Fig. 47. Principle of Sustainability.

3. Indian Scenario

Globally, approximately 1.7 billion poor people are below the poverty line and they do not have access to finance due to a lack of physical collateral. Banks are not willing to lend loans to the poor due to information asymmetry, as banks do not have information about the micropoor. In 1992, NABARD introduced the SHG bank linkage scheme to provide financial services to the poor. However, this scheme has been fraught with challenges including financial and institutional unsustainability (Das & Guha, 2019). There is a need for assessment of the resources and financial planning to achieve the objectives of the groups. Zeller & Meyer (2002) refer to the triangle of microfinance as financial sustainability, outreach, and impact. The author argues that there are two approaches to microfinance. One is the minimalist approach, in which only microcredit is provided to the rural poor and there is a holistic approach, which aims at providing microcredit and other services such as insurance and other financial services. von Pischke (1996) argues that matching the demand for microfinance with the supply has been a constraint for the MFIs due to the lack of collateral and lack of trustworthiness. Further as per Yaron and Benjamin (1997), the traditional approach to finance which is composed of the donor or subsidy-based model has been replaced with a new paradigm that emerged in (Adams et al., 2008) the 1990s and was mainly aimed at sustainable finance to serve the poor. The success of microfinance initiatives such as the Unit Desa system of Bank Rakyat Indonesia, Grameen Bank, and Banc Sol in Bolivia gave rise to sustainable finance. As per the extant literature, the new paradigm attributes the financial unsustainability of microfinance to information asymmetry (Stiglitz & Weiss, 1981). The challenge of information asymmetry has been identified as moral hazard and adverse selection. As per the researchers, the institutional innovation of joint group lending provides a panacea to the issues of moral hazard and adverse selection. As per the joint group lending is as per (Mosley & Hulme, 1998) the joint group lending is based on trade off between the depth (reach poorest of the poor) and becoming financially sustainable. Group lending is based on the rationale of declining average transaction cost per borrower, which leads to an optimal trade-off between outreach and financial sustainability.

3.1. Trade-off Between Outreach and Financial Performance

There are various approaches to study the issue of sustainability, that is, the old paradigm that refers to the donor-based subsidized model and the newer paradigm which refers to the sustainable finance. Till 1980s, the approach adopted by the rural financial system was the poverty lending approach which works on the principle of reduction of poverty and social welfare. Most of the formal financial institutions are unwary to lend to the poor due to the lack of the information about the poor, lack of adequate return, lack of physical collateral, and increasing cost of lending to the poor (Armendariz & Morduch, 2010). Lender perspective refers to the need for a collateral and adequate return with information about the borrower and borrower perspective is access to finance at lower rates. In light of this argument, the first objective of the microfinance is to reach to the poorest of the poor, which is referred to as outreach. And hence, most of the formal financial institutions including MFIs are wary to lend to the poor. Most of the formal financial organizations are not willing to lend to the poor due to the lack of return on investment (ROI) (Mosley & Hulme, 1998). This leads to the mission drift and most of the formal financial institutions have to choose between the ROI and the outreach to the poor. Conning (1999) highlights the trade-off between outreach and sustainability. Despite all the perils of operating in a high-cost industry like MFIs in the form of interest rates, most of the MFIs are able to achieve the higher rate of repayment from the clients. Most of the literature highlights the trade-off between the outreach and financial performance. The authors (Navajas et al., 2000; Schreiner, 2002) assert that due to the small size of the loans, the transaction cost of the smaller loan is on average higher than the larger loans. Lélé (1991) highlighted the role of financial intermediation in achieving sustainability.

Most of the microloan borrowers do not have the physical collateral and they lack information about the creditworthiness of the poor. It is highlighted that the social innovation like group lending drastically reduces the cost of the lending to the poor. Overall, the issue of outreach has been further discussed as the breadth and the depth of outreach. Breadth of outreach refers to the number of people reached by the MFIs and expressed as the fraction of total borrowers. Depth of outreach is the measure of reaching out to the poorer of the poor and it also refers to the lack of information about the poor client. The proxy used for the outreach is the average loan per borrower (ALBG). Hisako (2009) makes use of the average loan size per borrower as the proxy for the outreach. Though, with the emergence of new paradigm there is a shift towards the attainment of the goal of financial sustainability; most of the MFIs, despite commercialization and market access, do not possess any kind of information about the poor, which leads to lack of financial sustainability. Markets have yet not fully developed to facilitate the access to finance for the poorest of the poor. Mahapatra and Dutta (2016) highlight the size of loan per borrower and ALBG, cost per borrower, and yield per portfolio as indicators of sustainability. Srinivasan (2008) mentioned the frequency of loans or number of active borrowers (NAB) as indicator of sustainability, and Armendariz and Morduch (2010) highlight the gross loan portfolio or amount of loan as indicator of financial sustainability. In addition to this, Pati (2008) identified the operational self-sufficiency ratio (OSSR) and financial self-sufficiency ratio (FSSR) which refer to the ratio of operating profits to cost as an indicator of financial sustainability. In light of difficulty in earning ROI, the extant literature (Hisako, 2009; Weiss & Montgomery, 2005) argue that the MFIs have to eventually decrease the depth and increase the credit to large clients to meet their ROI. Yaron and Manos (2010) highlight that MFIs have over the period of time started evolving business models to reduce the cost of lending and monitoring to the poor.

Indian MFIs have been able to achieve higher repayment despite high transactions costs. This does not take into account the administrative costs. Reaching the poor is an extremely difficult proposition and microfinance offers an opportunity. Indian banks lend to the SHGs and there is a higher default rate as far as the external funds are concerned. SHGs are linked to the Federations and collect savings from the members. Deininger and Liu (2013) highlight the importance of economic and non-economic indicators in enhancing the outreach and impact of the microfinance. Norton (1992) defines the financial sustainability of an organization as its ability to be operational even when donor aid is withdrawn. Fowler (2000) has defined financial sustainability as continuity and security. He defines financial sustainability as the recognition of the work of the semi-formal organizations to the extent that there is no need to raise the funds. The author highlights that only financial sustainability is not sufficient for the success of the business model of semi-formal institutes like SHGs, there is a need for impact, resource management, and resource reorganization. There is a need for a core financial strategy based on financial discipline, ethics, skill-building, and communication to ensure financial sustainability. Besides ensuring the regular inflow of funds that is commensurate with the outflow of funds, there is a need for the monitoring of the activities to ensure the financial sustainability of the system. Often, many researchers call the basic principles of financial sustainability as access to capital, profitability, reporting, planning, and monitoring. León (2001) in her report has mentioned that semi-formal organizations are unable to achieve financial sustainability not due to the lack of creativity but due to the lack of vision and commitment. León (2001) argues that the basic pillars of financial sustainability are strategic and financial planning, income diversification, sound administration of finance, and own income generation. Thus, it highlights the need for budgeting, financial control, administration, and bookkeeping to achieve financial sustainability. Strategic planning helps to achieve the goals. Operational self-sufficiency is calculated as a ratio of operating profit to the net profit and FSS is the total expenses divided by the net profit, and it is used as the indicator of operational self-sufficiency (Pati, 2008).

4. Objectives of Sustainability

As per Yaron and Benjamin (1997), the traditional approach to microfinance depended mostly on donor-based finance, and in this scenario as per Zeller and Meyer (2002), the MFIs faced the trade-off between financial sustainability and depth outreach. In quantitative terms, it referred to the trade-off between the social benefits and social costs. Most of the research studies have adopted the subsidy operational index as the measurement tool for this objective. Microfinance leads to social benefits such as poverty reduction, gender empowerment, and social costs and is the alternative use of the funds deployed for microfinance. Most often than not, literature refers to financial sustainability as synonymous with economic sustainability. However, financial sustainability refers to the financial viability of the institution of microfinancing, or joint liability groups, which

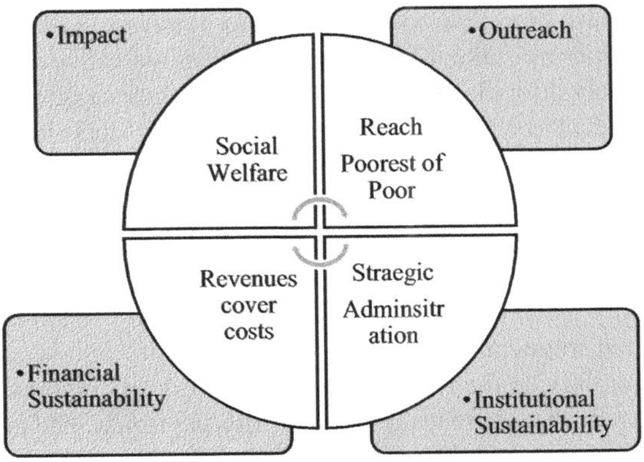

Fig. 48. Objectives of SHGs.

implies the profits and costs. Whereas economic sustainability refers to the economic impact of microfinancing.

In this study, we propose a hybrid model of sustainability that combines the financial and economic sustainability of joint liability groups. Another aspect of sustainability is institutional sustainability that refers to organizational resilience and regeneration. Thus, the study proposes a four-dimensional quadrant of sustainability, which includes outreach, impact, financial sustainability, and institutional sustainability. As per the authors, the microfinancing initiatives always strive to achieve a trade-off between these four objectives.

Fig. 48 describes the objectives of the SHGs.

4.1. Environment and Macroeconomic Conditions

In this research study, we have adopted a four-pronged approach to sustainability, which comprises assessment of financial sustainability, institutional sustainability, impact, and outreach. Financial sustainability refers to operational self-sufficiency. Institutional sustainability refers to the adherence to the group norms, which comprise maintenance of books of accounts, record keeping, and attendance. Outreach refers to the breadth or number of microborrowers catered to and depth refers to the poorest of the poor. Impact refers to the contribution to social welfare in terms of social equity and equitable distribution of wealth.

Thus, MFIs can achieve high depth and breadth simultaneously. The literature argues that the financial sustainability of MFIs depends on the characteristics of MFIs and the macroeconomic environment. Robinson (2001) has highlighted the trade-off between financial sustainability and welfare. Hermes and Lensink (2011) emphasize that the institutions seeking financial sustainability tend to achieve this by reducing the cost of operation and generating enough income to meet the cost of loan outstanding. Rajdev et al. (2013) and Woller, Dunford and Woodworth (1999) argue that the financial institutions seeking financial sustainability do not cater to the poor people and divert funds to meet the demand of the rich entrepreneurs. As per the literature, there is no unanimity on the trade-off between outreach and sustainability. Hermes and Lensink (2011) argue that there is a trade-off between financial sustainability and outreach. Other studies such as Ayayi and Sene (2008) do not find a trade-off between sustainability and outreach.

4.1.1. Measured to Achieve Institutional Outreach and Financial Sustainability

The authors (Ayayi & Sene, 2008; Honohan, 2004; Mersland & Strøm, 2009; Narayana & Pati, 2012) examine the impact of firm size, expenditure control, and mode of governance to explain financial sustainability. Besides the characteristic of MFIs, literature also examines the role of the macroeconomic environment through factors such as inflation status, economic growth per capita, and human capital development on financial sustainability (Cull et al., 2009; Kai, 2009). Hartarska (2005) and Mersland and Strøm (2009) define the role of size, management quality, and governance in impacting outreach and financial sustainability. There are very few studies that seek to analyse the impact of macroeconomic factors such as competition on the financial sustainability of the poor. McIntosh and Wydick (2005) and Olivares-Polanco (2005) highlight that competition adversely impacts the outreach of financial services to the poor. There is a lack of studies that measure the impact of various factors such as PAR, financial revenue ratio, personnel ratio, age of MFI, loan balance, and percentage of women staff on the financial sustainability of MFIs in India.

5. Indicators of Financial Sustainability

Most MFIs measure financial sustainability through the OSSR which is aimed at ensuring that the cost of finance or cost of loans is covered by the number of profits or the income generated (Hartarska & Nadolnyak, 2007). The other measures of financial sustainability are return on assets (ROA) and return on equity (ROE). To measure the depth and outreach, different measures are used. One of the important measures for depth is the average amount of loan outstanding (Luzzi & Weber, 2007; Olivares-Polanco, 2005) and breadth of outreach is the number of female borrowers (Hartarska & Nadolnyak, 2007; Mersland & Strøm, 2009).

6. Synergies Between the Sustainability Objectives

Nguyen et al. argue that there is an apparent synergy between the varied objectives of group lending institutions in terms of outreach, impact, financial sustainability, and institutional sustainability. Zeller et al. (1997) discuss the social benefit–cost ratio as the indicator of the economic sustainability or impact of an institutional innovation like group lending. As per the extant literature, there are three major ways to achieve financial sustainability through credit generation for undertaking income-generating activities, strategic financial management of assets with the group, promoting the saving and thrift habits among the poor, and strategic financial planning to plan for future through the preparation of budgets. Yaron (1992) and Christen et al. (1995) argue that most of the indicators of financial sustainability mainly assume the breadth of financial services or the number of loans made as to the indicator of financial sustainability. There is no study on the depth of financial sustainability or the impact of these loans. Navajas et al. and Zeller et al. (1997) provide the index to measure the depth of the financial sustainability of the microfinance initiatives like joint liability groups. Diagne (1999) highlights the impact of microfinance initiatives on the welfare of the members of the joint liability groups.

As per many research studies, the impact of microfinance can be gauged through the increase in income and increased acquisition of income-generating assets. As per the literature (Zeller et al., 1997) considering the depth of sustainability, the stakeholders for microfinance are the 'Poorest of the Poor'. These people do not have access to finance and suffer from a lack of physical collateral. The formal financial institutions do not have information about the creditworthiness of the poor. These people need the microfinance for (1) credit requirement for income generation and microfinance to provide for insurance as well, (2) savings requirements, and (3) microcredit for consumption. Diagne (1999) mentions that in the rural areas the poorest of the poor mainly depend on informal savings, and microfinance helps to replace informal finance with formal finance.

Microloans given for consumption purposes have a higher probability of default and cannot be monitored. And loans given for the production purpose can be diverted to consumption purposes.

7. Research Problem

This study mainly deals with the impact of various factors such as outreach, capital asset ratio, size of firm, maturity of firm, deposits, type of MFIs, and regions on financial sustainability of MFIs. It also seeks to measure how in context of Indian economy yield impacts the financial sustainability and operational sustainability of firm. It seeks to measure the impact of yield and delinquency on PAR for the MFI. PAR is mentioned as loan greater than 30 days.

H1. Financial sustainability does not necessarily lead to the outreach of microfinance. This hypothesis seeks to measure the impact of financial sustainability on the outreach of the firm.

H2. In the case of the Indian economy, yield does not have any impact on OSSR and FSSR.

H3. Delinquency and yield on portfolio do not have any impact on PAR.

H4. PAR, financial revenue ratio, personnel expense ratio, the age of MFIs, the average loan balance, the percentage of women borrowers, and the number of women borrowers per loan on operational sustainability of MFIs do not have an impact on operational sustainability of MFIs.

8. Data Methodology

The data for the research have been downloaded from the MIX Market database provided by the World Bank. This database seeks to compare and analyse the performance of MFIs in most of the developing nations of the world. After the transition from the mix market dataset to the World Bank Catalogue, this database is the largest information provider. Data about the performance indicators of the MFIs are provided in this database.

9. Data Analysis

H1. Various factors such as type of MFIs, geographic regions, age of the MFIs, asset, loan portfolio, deposits, and loans do not have any impact on financial sustainability (financial sustainability is in form of average loan GDP per capita, percentage of female borrowers, and NAB).

9.1. Dependent Variables

In this study, we have taken two dependent variables: sustainability and outreach. Sustainability refers to the financial performance that is endured forever. To design an indicator for sustainability, one has to assume that sustainability refers to a scenario, where MFIs can operate profitably and does not require the support of donor-based or subsidy-based funds. Operating self-sufficiency (OSS) refers to the ability of the MFI to meet its expenses within its operational revenues (Hartarska & Nadolnyak, 2007). In the study, we have used two measures for outreach, depth, and breadth. The average loan outstanding is used to measure the depth and the number of female borrowers is used to measure the breadth of the microfinance. We have used the average loan outstanding as the depth and number of female borrowers as the measure of the breadth of the MFIs (Luzzi & Weber, 2007; Olivares-Polanco, 2005).

9.2. Independent Variables

The governance mechanism has an impact on the financial sustainability of the MFIs. The researches (Ahlin et al., 2011; Cull et al., 2013; Hartarska & Nadolnyak, 2007; Hermes et al., 2011) in their study have mentioned the importance of the governance mechanism in defining the performance of the MFI. Ownership structure, lending methodology, and governance mechanism are taken into account for analysis.

9.3. Descriptive Statistics

Descriptive statistics for the financial sustainability of MFIs are mentioned above. The table mentions the descriptive statistics for the OSSR, ALBG per capita, percent of female borrowers, NAB, capital asset ratio, assets as a proxy for the size of the MFI, deposits, and gross loan portfolio of total assets.

Table 18. Definition of Variables.

OSS refers to operational self-sufficiency as a measure of how well the revenues or the profits cover the cost of the project.

Average loan per capita refers to the average loan balance per borrower/GNI per capita.

Percentage of female borrowers refers to the NAB who are women.

NAB refers to the logarithm of the NAB, which refers to the number of borrowers who have active loans with the MFIs.

Profit refers to the number of MFIs that are being operated at profit.

Capital refers to the ratio of capital to total assets.

Age refers to the maturity of the group. If the group is formulated after 2010 it is called the mature group; otherwise, it is called the young group.

Loans refer to the ratio of outstanding loans to total assets.

Size refers to the logarithm of the total assets.

Deposits refer to the amount of deposit taken by the members of the group.

Region for each of the regions, the dummy variable was created. In total there are five regions, and Africa is taken as the dummy and all the other regions are taken as dummy variable or dichotomous variable.

	Mean	Median	Minimum	Maximum	Standard Deviation	C.V.	Skewness	Kurtosis
OSSR	1.147	1.108	−1.276	18.436	0.627	0.547	11.10	215.43
Average loan per borrower per capita	312.61	7.12	0.	30,429	1,854.5	5.93	8.86	93.62
Percent of female borrowers	0.7887	0.9301	0	18.50	0.374	0.474	21.11	1,018.8
NAB	2,459.1	2,338.5	1	5,568	1,708.9	0.694	0.156	−1.237
Capital asset ratio	0.2702	0.1972	−18.53	17.75	0.447	1.655	−2.153	873.3
Assets	7.54	7.64	0.00	11.64	1.31	0.173	−1.97	10.46
Deposits	5.06	6.75	0.00	13.43	3.66	0.724	−0.494	−1.412
Gross loan portfolio total assets	0.884	0.785	0.000	126.82	3.06	3.46	36.19	1,376.3

9.4. Outreach of MFIs

> ***H1***. Financial sustainability (operational self-sustainability) does not necessarily lead to the outreach of microfinance. This hypothesis seeks to measure the impact of financial sustainability on the outreach of the firm. Outreach is measured through average loan per GDP, percentage of female borrowers, and NAB.

Table 18 measures the impact of type of MFIs, regions and size, age and deposits on outreach. Outreach as per the literature can be measured as breadth and depth. In our study, we have included a binary variable, that takes the value of '1' if the entity is a profit organization and '0' if it is a non-profit organization. A dummy

Table 19. Outreach of MFIs.

	Average Loan Per GDP Per Capita	**Percentage of Female Borrowers**	**NAB**
Constant	−3,994.26***	0.92***	−372.41**
Profit	90.09**	0.03***	−14.67
Bank		*Base*	
Credit Union	413.06***	−0.065**	−234.57***
NBFI	300.93**	0.100***	240.99***
NGO	382.99***	0.156***	157.06**
Other	506.99**	−0.007	172.98
Rural Bank	2,086.69***	−0.13***	−154.34**
Africa		*Base*	
East Asia and the Pacific	137.65	−0.078*	779.59***
Eastern Europe and Central Asia	−646.65**	−0.071	1,663.23***
Latin America and The Caribbean	−355.65	0.00	2,361.73***
South Asia	−38.51**	−0.06	3,595.92***
Young	299.56***	−0.061***	−333.58***
Capital asset ratio	243.89**	−0.148***	26.77
Size	423.07***	−0.03***	79.17***
Deposits	10.75	0.012***	−2.94
Loans	0.63	0.000	2.48
OSS	146.55***	0.006	−46.23**
Adj. R^2	0.2218	0.096	0.578

***represents significance at 1%; **represents significance at 5%; and ***represents significance at 10%.

variable is also included for the type of banking technology. A dummy variable is included for the individual and solidarity group. Hartarska and Nadolnyak (2007) have prescribed various control variables for financial sustainability and outreach. All the MFIs before the year 2010 are considered to be 'Young' and all the MFIs after the year 2012 are considered to be 'Mature'. Various research studies highlight that the size of the loan has an impact on the financial sustainability of MFIs. The logarithm of total assets is included as a variable to measure the impact of loan size on the financial sustainability of the MFIs (D'Espallier et al., 2011). As per the literature, the deposit taking has a positive impact on the financial sustainability of the MFIs (Caudill et al., 2009). To proxy for this control variable, the ratio of deposits to total assets is taken as the proxy. From the analysis of the data, it becomes apparent that as compared to banks, besides other formal institutions, Credit Union and Rural Bank have maximum impact on the average loan per capita, NBFI and NGO have maximum impact on the NAB and percentage of active borrowers. However, the Credit Union has a negative impact on percentage of female borrowers.

From Table 19, capital asset ratio, size of the microfinance, and OSSR have positive impacts on average loan GDP per capita or institutional outreach of the MFIs. Deposits have a positive impact on the percentage of female borrowers, and size, capital, and young MFIs have a relatively lesser percentage of female borrowers or the outreach. Deposits have a positive impact and young firms are negatively related to the NAB. As compared to Africa, the other four regions have a positive and significant impact on institutional outreach in terms of the number of borrowers. MFIs are more operationally self-sufficient with a smaller NAB and more average GDP per capita.

Thus, we can conclude that there are regional differences in terms of institutional outreach among MFIs. Type of MFIs, capital asset ratio, size of the MFI, deposits, and operational self-sufficiency impact the institutional outreach of the firm.

H2. In the case of the Indian economy, yield does not have any impact on OSSR and FSSR.

Table 20 highlights the empirical analysis for financial sustainability of MFIs and Table 21 highlights the empirical analysis for the impact of yield on PAR.

9.5. Data

For analysis, the data were downloaded for the Indian economy. It comprises a total 562 observations. The dependent variable is the OSSR and FSSR. Independent variables are the age of MFIs, ROAs, NAB, assets, capital ratio, loan to total asset portfolio, yield, and the number of loans outstanding to the SHG.

9.6. Analysis

The objective of the regression is to analyse why some MFIs are more financially sustainable than others. It takes into account the age, ROAs, NAB, assets of the

Table 20. Financial Sustainability of the MFIs.

	OSSR	FSSR	OSSR
Constant	1.18***	0.178***	1.11***
Age	−0.001	−0.001***	−0.005*
ROA	0.61***	0.029***	2.77***
NAB	0.000	−0.000	0.000***
Assets		0.000	−0.000*
Capital ratio	0.09**	0.040***	−0.037
Loan to total asset portfolio	0.001	0.045***	0.00
Yield			0.24**
Number of loans outstanding to SHG			−0.00
Adj. R^2	0.159	0.28	0.65

*** represents significance at 1%; ** represents significance at 5%; and * represents significance at 10%.

Table 21. Impact of Yield on PAR.

	Coefficient
Constant	−3.44***
Log loan delinquency	0.67***
Log NAB	0.76***
Capital asset ratio	0.000
Yield on gross portfolio	−0.49
East Asia Pacific	0.244***
Eastern Europe and Central Asia	−0.156**
Latin America and the Caribbean	−0.833***
Middle East and North America	−0.101
Adj R^2	0.2387

*** represents significance at 1%; ** represents significance at 5%; and * represents significance at 10%.

firm, capital asset ratio, loan to asset portfolio, the yield of the firm, and number of loans outstanding to SHGs. The results show that ROAs positively impact the financial and operational sustainability of MFIs. And older the firm the lesser is the financial sustainability of the firm. Loan to asset portfolio positively impacts the financial sustainability of the MFI and yield has a positive impact on the operational self-sustainability of the MFI. This implies that increase in scale of business for MFIs is supplemented by better repayment rates.

9.7. Delinquency and PAR

H3. Delinquency and yield on portfolio do not have any impact on PAR.

In this analysis, the dependent variable is PAR > 30 days and the independent variables are Log loan delinquency, NAB, capital asset ratio, the yield on the gross portfolio, and different regions of the world. From the analysis of the regression results, it becomes apparent that loan delinquency has a positive impact on PAR. Net active borrowers do have a significant impact on PAR. Both loan delinquency and NAB have been taken as logarithm of the variable.

East Asia Pacific has the highest rate of PAR, whereas Eastern Europe & Central Asia, Latin America, and the Middle East do have a negative impact on the PAR. A portfolio is a challenge in the East Asia Pacific and not a challenge in Eastern Europe, Latin America, and the Middle East.

H4. Operational self-sufficiency is positively related to capital asset ratio, gross loan portfolio to asset ratio, number of borrowers, ROAs, ROE, and yield in gross loan portfolio and negatively related to operating expenses to loan portfolio, PAR, and debt to equity.

OSSR refers to the ratio of operational profits on loan and investment and the operational costs, finance costs, and provision. This operational self-sufficiency is determined by factors such as capital asset ratio, operating expenses to loan ratio, NAB, PAR, gross loan portfolio to total assets, debt to equity, ROAs, ROE, yield in gross loan portfolio. Data for the purpose of analysis were taken from MIX database and composed of observations from the countries of Afghanistan, Bangladesh, Brazil, China, India, Indonesia, Mexico, Nepal, Pakistan, Philippines, Russia, South Africa, Sri Lanka, and Zimbabwe for period 2005–2019.

Table 22 provides an empirical analysis of factors impacting the OSSR.

Table 22. Empirical Analysis of Factors Impacting OSSR.

	Coefficient	**Std. Error**
CAR	0.0499	(0.0362)
OPELP	0.000	(0.0187)
ACTBRW	0.000	(0.000)
PRTRSK	−0.099***	(0.032)
GLPTA	0.0108	(0.0117)
DBTEQ	−0.000**	(0.000)
ROA	1.725***	(0.080)
ROE	0.000	(0.000)
YDGLP	0.150***	(0.064)
CONSTANT	1.062***	(0.280)
Rho	0.565	

*** represents significance at 1%; ** represents significance at 5%; and * represents significance at 10%.

CAR refers to capital asset ratio, OPELP refers to operating expenses to loan portfolio, ACTBRW refers to the active borrowers, PRTRSK refers to PAR > 30 days, GLPTA refers gross loan portfolio to total assets, DBTEQ refers to debt to equity, ROA refers to return to assets, ROE refers to ROE, and YDGLP refers to yield on gross loan portfolio. From the analysis of data, it becomes apparent that the operational self-sufficiency is positively related to the capital asset ratio, ROE, ROAs, yield to gross loan portfolio, and gross loan portfolio to total assets. The results are substantiated by the findings. And results establish that the operational self-sufficiency of MFIs is negatively related to the debt equity ratio, PAR >30 days.

9.8. Model Specification

The fixed effect model has been used in this panel regression model. In this model, the individual effect is the result of a large number of non-observable individual effects in the model; in that case the fixed effect model in the Panel regression has been used. In this model, the '*I*' index denotes the cross section and '*t*' denotes the time series of regression. The constant term basically captures the constant individual effects. This constant basically assumes that the individual characteristics remain constant over the period of time (Blanchard & Sevestre, 1996). In a panel, the fixed effects are allowed to vary from individual to individual, while the slope parameters are assumed to be constant in both the time and the individual dimension. The fundamental assumption of the fixed effect is that

$E(\varepsilon_{it}) = 0$, the expected value of the error terms is 0. $\mathrm{Cov}(\varepsilon_{it,}\ \varepsilon_{jt}) = 0$ and the $\mathrm{Var}(\varepsilon_{it})$ is constant over the period of time. Under these assumptions, the panel with instrumental variables has been used for the purpose of analysis:

$$Y_{it} = \alpha_i + \beta_1 X_{1it} + \beta_2 X_{2it} + \ldots + \beta_k X_{kit} + \varepsilon_{it}$$

or in *matrix* notation:

$$Y_{it} = \alpha_{it} + X_{it}\beta + \varepsilon_{it}$$

This analysis deals with the sustainability, through the dimensions of OSS and outreach in terms of breadth and depth. The FSS of MFIs is measured through the indicator of OSS. Outreach refers to the number of people who are reached and, in this study, we have used outreach using two different dimensions: the breadth, which refers to the number of people reached, and depth, which refers to the quality of credit. Depth of outreach in this study is measured through the variable ALBG/per GNI and breadth of outreach is measured through the NAB. For model specification, we have taken the log average loan borrower group, gross loan portfolio, cost per borrower, and total equity as suggested by previous studies (Ahlin et al., 2011).

From the extant literature it is established that the financial sustainability leads to better outreach of an MFI. The simple model specification using panel regression is defined as

$$\ln ALBG_{it} = \alpha_{0} + \alpha_{1}. \ln GLP_{it} + \alpha_{2} \ln TEQ_{it} + \gamma_{1} FSS_{it} + \alpha_{3} DER_{it} + \alpha_{4} TERit_{I} + \alpha_{5} \ln CPBit + \delta_{1} WBR_{it} + \varepsilon_{it}$$

$$\ln OSS_{i} = \alpha_{0} + \alpha_{1}. \ln GLP_{i} + \alpha_{2} \ln TEQ_{I} + \gamma_{1} LLR_{i} + \alpha_{3} DER_{I} + \alpha_{4} TER_{I} + \alpha_{5} \ln ALBG_{I} + \delta_{1} NAB_{I} + \varepsilon_{i}$$

In this study, α_0 is the intercept from α_1 to α_5 and represents the coefficients of the explanatory variable. The detailed description of the explanatory variable is given Table 23.

The research question in this study is to measure the impact of financial sustainability on the depth of outreach (see Tables 24 and 25), measured by the ALBG per GNI. This implies that when the depth of outreach increases, the average loan size declines. This is because monitoring of the small loans requires a large amount of expenditure and MFIs do not find that viable. The motivation for using the Panel Instrument variable in the model is that the initial OLS model is fraught with endogeneity, which states that while the financial performance depends on the depth outreach, the depth or outreach also depends on the financial performance. The problem of endogeneity is handled in the model, using the instrument variable in the panel model with the fixed effects. At first, we run an OLS model and then estimated the Shapiro–Wilk *W* test for normality of distribution, which through the graphical distribution of plot shows that the data distribution is normal. In order to control for heteroscedasticity in the model, we have used the VCE (robust) errors. The test for heteroscedasticity is done using the IM test. Variance of inflation factor ranges from 1 to 4 and there is no multicollinearity problem in the data. In this model in order to provide

Table 23. Description of Variables for Empirical Analysis.

Financial Sustainability	
Operating self-sustainability	OSS > 1 (operating revenue/loan loss provision + financial expense + operating expense)
Outreach	
Active borrowers	NAB – number of active borrowers
Average loan size	ALS which refers (gross loan portfolio/NAB)
Other control variables	
Gross loan portfolio	GLP – gross loan portfolio
Financial self-sustainability	FSS – financial self-sustainability
Debt equity ratio	DER – debt equity ratio
Total expense ratio	TER – total operating expense ratio
Cost per borrower	CPB – cost per borrower
Woman borrower ratio	WBR – number of female borrowers/NAB

for the endogeneity, we have used the women borrow rate, which is the number of women borrowers divided by the NAB as the instrument variable. When we regressed the instrument variable, women borrower as of the independent variable OSSR, the results were relevant. Age of the age MFI has an impact on the financial sustainability of the firm. Extant literature highlights that the firm with more age reap benefits in the form of the economy of scales and will be more sustainable due to its operation. If older firms do not innovate and improve, they will have to reap higher costs. Higher PAR highlights the higher potential loss in revenue. Ayayi and Maty (2010) propound that the PAR > 30 days has a negative impact on financial sustainability. In our model PAR leads to a 0.04% decline in the average loan size of borrowers which is a proxy for the depth of the outreach. If the PAR > 30 days is higher it leads to a decline in disbursal of small size loans. The capital structure of the firm has an impact on the financial performance of the firm. From the study of extant literature, we find that the capital structure can have both positive and negative impacts on the sustainability and outreach of the

Table 24. Impact of Financial Sustainability on Outreach of Financial Firms.

	Fixed Panel	**Dynamic Panel**	**Anderson Hsiao**
Dependent Variable			
Logglp	0.194*** (0.0222)	0.176*** (0.0347)	
Log ALBG L1		01.47** (0.079)	
Debt equity	0.0003** (0.0001)	0.0002 (0.00017)	
D1. debt equity			−0.0004 (0.002)
Log CPB	0.327*** (0.086)	0.296*** (0.0952)	
D1. operating expenses			
LD. log ALBG			−0.183*** (0.0652)
D1. log OSSR			0.1400 (0.099)
D1. log GLP			0.255*** (0.038)
D1. log CPB			0.150*** (0.061)
DI. PAR			0.001 (0.001)
PAR	−0.0004 (0.000)	−0.003 (0.004)	
Log OSSR	0.261*** (0.090)	0.173 (0.158)	
Constant	−2.801*** (0.747)	−2.34*** (0.962)	0.052*** (0.019)
Rho	0.96	0.95	0.97
Number of observations			

*** represents significance at 1%; ** represents significance at 5%; and * represents significance at 10%.

firm. From the analysis, we find that our results support the argument by Briggs and Coleman (2007) who propound that the capital structure or the debt equity ratio has a positive impact on sustainability and outreach of the MFIs.

9.9. Correlation Matrix

Table 25. Correlational Matrix Provides the Correlation Between Various Variables.

	Log ALBG	Log GLP	Debt Equity	Operating Expenses	Log CPB	Age	OSSR
Log ALBG	1						
Log GLP	−0.320	1					
Debt equity	0.029	−0.0504	1				
Operating expenses	−0.258	−0.295	−0.106	1			
Log CPB	0.004	−0.005	−0.114	0.622	1		
Age	−0.200	−0.086	−0.025	0.091	−0.235	1	
OSSR	−0.278	0.290	0.035	−0.338	−0.30	−0.0039	1

9.10. Fixed Panel Model

In a panel regression model,

$$Y_{it} = \beta_0 + \beta_1 X_{it} + \beta_2 Z_i + u_{it}$$

where Z_i are unobserved time invariant heterogeneities across the entities $i = 1, \ldots, n$. This model aims to estimate β_1, the effect of Y_i of a change in X_i holding constant Z_i. With $\alpha_i = \beta_0 + \beta_2 Z_i$ we obtain the model $Y_{it} = \beta_0 + \beta_1 X_{it} + u_{it}$. With the individual fixed intercepts α_i $i = 1, \ldots, n$, where each of these can be interpreted as fixed effect of entity i, this model is called as the fixed model taking average on both sides of the model:

$$\frac{1}{n}\sum_{i=n}^{n} Y_{it} = \beta 1.\frac{1}{n}\sum_{i=n}^{n} X_{it} + \frac{1}{n}\sum_{i=n}^{n} a_i + \frac{1}{n}\sum_{i=n}^{n} u_{it}$$

This is often expressed in the form of the demeaned version:

$$(Y_{it} - \overline{Y_i}) = \beta_1((X_{it} - \overline{X_{it}}) + (u_{it} - \overline{u_{it}})$$

In this model, we have taken the data from 2012 to 2019, for MFIs across five nations of India, China, Philippine, Bangladesh, and Indonesia. The nations were selected on the basis of the diamond rating of MIX microfinance database.

Our main equation is as follows:

$$\text{Log Average Loan Per Borrower}_{it} = \alpha_0 + \beta_1.\ \text{Lag1. Log Average loan per borrower} + \beta_2.\ \text{Log Operational Self-Sufficiency ratio} + \beta_3.\ \text{Log Gross Loan Portfolio} + \beta_4.\ \text{Log Cost Per Borrower} + \beta_5.\ \text{Portfolio at Risk} + \beta_6.\ \text{Debt Equity ratio} + \beta_7.\ \text{Age} + \varepsilon_{it}$$

In this equation, the dependent variable is the measure of the depth of outreach or the ALBG. The endogenous variable is the lag of ALBG and the explanatory variables are the log of operational self-sufficiency, debt at equity, PAR, log gross loan portfolio, log cost per borrower, and age is the control variable. In this model, we are using a few instruments. Internal instruments include the first lag of log of the ALBG and the log of operational self-sufficiency and the external instruments include the NAB. In this model, we have used the dynamic panel model to provide for any kind of correlation between the existing ALBG and the ALBG in the previous year. However, this dynamic panel without the use of appropriate instruments lead to the problem of serial correlations between the error terms or the reverse causality. With the use of the first difference in the second model, we intend to provide for any kind serial correlation between the residuals. However, if the residual serial correlation of the model does not follow the random walk, the first difference regressions are still biased. To check for the reverse causality, in a short panel, we use the Arellano Bond GMM, which are more efficient in case of a short panel.

GMM is a generic method for estimating the parameters in statistical models. This method uses the moment conditions that are the function of the model parameters and data such that their expectation is zero at the parameters' true value and is a dynamic panel estimator. In this model, we use a longitudinal panel data over eight years. GMM is a dynamic panel data estimator that controls for the endogeneity of the lagged dependent variable in a dynamic panel model, where there is correlation between the explanatory variable and the error. This model with GMM controls for the endogeneity of the lagged dependent variable, where there is correlation between the explanatory variable and the error term in a model, omitted variable bias, unobserved panel heterogeneity, and the measurement errors.

In a linear regression model, if there is an endogenous regressor

$$Y = X'\beta + u$$

where y and u are $N \times 1$ vectors, β is a $K \times 1$ vector of unknown parameters; X is a $N \times k$ matrix of explanatory parameters. Due to the assumption of endogeneity, there is another matrix Z that is $N \times L$, where $L > K$. The Z matrix is assumed to comprise a set of variables that are highly correlated with X but are orthogonal to u (i.e. a set of valid instruments). GMM specifies that N (cross sections of group) $> t$ (time span) and we use instrumental variables Z that are exogenous such that $E\,(Z'u) = 0$ and the number of instruments $Z \leq$ number of groups, N. GMM can be system or difference estimators. GMM is suitable for dynamic panel with small t and large N and the independent variables are not strictly exogenous and arbitrarily distributed fixed effects that have heteroscedacity and autocorrelation within panels (Arellano & Bond, 1991; Blundell & Bond, 1998). This model uses the internal and the external instruments. Arellano and Bond (1991) provide that the difference GMM corrects for the endogeneity by transforming all regressors through differencing and controls for the endogeneity. However, this model with first difference transformation magnifies gap in an unbalanced panel. To correct for the endogeneity, by introducing more instruments to improve the efficiency, we transform the instruments to make them uncorrelated with the fixed effects. It uses two equations: the original equation and the transformed ones. It uses the orthogonal deviations:

$$\text{Initial model: } \ln Y_{it} = \varphi \ln Y_{it-1} + \beta X'_{it} + (\delta_i + \varepsilon_{it})$$

$$\text{Transformed model: } \Delta \ln y_{it} = \Delta \ln y_{it-1} + \beta \Delta X'_{it} + \Delta\varepsilon_{it}$$

By transforming the regressors through first differencing the fixed effect is removed as it does not vary with time but the problem of endogeneity remains in the model. From the model:

$$\Delta u_{it} = \Delta \eta_i + \Delta\varepsilon_{it}$$

$$u_{it} - u_{it-1} = (\eta_i - \eta_i) + (\varepsilon_{it} - \varepsilon_{it-1}) = \varepsilon_{it} - \varepsilon_{it-1}$$

Unobserved fixed effects no longer enter the equation as they are by the assumption constant between the periods. Also, the first differenced lagged dependent variable is instrumented with its past levels and now changes in the dependent variable are assumed to be represented by the transformed equation. Let's assume that the equation is a random walk model and Y is persistent. In these conditions, the application of the difference GMM estimator yields both biased and inefficient estimate of φ in finite samples, and this is particularly acute when T is short. Poor performance of the difference GMM estimator in such circumstances is attributed to the use of the poor instruments (Blundell & Bond, 1998). System GMM is used when one equation is expressed in level forms with first differences as instruments. The second is expressed in first-differenced form with levels as instruments. This model uses a large number of moment conditions where T is short and the dependent variable is persistent, these are gains in precision and small sample bias is reduced. To further provide for the heteroscedacity and serial correlation, a two-step GMM estimator will be used by exploiting a weighing matrix using residuals from the first model. System GMM is preferable in case of the random walk in the errors.

This study seeks to measure the impact of self-sufficiency on the outreach of microfinance. In the model specified, the ALBG is used as a dependent variable of the lagged ALBG. Persistence of credit disbursal and loan size and financing constraints depend on observable MFI characteristics. A spurious state dependence arises, if these unobserved factors are correlated over time and not controlled for (Heckman, 1981). The most widely used measure of depth of outreach is average loan size per borrower and as a policy many a times this average loan size per borrower depends on the previous year value. There is an endogeneity between the outreach which is the average loan size and the sustainability of the firm which depends on previous year values.

In this study, the second model is the one-step GMM model. Model specification for the Arellano Bond Estimator is given as follows.

9.11. Model Specification for the Arellano Bond Estimator

Model 1: $\log \text{Average Loan Per Borrower}_{it} = \alpha_0 + \beta_1 \log glp + \beta_2 \log ossr + \beta_3 \text{ debt equity} + \beta_4 \log cpb + \beta_5 \log. \text{ Portfolio at Risk} + \beta_{5\cdot} \text{ Age} + \epsilon_{it}$

Model 2: $\log \text{Average Loan Per Borrower}_{it} = \alpha_0 + \beta_{1\cdot} \log \text{Average Loan per borrower} + \beta_2 \log glp + \beta_3 \log ossr + \beta_4 \text{ debt equity} + \beta_5 \log cpb + \beta_6 \log. \text{ Portfolio at Risk} + \beta_7 \text{ Age} + \epsilon_{it}$

Model 3: xtabond2 logalbg l. logalbg logglp logossr portfolioatrisk30days logcpb y, gmm (l. logalbg logossr, collapse) iv (logcpb y*, equation (level)) robust small*

In this model, we have used the Arellano Bond GMM estimator. The sustainability of the MFIs and the depth of outreach in the form of the average loan size per borrower are endogenous. This is due to the reverse causality that flows from the ALBG to operational self-sustainability and vice versa – these regressors may be correlated with the error term. Time invariant characteristics of the MFI such as the age and geography may be correlated with the explanatory variables. The fixed effects are contained in the error term in eq. (1) which consists of the unobserved country specific effects v_i and the observation specific error e_{it}:

$$u_{it} = v_i + e_{it}$$

Moreover, the presence of the lagged dependent term leads to auto correlation in model and panel dataset has a short time dimension, eight years for approximately 104 MFIs across 5 nations.

Table 26 explains the empirical results for GMM analysis of the impact of microfinance on the sustainability of the community lending groups.

10. Conclusion

As per this study, financial sustainability is an important concept and is negatively impacted by the PAR, some female borrowers, and personnel expenses. And it is positively impacted by the financial revenue. PAR > 30 days is highest for the East Asian economy and negative for other parts of the world. And PAR is impacted

Table 26. Empirical Results for GMM Analysis and Impact of Microfinance on Sustainability of Community Lending Groups.

	Fixed Panel Model Model (1)	**Dynamic Panel (Model 2)**	**Arellano Bond Model (Model 3)**
Dependent Variable	log. albg		log. albg
Logglp	0.180*** (0.028)	0.1667*** (0.229)	0.030 (0.124)
Log OSSR	0.300*** (0.109)	0.198** (0.092)	0.984 (0.687)
Log ALBG L1			1.04*** (0.072)
Debt equity	−0.0003*** (0.00004)	−0.0002*** (0.000)	
PAR		−0.001 (0.001)	−0.0004 (0.006)
D1. debt equity			
Log CPB	0.444*** (0.0841)	0.304*** (0.064)	−0.003 (0.068)
LD. Log ALBG			
D1. Log OSSR			
D1. Log GLP			
D1. Log CPB			
DI. PAR			
PAR	−0.0001 (0.000)		
Log OSSR			
Age	−0.0211** (0.0124)		
Year			0.009 (0.042)
Year 2012			
Year 2013			0.156*** (0.055)
Year 2014			
Year 2015			0.080*** (0.037)
Year 2016			0.032 (0.044)
Year 2017			0.107*** (0.045)
Year 2018			
Year 2019			−0.094 (0.071)
Sargan test			
AR (1)			−4.17 (0.000)
AR (2)			0.09 (0.928)
Sargan test			14.79 (0.253)

(Continued)

Table 26. (*Continued*)

Hansen test			11.29 (0.504)
Constant	−0.605 (1.10)	−1.383*** (0.558)	−25.27 (80.87)
Rho	0.994	0.992	
F statistics (10,99)			6977.06 (0.000)
Number of observations	**681**	**579**	**579**

*** represents significance at 1%; ** represents significance at 5%; and * represents significance at 10%.

by the delinquency of loans, several active borrowers, and regions of the world. OSS is impacted by ROAs and capital assets ratio. The financial sustainability of a MFI is impacted by profit, size, capital asset ratio, region of the world, type of MFI, and the maturity and age of the MFIs. The East Asia Pacific region positively impacts the financial sustainability of MFIs. Rural Bank and Credit Union impact the financial sustainability of the MFIs. MENA region has the highest level of financial revenue rate among all the regions of India. East America has the highest rate of personnel expenses and PAR > 30 days is higher for 30 days.

References

Ahlin, C., Lin, J., & Maio, M. (2011). Where does microfinance flourish? Microfinance institutions performance in macroeconomic context. *Journal of Development Economics, 95*, 105–120. 10.1016/j.jdeveco.2010.04.004

Arellano, M., & Bond, S. (1991). Some tests of specification for panel data: Monte Carlo evidence and an application to employment equations. *Review of Economic Studies, 58*, 277–297. https://doi.org/10.2307/2297968

Ayayi, A. G., & Sene, M. (2008). What drives microfinance institution's financial sustainability. *The Journal of Developing Areas, 44*(1), 303–324. https://ssrn.com/abstract=1954114

Adams, W. M., Jeanrenaud, S., & International Union for Conservation of Nature and Natural Resources. (2008). *Transition to sustainability: Towards a humane and diverse world.* IUCN.

Ayi, G. A., & Maty, S. (2010). What drives microfinance institutions' financial sustainability. *The Journal of Developing Areas, 44*(1), 303–324. https://doi.org/10.1353/jda.0.0093

de Aghion, B. A., & Morduch, J. (2010). *The economics of microfinance* (2nd ed.). The MIT Press. https://econpapers.repec.org/bookchap/mtptitles/0262513986.htm

Barbier, E. B. (1987). The concept of sustainable economic development. *Environmental Conservation, 14*(2), 101–110. https://doi.org/10.1017/S0376892900011449

Barney (1991). Firm resources and sustained competitive advantage. *Journal of Management, 17*(1), 99–120. https://doi.org/10.1177/014920639101700108

Baumgartner, T. A., & Hensley, L. D. (2006). *Conducting and reading research in health and human performance* (4th ed.). McGraw-Hill.

Bell, S., & Morse, S. (2008). *Sustainability indicators: Measuring the Immeasurable? Earthscan.*

Berenbach, S., & Guzman, D. (1994). Financial services for micro enterprises: Principles and institutions. In M. Otero & E. Rhyne (Eds.), *The new world of micro enterprise finance*. IT Publications

Blanchard, P., & Sevestre, P. (1996). Présentation générale. *Économie et Prévision, Programme National Persée, 126*(5), 1–9. https://ideas.repec.org/a/prs/ecoprv/ecop_0249-4744_1996_num_126_5_5818.html

Blundell, R., & Bond, S. (1998). Initial conditions and moment restrictions in dynamic panel data models. *Journal of Econometrics, 87*, 115–143. http://dx.doi.org/10.1016/S0304-4076(98)00009-8

Briggs, A. R. J., & Coleman, M. (2007). *Research methods in educational leadership and management* (2nd ed.). Sage.

Christen, R. P., Rhyne, E., Vogel, R. C., & McKean, C. (1995). Maximizing the out reach of microenterprise finance: An analysis of successful microfinance programs (USAID Program and Operations Assessment Report No. 10). Washington, DC

Caudill, S., & Gropper, D., & Hartarska, V. (2009). Which microfinance institutions are becoming more cost effective with time? Evidence from a mixture model. *Journal of Money, Credit and Banking, 41*, 651–672. 10.1111/j.1538-4616.2009.00226.x

Conning, J. (1999). Outreach, sustainability and leverage in monitored and peer-monitored lending. *Journal of Development Economics, 60*, 51–77. https://doi.org/10.1016/S0304-3878(99)00036-X

Cull, R., Demirg€uç-Kunt, A., & Morduch, J. (2009). Microfinance meets the market. *The Journal of Economic Perspectives, 23*(1), 167–192. https://doi.org/10.1257/jep.23.1.167

Cull, R., Demirgüç-Kunt, A., Morduch, J. (2013, February 7). *Banks and microbanks*. NYU Wagner Research Paper No. 2232170, https://dx.doi.org/10.2139/ssrn.2232170

Das, T., & Guha, P. (2019). Measuring women's self-help group sustainability: A study of rural Assam. *International Journal of Rural Management, 15*(1), 116–136. https://doi.org/10.1177/0973005219836040

Deininger, K., & Liu, Y. (2013). Economic and social impacts of an innovative self-help group model in India. *World Development, 43*, 149–163. https://doi.org/10.1016/j.worlddev.2012.09.019

D'Espallier, B., Guérin, I., & Mersland, R. (2011). Women and repayment in microfinance: A global analysis. *World Development, 39*(5), 758–772. https://econpapers.repec.org/article/eeewdevel/v_3a39_3ay_3a2011_3ai_3a5_3ap_3a758-772.htm

Diagne, A. (1999). *Determinants of household access to and participation in formal and informal credit markets in Malawi*. FCND discussion papers 67, International Food Policy Research Institute (IFPRI). https://ideas.repec.org/s/fpr/fcnddp.html

Ferro-Luzzi, G., & Weber, S., (2007). *Measuring the performance of MFIs: An application of factor analysis*. 10.1057/9780230300026_9

Fowler, A. (2000). *Civil society, NGDOs and social development: Changing the rules of the game*. http://www.unrisd.org

Hartarska, V. (2005). Governance and performance of microfinance organizations in Central and Eastern Europe and the newly independent states. *World Development, 33*, 1627–1643. https://doi.org/10.1016/j.worlddev.2005.06.001

Hartarska, V., & Nadolnyak, D. (2007). Do regulated microfinance institutions achieve better sustainability and outreach? Cross-country evidence. *Applied Economics, 39*, 1207–1222. https://doi.org/10.1080/00036840500461840

Heckman, J. (1981). *Heterogeneity and state dependence in NBER Chapters*. National Bureau of Economic Research, Inc. https://econpapers.repec.org/bookchap/nbrnberch/8909.htm

Hermes, N., & Lensink, R. (2011). Microfinance: Its impact, outreach, and sustainability. *World Development, 39*(6), 875–881. https://doi.org/10.1016/j.worlddev.2009.10.021

Hermes, N., Lensink, R., Meesters, A. (2011). Outreach and efficiency of microfinance institutions. *World Development*, *39*(6), 938–948. https://doi.org/10.1016/j.worlddev.2009.10.018.

Hisako (2009). *Competition and wide outreach of microfinance institutions*. MPRA Paper 17143, University Library of Munich, Germany. https://ideas.repec.org/s/pra/mprapa.html

Honohan, P. (2004). *World Bank policy research* [Working Paper 3203]. http://econ.worldbank.org.Acknowledgments

Hulme, D., & Mosley, P. (1996). *Finance against poverty, 1 and 2*. Routledge.

Kai, H. (2009). *Competition and wide outreach of microfinance institutions*. Munich.

Kidd, C. V. (1992). The evolution of sustainability. *Journal of Agricultural and Environmental Ethics*, *5*(1), 1–26.

León, P. (2001). Four pillars of financial sustainability. The nature conservancy. *Open Journal of Business and Management*, *11*(6).

Lélé, S. M. (1991). Sustainable development: A critical review. *World Development*, *19*(6), 607–621. http://dx.doi.org/10.1016/0305-750X(91)90197-P.

Mahapatra, M. S., & Dutta, S. (2016). Determinants of sustainability of microfinance sector in India. *Journal of Rural Development*, *35*(3), 507–522. https://nirdprojms.in/index.php/jrd/article/view/104700

Maher, L., Gustafson, D., & Evans, A. (2010). *NHS sustainability model institute for innovation and improvement*. http://www.institute.nhs.uk/sustainability

McIntosh, C., & Wydick, B. (2005). Competition and microfinance. *Journal of Development Economics*, *78*(2), 271–298. https://doi.org/10.1016/j.jdeveco.2004.11.008

Mersland, R., & Strøm, R. Ø. (2009). Performance and governance in microfinance institutions. *Journal of Banking and Finance*, *33*(4), 662–669. https://doi.org/10.1016/j.jbankfin.2008.11.009

Mosley, P., & Hulme, D. V. (1998). Microenterprise finance: Is there a conflict between growth and poverty alleviation? *World Development*, *26*(5), 783–790.

Mosley, P., & Mayoux, L. (1999). Questioning virtuous spirals: Micro-finance and women's empowerment in Africa. *Journal of International Development*, *11*(7), 957–984. https://econpapers.repec.org/article/wlyjintdv/v_3a11_3ay_3a1999_3ai_3a7_3ap_3a957-984.htm

Narayana, S. A., Pati, R. K., & Vrat, P. (2012). Research on management issues in the pharmaceutical industry: A literature review. *International Journal of Pharmaceutical and Healthcare Mark*.

Navajas, S., Schreiner, M., Meyer, R., Gonzalez-Vega, C., Rodriguez Meza, J., Conning, J., Morduch, J., Sievers, I., & Zeller, M. (2000). Microcredit and the poorest of the poor: Theory and evidence from Bolivia. *World Development*, *28*, 333–346. 10.1016/S0305-750X(99)00121-7

Norton, B. (1992). Sustainability, human welfare, and ecosystem health. *Environmental Values*, *1*(2), 97–111.

Nurmakhanova, M., Kretzschmar, G., & Fedhila, H. (2015). The trade-off between financial sustainability and outreach of microfinance institutions. *Eurasian Economic Review*, *5*(2), 231–250. https://doi.org/10.1007/s40822-015-0016-7

Olivares-Polanco, F. (2005). Commercializing microfinance and deepening outreach? Empirical evidence from Latin America. *Journal of Microfinance/ESR Review*, *7*(2), Article 5.

Pati, A. P. (2008). Subsidized micro financing and financial sustainability of SHGs. *The Indian Journal of Commerce*, *61*(4), 137–150.

Rajdev, A., Amit, M., Rajdev, A., & Bhatt, M. K. (2013). *An Analysis of sustainability of microfinance institutions & its determinants: Using institutionalists approach sustainability and creativity (Fintech) view project*. https://www.researchgate.net/publication/299512526

Robinson, M. S. (2001). *The microfinance revolution: Sustainable finance for the poor*. World Bank.
Senge, P., et al. (1994). *The fifth discipline field book strategies and tools for building a learning organization*. Currency Doubleday.
Schaller, M., & Maass, A. (1989). Illusory correlation and social categorization: Toward an integration of motivational and cognitive factors in stereotype formation. *Journal of Personality and Social Psychology*, *56*(5), 709–721. https://doi.org/10.1037/0022-3514.56.5.709
Schreiner, M. (2002). Aspects of outreach: A framework for the discussion of the social benefits of microfinance. *Journal of International Development*, *14*, 591–603. https://doi.org/10.1002/jid.908
Soyibo, A. (1996). *The transmission of savings to investment in Nigeria*. Papers 48, African Economic Research Consortium. https://ideas.repec.org/p/fth/afrirc/48.html
Spangenberg, J. H. (2002). Environmental space and the prism of sustainability: Frameworks for indicators measuring sustainable development. *Ecological Indicators*, *2*, 295–309. http://dx.doi.org/10.1016/S1470-160X(02)00065-1
Stiglitz, J. E., & Weiss, A. (1981). Credit rationing in markets with imperfect information. *The American Economic Review*, *71*(3), 393–410.
Thomas, K. W. (1992). Conflict and conflict management: Reflections and update. *Journal of Organizational Behavior*, *13*, 265–274. http://dx.doi.org/10.1002/job.4030130307
von Pischke, J. D. (1996). Measuring the trade-off between outreach and sustainability of microenterprise lenders. *Journal of International Development*, *8*(2), 225–239.
Weiss, J., & Montgomery, H. (2005). Great expectations: Microfinance and poverty reduction in Asia and Latin America. *Oxford Development Studies, Taylor & Francis Journals*, *33*(3–4), 391–416. https://ideas.repec.org/s/taf/oxdevs.html
Woller, G. M., Dunford, C., & Woodworth, W. (1999). *Where to microfinance?* Draft Paper, 25 p.
Yaron, J. (1992) Assessing development finance institutions: A public interest analysis. World Bank Policy Research Working Paper, Paper No. 174, Washington DC.
Yaron and Benjamin (1997). *Developing rural financial markets*. Finance & Development.
Yaron, J., & Manos, R. (2010). Information transparency and agency costs in the microfinance industry: The adequacy of the operational self-sufficiency index. *Review of Market Integration*, *2*(1), 87–99. https://doi.org/10.1177/097492921000200106
Yaron, Y., Benjamin, M. D., & Charitonenko, S. (1998). Promoting efficient rural financial intermediation. *The World Bank Research Observer*, *13*, 147–170. https://doi.org/10.1093/wbro/13.2.147
Zeller, M., & Meyer, R. L. (2002). *The triangle of microfinance: Financial sustainability, outreach, and impact*. Johns Hopkins University Press.
Zeller, M., et al. (1997). Rural finance for food security for the poor: *Implications for research and policy* (p. 29). IFPRI.

Printed and bound by CPI Group (UK) Ltd, Croydon, CR0 4YY

16/09/2026

14963577-0001